OXFORD THEOLOGICAL MONOGRAPHS

Oxford Theological Monographs

BECOMING AND BEING

THE DOCTRINE
OF GOD IN
CHARLES HARTSHORNE
AND KARL BARTH

COLIN E. GUNTON

1978

OXFORD UNIVERSITY PRESS

Oxford University Press, Walton Street, Oxford OX2 6DP

OXFORD LONDON GLASGOW
NEW YORK TORONTO MELBOURNE WELLINGTON
KUALA LUMPUR SINGAPORE JAKARTA HONG KONG TOKYO
DELHI BOMBAY CALCUTTA MADRAS KARACHI
IBADAN NAIROBI DAR ES SALAAM CAPE TOWN

British Library Cataloguing in Publication Data
Gunton, Colin E.
  Becoming and being – (Oxford theological monographs)
  1. Barth, Karl 2. Hartshorne, Charles
  3. God – History of doctrines – 20th century
  I. Title II. Series
  231'.092'2   BT101.B2718   77–30287
ISBN 0 19 826713 4

*Printed in Great Britain
at the University Press, Oxford
by Vivian Ridler
Printer to the University*

PREFACE

THIS book began life as a thesis presented for the degree of Doctor of Philosophy in the University of Oxford. Its revision for publication represents a further stage in an already long process of concentration on the central philosophical and theological issues to arise out of a comparison of two different approaches to the doctrine and knowledge of God.

Grateful thanks are due to many who have assisted along the way, above all to Professor Robert Jenson, from whom came the initial ideas for direction and structure, as well as continuing interest from abroad. When he returned to America, the supervision was taken over by Principal John Marsh, to whom, along with his successor as Principal of Mansfield College, Professor George Caird, I owe so much of my early and crucial theological development. On the retirement of John Marsh, Professor John Macquarrie took over the scarcely exciting task of being third supervisor of a work near to completion, and contributed many helpful suggestions. Of my colleagues and students at King's College who have assisted in many ways, special mention must be made of Sophie Laws, who read the whole thesis in draft and contributed many characteristically penetrating comments, Keith Ward, and Professor H. P. Owen.

The book is dedicated with love and thanks to my wife, who has patiently lived with the work for nearly ten years.

C. E. G.

King's College, London
Advent 1976

LIST OF ACKNOWLEDGEMENTS

THANKS are due to the following for permission to quote from copyright works:

T. & T. Clark Limited	Karl Barth, *Church Dogmatics*
Harper & Row, Publishers	Charles Hartshorne, *Man's Vision of God* (reprinted by Archon Books, The Shoe String Press)
Open Court Publishing Company	Charles Hartshorne, *Anselm's Discovery* and *The Logic of Perfection*
SCM Press	Karl Barth, *Anselm: Fides Quærens Intellectum* Charles Hartshorne, *Creative Synthesis and Philosophic Method*

CONTENTS

ABBREVIATIONS

References to the works listed below are directly followed by a numeral, giving the page reference, except in the case of the *Church Dogmatics*, where the volume and part numbers (Roman and Arabic numerals respectively) are directly followed by numerals giving page references. Repeated references to the *Church Dogmatics* will give only volume and part numbers, followed by page reference. References to works of Barth are to the English translation listed in the Bibliography.

AD	Charles Hartshorne, *Anselm's Discovery* (1965)
BH	Hartshorne, *Beyond Humanism* (1937)
CD	Karl Barth, *Church Dogmatics*, E.T. edd. G. W. Bromiley and T. F. Torrance (1956–75)
CSPM	Hartshorne, *Creative Synthesis and Philosophic Method* (1970)
DR	Hartshorne, *The Divine Relativity* (1948)
FQI	Barth, *Anselm: Fides Quaerens Intellectum*, E.T., by I. W. Robertson (1960)
LP	Hartshorne, *The Logic of Perfection* (1962)
MVG	Hartshorne, *Man's Vision of God* (1941)
NTOT	Hartshorne, *A Natural Theology for Our Time* (1967)
PSG	Hartshorne, with W. L. Reese, *Philosophers Speak of God* (1953)
RSP	Hartshorne, *Reality as Social Process* (1953)

Full details of these books are given in the Bibliography.

INTRODUCTION

THE CLASSICAL CONCEPT OF GOD

THE decline of belief in God in the Western world has been documented and analysed in many ways. The cultural aspect of the decline, so vigorously welcomed and preached by Nietzsche as the death of God, has received the bulk of the attention, and is often the presupposition of modern Christian apologetic. Given that man is irreversibly secularized, runs the argument, how best may elements of the Christian gospel still be made real to him, so that he may at least find them interesting enough to take up some kind of attitude to them?

This study is written in the belief that the situation is by no means as simple as it is sometimes made to appear, and that much light can be thrown by looking at it from a different angle. It is a theological as well as a cultural development, and while this aspect has by no means been entirely neglected, it remains true that in most secular writing, and certainly in the mainstream of philosophy since Descartes, by and large only one concept of God has been under review. However great an exception is provided by nineteenth-century German philosophy, the pattern of most discussion of the nature and existence of God was laid down in the Middle Ages, classically in the *Summa Theologica* of St. Thomas Aquinas. Modern philosophy of religion in the Anglo-Saxon world is still conducted largely against a background of Aquinas's concept and the great critiques of its central doctrines and assumptions in Descartes, Spinoza, Hume, and Kant.

The two subjects of this study have a different relation to the classical concept. Both are radicals, in the sense that they reach down to what they understand to be the roots of rational theology. They are at once critics and innovators, and their rejection of the classical concept is made on the basis of their own ways of speaking about God. But both positive and negative aspects of their proposals will be more clearly comprehensible if they are seen against a background of the chief characteristics of the classical concept and some of the reasons for its decline.

First, there is its supernaturalism. Like so many of the words that appear in the course of modern theological debate, this admits of a variety of meanings. To reject some forms of supernaturalism is not to reject all. For example, Karl Barth's concept of revelation requires that some historical events be interpreted in terms of divine agency, even though they may also be susceptible of a natural interpretation. Here 'supernatural' agency is not exclusive of or necessarily alternative to—say—human agency. The story of Jesus is both the account of God's dealings with man and the description of the life of a man. Clarity would probably be served if the word 'theological' were used in this context, because this conception lacks many of the connotations of traditional supernaturalism. Therefore 'supernatural' is best used of that conception of God developed, as it was developed in the classical tradition, by the use of the 'negative way'. According to Aquinas, 'we cannot know what God is, but only what he is not'.[1] He therefore arrives at a concept of God by denying the characteristics of the natural world, or the effects, to use his Aristotelian terminology. Before we can say anything else about God—and Aquinas does want to speak positively also, though only of the ways in which we know and describe God, not of how he is in himself—we have to describe him by means of negative abstractions.

The outcome is that, first, 'supernatural' reality begins where nature's leaves off, and, second and more important, it is defined *in terms of its opposition to nature*. It is precisely what nature is not, and therefore its relations with nature are necessarily problematic, just as Descartes found it impossible to reach a satisfactory understanding of the relation between mind and matter precisely because he had begun by defining them in terms of their opposition to one another. In particular, any historical activity of God will tend to take the form of an isolated intervention which is also a violation of the natural.

Second, the classical conception of God holds him to be timeless. Because the natural is necessarily temporal, and because God is the negation of the natural, his relation to time

[1] St. Thomas Aquinas, *Summa Theologica* 1a.2.3.

will be that of the timelessly eternal. Once again, acute logical difficulties are raised for those, like Christians, who would speak of the historical relations of this God to the world. The paradigm relation is the metaphysical or even logical, analogous to the relation of form and particular. All hangs upon a conception of cause and effect that is not in terms of temporal regularities, but essentially metaphysical and timeless. Difficult though it may be for the modern mind to conceive after centuries of natural science, when Aquinas understands God to be the cause of the world, or the stick to be the cause of motion in the stone,[2] he is always thinking of instantaneous causation. God is then not a deist God belonging to the beginning of time, but a timeless absolute on which all temporal reality depends. Just as, to use an example from Plato that is crude but intelligible, the bed on which I sleep only remains in being so long as the matter of which it is composed participates in the reality of the timeless form of the bed, so the temporal, contingent world exists only in so far as it hangs in causal dependence on that which is essentially timeless.

Third, the classical conception of God depends upon a hierarchical ordering of reality. Entities are higher or lower in a scale of beings, the lower depending to a greater or lesser degree on the higher. The hierarchy is to some extent perspicuous to reason, and so lower reality—the only reality we directly experience—is believed to point beyond itself, to mirror a highest being which is both the tip of the pyramid and radically different from it, in being of another order entirely.

Aquinas's Five Ways illustrate all these points.[3] They also determine once and for all the shape of his concept of God.[4] The opposition of nature and supernature is revealed in the first three ways, in the way in which each argument develops. Nature contains motion, it is moved, and by negation it emerges that God is the sole unmoved mover; nature is caused, God the causeless cause, untouched by finite cause and effect; nature is contingent, God the timeless necessity. Second, each of the Ways represents a version of the classical Greek quest to find the timeless in the midst of time. Together they build up

[2] Aquinas, op. cit 1a.2.3. [3] Ibid.
[4] R. W. Jenson, *The Knowledge of Things Hoped For* (London and New York, 1969), pp. 58–89.

a pictute of the one changeless, infinite, perfect, abstract absolute.[5] Third, all of the Ways, with the possible exception of the fifth, presuppose and depend upon a hierarchical ordering of reality. Each is an argument to absurdity, to the absurdity of the infinite logical regress that results if a chain of beings, each dependent on the higher, is not crowned by a highest being that both upholds and is yet of a radically different nature from the beings below it.[6] Without some such neoplatonic view of the world arguments of this type either fail or beg the question. To the modern reader, the arguments often appear to beg the question, but this is because he either misunderstands or cannot accept their premises; nor can he understand that Aquinas seeks to move from the contemporary world-view to the Christian God.

The Third Way is here of particular interest. It depends upon a hierarchy of beings,[7] from the purely contingent, through the conditionally necessary, to God, the absolutely necessary. Without the hierarchy there is no reason why, as Hume suggested, the universe should not be the necessary being. And the resulting concept of God sums up all the difficulties which both Hartshorne and Barth find in the classical concept. Unlike the conditionally necessary beings below him on the scale, this God is wholly necessary. Now, what Aquinas intends by 'necessary' is disputable: he certainly appears in this argument to confuse logical and ontological necessity.[8] But whether or not he would have been able or willing to distinguish between the two—and it may be the case with him, as it is with Hartshorne, that his whole metaphysical enterprise requires the equation of the two—the fact remains that, if God is wholly and utterly necessary, and if his relation to the world is that of the timeless to the temporal, it is difficult to understand how contingency is possible at all. Logic would appear to be on the side of Spinoza who, taking this aspect of the concept, and, in line with the presuppositions of Newtonian science radicalizing the equation of cause and logical implication, produced a pantheistic system in which everything takes

---

[5] Aquinas, op. cit. 1a.13.11.

[6] Anthony Kenny, *The Five Ways* (London, 1969), pp. 41–5, documents the astrological beings that people the higher reaches of the hierarchy.

[7] Kenny, op. cit., pp. 67 f.   [8] Kenny, op. cit., p. 68.

place through the necessity of a timeless logic. The universe as a whole is conceived on the analogy of a geometrical theorem, and both meaningful history and Christian theology become impossible. That is to say, the classical concept of God, allied with a more forthright rationalism than Aquinas's and with certain assumptions of modern science, collapses into a far from Christian pantheism.[9]

Other influences associated with the development of modern science hastened the decline of classical theism. The heart of the latter's supernaturalism consists in its taking the supernatural more seriously than it takes the natural, an interest which derives from the Greek concern with form and its tendency to assume the unreality of matter.[10] Nature, on this view, is interesting and comprehensible for what can be seen within and beyond it. A hierarchy gains its significance from its head. But modern science finds nature to be interesting *in itself.*[11] That the development of modern science owes much to theological influences is increasingly coming to be accepted.[12] This suggests that the disputes between scientists and the church at the end of the Middle Ages represent not so much a struggle between religion and science as one between a medieval and a more biblically oriented theology. Classical theology, with its doctrine of analogy and its negative theology, sees nature as being semi-independent of God. On the other hand, 'the idea of a divine creator implies the absolute dependence of the created things on him and also their total differentiation from him.'[13] If this is correct, not only can we claim that Christian belief does not stand or fall with the classical concept of God; but in this context the cultural phenomenon, so often held to be universal in modern thought, that men do not expect nature to offer up the kind of secrets that Aquinas did, need not dismay us. Both modern science and Christian theology have taught us to look at the world differently.

---

[9] To Hartshorne's manifest delight: *PSG* 189–91.

[10] M. B. Foster, 'The Christian Doctrine of Creation and the Rise of Modern Natural Science', *Mind* 43 (1934) 446–68, esp. 454 f.

[11] M. B. Foster, art. cit., and R. Hooykaas, *Religion and the Rise of Modern Science* (Edinburgh, 1972).

[12] '. . . his [sc. Francis Bacon's] attitude, as Professor B. Farrington says, might be summarized in the slogan: "Out with Aristotle and in with the Bible".' R. Hooykaas, op. cit., p. 39.

[13] Op. cit., p. 12.

A third destructive influence upon the classical concept is provided by those philosophers who helped to provide the theoretical background to pre-twentieth-century natural science and the cultural atmosphere of much modern scepticism. In particular, both Hume and Kant produced radical critiques of classical theism. Their individual arguments are, like any arguments that are of philosophical interest, disputable. But what is surely not open to dispute is that, in the light of the kind of assumptions they make about the world and our relation to it, a proof and concept of God cannot be obtained by reasoning from the experienced world. For Aquinas the material world of itself mirrored the immaterial; that is to say, of its very nature it invited reasoning by analogy to a reality that was essentially unlike it. For Hume and Kant the whole procedure was illegitimate. The finite world gave knowledge of finite entities, and no more. There was no *logos*, no inbuilt rationality, in the universe that licensed the kind of conclusions that traditional metaphysics had drawn.

This is not, as yet, to draw any final conclusions about the truth of the classical way of conceiving God. It may still turn out to be the best or only way of giving a rational account of the God whom Christians worship. Many theologians, particularly in the Catholic tradition, believe that it is. But so far as the mainstream of Protestant and secular thought is concerned, the path after Kant splits in two. The idealists, and notably Hegel, develop a concept of God that, in its essential immanentism, stands in marked contrast to the supernaturalism of classical theism. God is increasingly understood in terms of the cosmic process, rather than as being an external explanation of it. According to Hegel, 'the God outside of us who saves us by his grace, is a misleading pictorial expression for saving forces *intrinsic* to self-conscious Spirit, wherever this may be present'.[14] An important outcome of this tendency is the stress it puts on time. Time is not something that thought must escape, for it is at the heart of the way things are. Much modern liberal theology is in this tradition, and it is as a consciously liberal theologian that Schubert Ogden adopts Charles Hartshorne as *the* philosopher for modern theology.[15]

[14] J. N. Findlay, *Hegel: A Re-examination* (London, 1958), p. 143.
[15] S. M. Ogden, *The Reality of God* (London, 1967).

The other path is taken by Karl Barth. For him, Kant's lesson to modern theology is that it must stand on its own rational feet: 'in modern theology recognising the point of departure for its method in revelation, just as decidedly as philosophy sees its point of departure in reason, and in theology conducting, therefore, a dialogue with philosophy, and not, wrapping itself up in the mantle of philosophy, a quasi-philosophical monologue'.[16]

In their different ways Hartshorne and Barth both stand at the end of the critique of classical theism. Each goes to his own fountain-head, the one in pure reason, the other in revelation. Hartshorne's rejection of the classical tradition is explicit, and a pillar of his programme. Barth's reasons for rejection emerge as his own concept is developed. And, despite their different paths, they will be seen to have other, illuminating, features in common.

[16] Karl Barth, *Protestant Theology in the Nineteenth Century*, E.T. by Brian Cozens and others (London, 1972), p. 307.

PART ONE

HARTSHORNE'S
NEOCLASSICAL THEISM

I

THE REJECTION OF CLASSICAL THEISM

i. *Philosophical*

CHARLES HARTSHORNE accepts wholeheartedly the quest of the classical theists, to derive by the use of reason a concept of God. He is a philosopher with a traditional, pre-twentieth-century conception of the philosopher's function. Whatever use he may make of the tools of logical analysis, it is only in the service of a higher end; there could never be any suggestion that logical analysis is an end in itself. He is what Strawson would classify as a revisionary metaphysician,[1] in that he wishes to persuade us to alter our understanding of the universe. This is not to deny that he continues to use much of the terminology of those he wishes to replace, but he does it in such a way that its meaning is overturned, and overturned on two grounds. The first and major ground is the alternative vision of the way things are, but the second is also important. For Hartshorne claims that the classical concept of God is internally incoherent, and must therefore be rejected on grounds of logic.

Here a comparison with an earlier rationalist philosopher is instructive. Baruch Spinoza in no way rejected the quest of his predecessor Descartes. But he had to reject his conclusions both because he found them to be radically inconsistent and because he approached his subject-matter from a different direction. The same is true of Hartshorne, and both motives will be seen working alongside each other in his critique of classical theism. That is to say, when he rejects his predecessors on grounds of logic, the logic is none the less employed against the background of a metaphysic, a distinctive view of reality.

Hartshorne's first attack on classical theism concerns the way

[1] P. F. Strawson, *Individuals: An Essay in Descriptive Metaphysics* (London, 1964), p. 9.

in which it conceives the relation of God to the world. He argues
that it is absurd to hold that God is totally unaffected by the
events that take place in the universe. The point is not merely
the general one that an unmoved God is unloving and distant,
but derives from deeper philosophical and logical considerations. There is a logical absurdity, and it lies in the fact that
classical doctrines of the absolute ascribe to God only the
characteristics that belong to objects of knowledge. Of course
God is, in part, the object of our knowledge. But if he is only
that, how can he be God? Surely, goes the argument, if God
knows his creatures, he must be a subject on the analogy of
human subjects. And if he is a subject, he cannot, logically
cannot, remain unaffected by what, in his omniscience, he
knows about the doing and suffering of his world.

The notion of the subjectivity of God is very important for
this philosopher. Indeed, as will emerge later, the doctrine that
to be is to be a subject and that the universe consists of experiencing entities, is the very heart of his philosophy. At this
stage we need to see that he takes the model of one entity's
perception of another, and asks what happens in, say, the
event of seeing. What does a simple statement of the type,
'Charles Hartshorne saw a Great Spotted Woodpecker',
describe? Analysis shows that it describes a momentary event,
or, more specifically, a relation between two entities, in which
one of them, the subject, is affected by an object, which itself
remains unaffected. (If the bird returned the glance, that is
not to say that it was affected by the original event. Its perception takes the form of a new relation, in which it is now the
subject, while the philosopher, the object, remains unaffected.)
In that particular relation the subject's relation to the bird is
said to be *internal*; its relation to him *external*. If the pattern is
generalized, it becomes a doctrine of relations, and it is on the
basis of this doctrine that Hartshorne both criticizes the traditional theology and erects an alternative theory. The doctrine
can be summarized as follows:[2]

(i) Relations between entities are either external or internal.

(ii) If entity A is externally related to entity B, A is not in any
way affected by that relation. In principle, anything may be

---

[2] See *DR* 60–75 for a fuller account of the doctrine.

externally related to something else; what determines extern-
ality is the position an entity happens to hold in any given
relation. For example, no concept can be affected by my
knowing or thinking about it, and is therefore externally
related to me the thinker. Thus, in any relation involving
perception or knowledge, it is the *object* of knowledge that is
externally related. All objects of knowledge are so related in
so far as they are objects of knowledge; and in so far as they
are objects of knowledge, Hartshorne would also say that they
are *absolute* in relation to the knower, the *relative*. It is important
to see that the terms absolute and relative are both logical
descriptions—in that they describe the logic of the statements
of relation—and refer to the real world. For Hartshorne
our language successfully describes the world as it really is.
This will be particularly important when we come to see
how Hartshorne wants to use both these terms in speaking
about God.

(iii) Internal relations are possible only for knowing entities,
that is, for those who are affected or altered by the act of
cognition. If I think of the number '2', or mentally recall some
past event or act, it is I, and not the concept or event, who am
affected by the conceiving or recollecting. Indeed, only present
subjects can be internally related; the past and the concept can
only be absolute, or externally related. Thus it is the *subject*
that is internally related: in its act of knowing it is *relative* in
respect of concepts, the past, and in general any object of
knowledge. Thus, in an example used by Hartshorne, Plato is
absolute with regard to Leibniz, for, by the time that the latter
comes to think about the former, the events which make up
Plato's life are past and unchangeable.[3] But by the very fact
that he thinks about his predecessor Leibniz at least in some
small respect becomes something that he was not before he did
that piece of recollecting.

It is to be noted that in this as in other aspects of the discussion, Hartshorne has his own very idiosyncratic approach.
The distinctiveness of what he is doing can be seen at this stage
in the importance of time in the understanding of the relations
he is describing: for the knowing subject is always related to
things in its past. This is clear enough in the case of Leibniz's

[3] *DR* 17.

reflections on Plato, but the case of the woodpecker is more revealing. When he sees the woodpecker, what he sees is in fact what happened in the immediate past, even though perception appears to be instantaneous. In other words, perception is a kind of remembering, and memory is 'the paradigm of realistic awareness'.[4] '. . . science tells us . . . that the events perceived, at least if outside our bodies, are in the past quite as truly as what we remember.'[5] All objects of knowledge of the real world are therefore in the past, and are as such changeless, as is the other chief class of known or externally related objects, the world of concepts. The known is always the absolute, static, and unchanging; the knower the relative, dynamic, and changing.

In the light of this, Hartshorne examines Aquinas's treatment of God, who must necessarily be the supreme member of a world of knowing entities. He finds that Aquinas has helped to develop the very theory of relations that he himself holds, but that, in order to uphold at all costs the classical concept, in the case of God he inverts the two terms of the relation, 'giving the "subject" the very role taken, in the ordinary case, by the object!'[6] As God is argued to be completely unaffected by his relation to the world ('unmoved') it follows that he is a superobject rather than a supersubject and that 'if God is supremely absolute, he must, it seems, be that which is most abstract and merely objective, or least concrete and least subjective or conscious'[7]. This criticism of the classical doctrine of God holds, then, not that God is made an analogically special case—which might be justifiable—but that the logic of knowing is turned on its head in the divine case. Aquinas teaches both that God is omniscient, and that his relation to the things he knows remains external. The only grounds for maintaining what amounts to a contradiction are those deriving from the axioms of classical theism.[8] But can those axioms be maintained in face of evident absurdity?

Defences against this attack have been made by classical theists, and help to bring out the point of what Hartshorne is saying. F. X. Meehan[9] suggests that the issue is not as simple as

---

[4] *CSPM* 218.   [5] *CSPM* 75.   [6] *PSG* 120.   [7] *PSG* 132.   [8] Ibid.
[9] 'Efficient Causality: A Reply and a Comment', *Journal of Religion* 26 (1946) 50–4.

Hartshorne makes out, for the divine knowing cannot be understood in isolation from the divine willing. M. Westphal[10] takes the way of analogy, and argues that God *is* really related to the world, but in a different way. Whether or not these defences can succeed will depend in large part on where we start in our thinking about God. If the axioms of classical theism are accepted, then they will be convincing. But Hartshorne has a very strong case, and on two grounds in particular. (i) If, with Hartshorne, we take it as axiomatic that any case of knowing must be recognizably analogous to his paradigm of internal relations, without appeal to additional factors like will, then his case is irresistible. If to be a knowing subject is to be internally related, then clearly any knowing subject is to some extent dependent, at least for the contents of his knowledge, on what he knows. (ii) Even if an addition is made, so that God is conceived not merely as knowing subject, but as subject who somehow wills all that he knows, it remains difficult to conceive that he can remain unaltered by what he knows and does, at least in the way that a concept or past event is unaffected by my knowledge of it. Perhaps that is not what the classical theists mean when they speak of God's absoluteness. But on Hartshorne's understanding of the matter, his logic is impeccable: for him the *absolute* is by definition the object, and therefore cannot be said to *know* in any recognizable meaning of the term.

And so Hartshorne's first attack on classical theism is a strong one. Other aspects of the concept are vulnerable to attack on grounds not so dependent on Hartshorne's own axioms. For example, the doctrines of the immutability and impassibility of God are both implied by and used to support the doctrine of relations developed by Aquinas. Hartshorne asks, quite justifiably, how these attributes can be reconciled with assertions of the love of God for the world. 'Complete non-relativity or immutability, and relations of loving, with contingent things as relata' are, he says, 'incompatible requirements' of the classical system,[11] while another classical theologian, Anselm, is forced to commit logical contortions

---

[10] 'Temporality and Finitism in Hartshorne's Theism', *Review of Metaphysics* 19 (1966) 550–64.
[11] *LP* 101.

when he tries to square the mercy and pity of God of which he knows with the lack of real concern that the concept requires.[12]

Related difficulties arise in connection with the classical conception of the perfection of God. True to his own lights, Hartshorne understands the idea of perfection experientially and aesthetically,[13] almost mathematically. An entity is perfect not, say, in its qualities of love or grace, but rather in that it has more experience of reality than another. 'This was indeed the old Platonic argument: the perfect, being complete or maximal in its value, could only change for the worse; but the capacity for such change being a defect, the perfect cannot change at all.'[14] Arguments of this kind, which appear to appeal to the quantitative perfection of God, still appear in the works of classical theists, and indeed it is difficult to understand how the metaphysical immutability or impassibility of God could be established in any other way.[15] Hartshorne continues to hold a quantitative view of perfection, but does not believe that the idea of a fixed totality is a possible one. First, if God is a subject as distinct from an object, then he must in some sense be subject to change. Second, the idea of a static and total perfection of experience does not admit of consistent realization. '. . . if all values are not "compossible", cannot all coexist, as seems an almost obvious truth, then a purely final or static perfection possessing all possible values is impossible.'[16] A fixed totality is impossible, because any given state of reality is necessarily exclusive of a number of other states of reality. No being can therefore experience every possible state of reality ('all possible values') at one and the same time. How can God experience this telephone as green as well as yellow?

Of course, the classical theist would immediately question what to him would seem to be the naïve view here held of the

---

[12] *PSG* 103 f.

[13] And perhaps he is not all that different from Aquinas: see *Summa Theologica* 1a.4.2.   [14] *AD* 29.

[15] See, e.g. H. P. Owen, *Concepts of Deity* (London, 1971), p. 23. Though the author is here speaking of immutability rather than perfection, the assumptions are the same: 'there is no form or degree of being that he can either acquire or lose.'

[16] *MVG* 21, cf. 'Reflections on the Strength and Weakness of Thomism', *Ethics* 54 (1943) 53, where Hartshorne argues that a being conceived as perfect in this sense could not add to reality, and so could not create.

relation between God and temporal phenomena. But on Hartshorne's view of the matter it is impossible, logically impossible, that God should be in perfect and actual possession not only of all that is actual, but of all that is possible as well. It is perfectly conceivable that an omniscient being should simultaneously perceive all that is real at any given time; but the idea of a timeless omniscience empties the ideas of necessity and possibility of all meaning.[17]

Traditional theism is found to generate difficulties also over the relation of the necessary and the contingent, and these difficulties are parallel to those involved in the notion of a static or timeless maximum of experienced reality. It was pointed out in the Introduction that supernaturalism's method of arriving at a concept of God by negating nature's characteristics entailed, among other things, that God is wholly necessary. Hartshorne accepts that if God is to be God, his existence must be necessary, but this is not to say that he is so in every respect. Necessity as traditionally conceived involves insuperable logical problems. If God is wholly necessary, then so are his acts of creation, and creation can in no sense be described as a free or contingent act. Logic demands either that we follow Spinoza and hold that everything happens by necessity,[18] or that we abandon one of the two following propositions:

'(i) God's action of willing simply *is* his character ("essence");
(ii) This action is free (he creates this world, but might have created a different one, or none.'[19]

But the classical theists wanted to maintain them both, and, as S. M. Ogden, following Hartshorne, has put it, 'if we take them at their own word, giving full weight to both of their assertions, we find ourselves in the hopeless contradiction of a wholly necessary creation of a wholly contingent world'.[20]

Elsewhere, and more characteristically, Hartshorne puts the problem of the relation of the necessary and the contingent in terms of knowledge rather than creation. Given the contingency of the world, or more specifically the fact that certain things have happened in or are true about the world that

---

[17] *MVG* 137, cf. *MVG* 121: 'The idea of "pure actuality" is the idea of the absolute realisation of potency where there is no potency to realise.'
[18] *PSG* 189 f.   [19] *RSP* 198.
[20] S. M. Ogden, *The Reality of God* (London, 1967), p. 17.

need not have happened or been true, must not the contents of the divine knowing be dependent—contingent—upon them? 'Thus he [God] knows that a certain world exists which might not have existed; but surely had it not existed, he would not have known it to exist; hence he has knowledge which he might not have had.'[21] Here, once again, it could be claimed that Hartshorne has been insufficiently subtle in conceiving of the relation between temporal phenomena and the divine knowledge that is outside time. But there can surely be no defence against the charge that a wholly necessary God and a free creation are logically incompatible. If God has to be free in order to create—or, for that matter, to reconcile, forgive, and redeem—then, however much the word *necessary* is qualified, it is impossible to reconcile this freedom with the demands of a thoroughgoing necessity.

ii. *Metaphysical*

Further philosophical difficulties arise from the view of reality underlying the doctrines of classical theism. Aquinas held that it was possible for the mind of man not only to comprehend rationally the unchanging 'being' of which the entities of our experience consist, but also to divide the material universe into individual substances, each of which could be classified in terms of genus and species and identified as a partially independent entity with its appropriate place in the hierarchy of being. The God of Aquinas's system was analogous to these separate entities, for it is they which form the starting-point of each of the Five Ways. He is vastly different, only known in what he is not, unchanged and unaffected by his relations with other entities, but none the less he is an object of thought like them.

This unique and infinite being became for Spinoza the whole universe, the one substance which was both God and material reality. Across the Channel the idea of substance suffered even more grievously at the hands of the British empiricists. For Locke the ideas of our experience are certainly supported by an underlying substance, but we can know nothing about its real nature. It is hardly surprising, then, that though this philosopher continues to rely on the cosmological argument, his

[21] *CSPM* 48.

formulation of it is so astoundingly vague and full of assumptions that go ill with the rest of his philosophy. Nor is it surprising that Locke's successor Berkeley made such short shrift of the vestiges of medieval realism that remain in Locke. The idea of substance as it appeared in Locke is easily shown by him to be a complete nonsense, capable of no coherent elucidation.[22]

This progressive weakening of the concept of substance has necessarily had its consequences for the way in which man thinks about the world. A modern philosopher like Ayer rejects the whole conception of philosophy; it is a waste of time to seek for entities that we cannot see, hear, taste, touch, or smell. Substance is one of these.[23] But while he rejects all attempts at a rational description of the world—*his* metaphysic is implicit and assumed—Process philosophers like Hartshorne wish to replace the notion of substance with an alternative metaphysical category, and one more in line with the way modern men look at the universe. Their contention is that physics has shown us the importance of the dynamic elements of the universe, its 'becoming'. The mistake of classical metaphysicians to favour 'being' or substance and to neglect becoming is not now excusable. Whereas the traditional way was to conceive events as 'the adventures of "things" or "persons" . . . science now considers nature as most fundamentally a complex of events related together in a space–time system.'[24]

The key categories are now to be event and relation, and in embarking on a programme to develop a metaphysic based on these terms, Hartshorne can claim, if not the actual justification of the programme, at least the support of the philosophical undermining of the traditional view, and its practical obsolescence.

iii. *Moral and Religious*

The criticisms of the tradition from the point of view of logic and the movement of thought would nearly all seem to have been well made. The attacks outlined in this section show Hartshorne hitting out in all directions, heaping obloquy on

[22] G. Berkeley, *Three Dialogues between Hylas and Philonous* (London, Everyman edn., 1910), pp. 229 ff.
[23] A. J. Ayer, *Language, Truth and Logic* (2nd edn., London, 1946), pp. 40, 42 f.
[24] *LP* 218 cf. *CSPM* 45 f.

the classical concept and blaming it as the cause of all kinds of moral distortions. But they have their underlying rationale, and sometimes strike the target. Basically they depend on the very reasonable point that if God is totally unrelated to the world, and, like the Epicurean gods, is totally unaffected by its suffering, the value of the created order is called in question, at least from the point of view of God.

First it is argued that if the reality of God remains unchanged whatever we do, there is really very little point in performing one act rather than another. Because 'traditional theism posits among the circumstances of all acts the existence of an absolutely perfect being', it would appear to follow 'that no act can, in its consequences, be better than any other', for the same unchanging reality remains in either case.[25] Here Hartshorne alludes to the conception of God's perfection, already outlined in § i above, as the sum total of reality, and would appear to make the point that, *sub specie aeternitatis*, as it were, no act of a finite being can make the slightest difference to the over-all state of affairs.

But, second, there are other charges to be laid than that of encouraging men to believe that ethical choice is of no ultimate importance. It has in fact encouraged them to regard themselves as something ultimate. If, it is argued, men's worship of God does not affect God, it can only be self-regarding. But man can never be something ultimate.[26] While this particular charge may appear to be rather far-fetched, there may be more substance in the related point that the notion of a self-sufficient God has tended to promote the cultivation of self-sufficiency in men as an ethical ideal[27] and 'the dangerous individualism of our Western world'.[28] Further, it is claimed, the idea of providence that has developed on the soil of classical theism 'has sometimes encouraged extreme conservatism . . . and sometimes doctrinaire progressivism . . .'[29]

Moreover, the cultural origins of this concept of God are not wholly respectable in the modern world, and reveal a relationship between God and man that is morally repugnant. The concept of a totally independent deity 'seems plainly an idealisation of the tyrant–subject relationship . . .'[30] Not only is it

[25] *MVG* 156.   [26] *DR* 130 f.   [27] *MVG* 160 f.   [28] *LP* 121.
[29] *MVG* 159 f.   [30] *DR* 44.

morally repugnant, but it contradicts basic insights of the Christian faith. 'How can anyone believe that being a follower of Jesus is like being an imitator of Aristotle's divine Aristocrat, who is serenely indifferent to the world's turmoil?'[31] If a defence is attempted along the lines of Anselm's that God is only compassionate in terms of our experience, but not of his, that 'is to mock us'.[32] Real compassion would seem to require genuine relation and even suffering. Otherwise, it is difficult to see how the compassion is anything but an act, a hollow sham.

The *cantus firmus* beneath all these points is Hartshorne's genuine and serious concern that the things men do and the choices they make should matter, particularly in the sense that they should make some real difference to the way things are. They should not merely be acts in some play that has been written from eternity, 'a single absolute world-plan, complete in every detail from eternity, and executed with inexorable power'.[33] What makes the situation worse is that there is no need to subscribe to the classical concept. As a matter of fact men have usually, throughout the history of religion, preferred what Hartshorne calls a dipolar conception of God. Like many of the terms already introduced in this chapter, what Hartshorne means by dipolar will become clearer as his positive doctrine is expounded. But, broadly speaking, what he means is that God is conceived to be such that in part of his being he is affected by the doings of other entities, and in particular that he is able to suffer with them, while in the other part he is such that his very existence cannot be threatened by what he suffers. He is indeed fully God in the security of his position in the universe, but this does not prevent him from participating in the lives of his creatures. The error of the classical theists is that in their concern for his godness, they stressed only one pole of the divine reality—their doctrine was *monopolar*—with the result that they neglected important aspects of what mankind has instinctively felt God to be.[34]

[31] Charles Hartshorne, 'The God of Religion and the God of Philosophy', *Talk of God*, ed. G. N. A. Vesey, (Royal Institute of Philosophy Lectures II, London, 1969), pp. 161 f.
[32] *DR* 55. For the reference to Anselm see *PSG* 103 f. [33] *LP* 205.
[34] See *PSG* 76–164, ch. 3, 'Classical Theism', *passim*. In this section the recurring judgement on the theists discussed is that their conceptuality is 'monopolar', and

If we examine the history of religion, and forget the dogmas on which traditional theism has been based, we shall see that the worshipper has in fact considered God to be dipolar rather than monopolar. Take, for example, the ancient religious thinkers who failed to conceptualize their beliefs philosophically, but whose understanding of God is distorted if it is forced into the classical mould. These early theists are represented by, among others, the pharaoh Ikhnaton, with his 'poetic outpourings',[35] the biblical writers, and Plato.[36] There are dipolar elements in them all, and Plato is held to be particularly important because in the final dialogues 'both categories—absolute fixity and absolute mobility—find expression'.[37] But, more important from the point of view of this study, we should note Hartshorne's judgement on the biblical writings.[38] Far from affirming a monopolar God, 'they often seem to imply a dipolar conception'.[39] But they are essentially naïve in what they affirm and must, we might say, be demythologized. For Hartshorne, and in this respect he has far more in common with the classical theologians than with Karl Barth, 'metaphorical expressions like "the wrath of God" or his "pity" ' may be characterized as 'wholly non-literal concessions to the weakness of the human understanding; still, it may be suggested that the minimum to be expressed by such metaphors is this: that God is not blankly neutral to the happenings in the world . . .'[40] God could not be supposed literally to love, pity, or be angry. The philosopher knows better. His very function is to provide a superior representation of the divine reality to the anthropomorphic, mythological representations of God in scripture. The error of the classical metaphysicians lies not in their undertaking a programme, but in their making a mess of it by their neglect of the second pole of the divine reality. Hartshorne believes that there is a test by which we can see the failure of their project. There should be a two-way relation between the 'religious' or uninterpreted ideas and the secular concepts employed by the philosopher. In the case of the classical

that had they found room for the other pole of the divine reality, their theology would not have been so distorted.

[35] *PSG* 29.   [36] *PSG* 29–57.   [37] *PSG* 54.   [38] *PSG* 34–8.
[39] *PSG* 38.   [40] *PSG* 34.

concept this is not so. While it may be possible to derive the religious tenets from the non-religious—though this is only possible 'after a fashion'—the reverse is not possible.[41]

In other words, it is not the function of the metaphysical theologian to force the intuitions of the worshipper into a procrustean bed of abstract ideas that have already been established *a priori*; rather, it is his job to purify the crude expressions of religion in such a way that there is a two-way logical relationship between the two sets of terms. The philosopher must reflect accurately, and indeed with a precision the original lacks, the beliefs of the ordinary religious person. Hartshorne thinks he has achieved this. In the dipolar doctrine of God 'the "personal" conception of deity required in religion is reconciled with the requirements of philosophic reason'.[42] In fact 'It is a belief of many today that the "new" theology is more, not less, religious than the old, at least if religion means "devoted love for a being regarded as superlatively worthy of love", which is the Christian conception and to some extent the conception of the higher religions generally.'[43]

So much then, for the chief objections of this philosopher to the doctrines of his predecessors. We move now to an exposition of his own 'neoclassical' conception. But some of the assumptions revealed in the previous paragraphs will have to be borne in mind. First, it appears to be assumed that there is, or could be, a single religious outlook that the philosopher can conceptualize, and, moreover that he can and must in a sense improve upon the original. Second, and specifically, Hartshorne appears to believe, rather than assume, that he can do a service for Christian theology. Does dipolar theism do what a Christian theology would require of it; does it, that is to say, do justice to the 'anthropomorphic' God of scripture, or does it, in the end, repeat the error of the classical theists?

[41] *MVG* 95 f., cf. 113.   [42] *DR* x.   [43] *MVG* 3.

II

A DIPOLAR DOCTRINE OF GOD

i. *The Possible Concepts of God*

IT is Hartshorne's contention that many of the errors of the classical era could have been avoided if the philosophers in question had only considered with an open mind all the possibilities offered to them. He himself believes that there are three main types of doctrine,[1] and claims that 'The almost complete overlooking of the second of the three main types of doctrine has some title to be called the greatest intellectual error mankind has ever made . . .'[2] That there are only three 'formally possible views' can, he believes, be shown by mathematical analysis, and by an elimination of those possibilities which are not, on examination, any more than theoretical possibilities. In approaching this analysis, however, it is more important that we should examine the assumptions made in it than that there should be a detailed exposition of all the possibilities. For there can be no doubt that Hartshorne does not produce by his method an exhaustive list of the possibilities for theistic belief. All depends upon his approach to classification, as is shown by the fact that H. P. Owen (for example), a classical theist, produces an entirely different method of classification, which yet finds room for Hartshorne's theism, as well as for various types of classical and other theist.[3] More important, Karl Barth's conception of God fits into none of Hartshorne's categories. As will be shown in the second major section of this study, it is as different from classical theism as is Hartshorne's, and in some ways more so.

The limitations of Hartshorne's approach derive from what has already been described as the quantitative conception of the divine perfection. It is as if the supremacy of God can only be understood in terms of the superiority of his experience or

---

[1] i.e. classical theism, neoclassical theism, and atheism.   [2] *MVG* 28.
[3] H. P. Owen, *Concepts of Deity* (London, 1971).

embrace of reality.[4] When, therefore, Hartshorne begins his analysis by asking about the possible meanings of the term 'God', he assumes that he can find them all simply by reflecting on the words 'perfection'[5] or 'greatness'[6] in the light of some such presupposition. This account of his method is confirmed by the word which he uses at the centre of his analysis of the terms. God is the 'unsurpassable'—and the word is the most characteristic of a cluster of terms that belong together in Hartshorne's concept—in his experience and possession of reality; that is the beginning and the end of the ways of God for neoclassical theology.

By definition the unsurpassable will be *in possession of* more reality than any other entity. How does he come into possession? The classical God, of course, was not conceived to come into possession at all, because he eternally *is* all that he is, the most real being. But, as we have seen, Hartshorne believes this to be logically incoherent, and just as his rejection of it derives from his belief that there is no knowledge without relation,[7] so here perfection lies in superiority of experience of reality. That superiority is obtained, if we may anticipate later exposition, by a kind of omniscient perception, a perception understood after the manner of Locke[8] and Berkeley, who appear to conceive the mind to be a kind of container for the ideas that are presented to it in experience. Despite their differences Locke and Berkeley both hold the mind to receive its ideas as the result of outside agency, and although Hartshorne does not share their use of the term 'idea', he does maintain the notion of outside agency and the belief that the mind is a container of what it perceives. It is the latter of these doctrines that concerns us now, and evidence for it can be found in a passage where he attacks 'the view that mind does not literally include its objects . . .'[9] God, the mind that is omniscient, will therefore include or contain everything. That this, too, is Hartshorne's teaching is revealingly demonstrated in his reply

---

[4] Notice Kant's summary characterization of the God of rational theism, the *ens realissimum*, beginning, 'By this complete possession of all reality . . .', *Critique of Pure Reason*, tr. by F. M. Müller (New York, 1966), p. 389.

[5] *MVG* 6, *LP* 4.   [6] *AD* 25 f.   [7] Ch. I, § i, above.

[8] See especially the metaphor of 'the yet empty cabinet', *An Essay Concerning Human Understanding*, I. ii. 15.

[9] *DR* 111 f.

to an objection by W. A. Christian that his classification of concepts of God is not exhaustive. He says: 'To be conditioned by *is* to include, *according to my logic*.'[10] On his understanding, then, God is unsurpassable as an *experiencer or container of reality*; and the claim is that only dipolar theism can make coherent sense of this notion.

But the claim can only be established by the elimination of rival candidates for the title of the 'unsurpassable', and that, in turn, waits upon the elucidation of the different possible meanings of the term.[11] The various senses can be set out by dividing the term up into its two logical components—'none' and 'greater'—and by showing that there are variations of meaning in each of the two. First, the negative 'none' is that which excludes any other entity from rivalry with God. The exclusion could be of two possible kinds. (i) God might be absolutely unsurpassable, already in a state of total and static perfection, as the tradition has believed. He cannot even improve upon himself, because he is already everything he can be. But (ii) he might also be unsurpassable in that he cannot be surpassed by anything else, but can himself admit of experience beyond his present reality. This latter is described as 'relative perfection' as opposed to the 'absolute perfection' of the former possibility.[12] Second, the word 'greater' admits of three meanings, and if they are each taken into account, it transpires that God cannot be surpassed (i) in some (but not all) respects, (ii) in all respects, or (iii) in no respects.[13]

Hartshorne then combines the two components of the term 'unsurpassable' in all the mathematically possible ways, and, after eliminating those meanings that are obviously trivial or nonsensical, emerges with three possibilities. First, 'There is a being in *all* respects absolutely perfect or unsurpassable, in no way and in no respect surpassable or perfectible.'[14] This is classical theism, that is, the God who contains within himself all actual and all potential reality as actuality, the wholly necessary being. Second, 'There is no being in all respects absolutely perfect; but there is a being in *some* respect or respects thus perfect . . . in some respects surpassable,

---

[10] 'Interrogation of Charles Hartshorne', *Philosophical Interrogations* edd. S. and B. Rome (New York, 1964), p. 343. My italics in the second clause.
[11] *MVG* 6–12.   [12] *MVG* 7.   [13] *MVG* 7 f.   [14] *MVG* 11.

whether by self or others being left open.'[15] It is a version of this that Hartshorne is going to espouse, when once he has established in what respects this being may be said to be surpassable. The third possibility is that 'There is no being in *any* respect absolutely perfect . . .'[16] Under this heading come 'Doctrines of a merely finite God, polytheism in some forms, atheism'.[17]

The first option has already, as we have seen, been excluded as impossible; Hartshorne hopes to be able to exclude the third, especially in its atheist version, by establishing the rationality and existence of a being in the second class. But first, this class must be looked at more closely, for various options appear to be possible within it.[18] However, this does not detain Hartshorne long, for all but one entail the attribution to God of imperfection in some form or other, and so are automatically excluded as definitions of perfection. There remains the concept of God that holds God to be 'Absolute perfection in *some* respects, relative perfection in all others.'[19]

ii. *The Twin Poles of the Divine Reality*

It is here that we come to the first step in distinguishing the two poles of the 'dipolar' God of neoclassical theism. First, God is absolutely perfect *in some respects*. Precisely what these respects are must await a later section, for here we are simply concerned to show how God can be conceived to have two poles to his reality. The absolute perfection describes one pole; Hartshorne does not wish to quarrel with the old theology's equating of the perfect and the absolute, so long as it is made clear in what limited sense God is correctly so described. In one of his poles, God is as classical theology described him: he is absolute. But what of the second pole, 'relative perfection' in the other respects? How can what is relative be perfect? The answer is that it can be perfect in its relativity. Hartshorne describes it thus, that 'in no possible state of affairs can there be anything in any fashion superior to God as he is in that same state of affairs'.[20] More simply, it can be expressed as follows. To be is to know; to know is to be relative to other entities; no entity can rival the perfect being in relativity, for none can have greater perfection of experience than the omniscient. And so

[15] *MVG* 12.   [16] Ibid.   [17] Ibid.   [18] Listed, *MVG* 8.
[19] *MVG* 8.   [20] *MVG* 48.

God is, in his two poles, supremely absolute and supremely relative, in the meanings of those terms that have previously been expounded.

It is possible to express the divine dipolarity in a second way, if we follow up the doctrine mentioned in the previous section, that our minds receive what they perceive through outside agency. Here we have manifestly an instance of what is known as the causal theory of perception. Our perceptions are the effects of causes outside ourselves.[21] 'The very idea of perception as a form of knowledge is that of a one-way dependence upon an independent reality. . . . In other words, the perceiving is an effect.'[22] A corollary of this doctrine, for Hartshorne at any rate, is that omniscience will necessarily receive more causal influences than anything else.

Traditionally, of course, God has been conceived to be the very opposite of this, the supreme uncaused cause who is free from every trace of 'effectness'. But once again Hartshorne asks us to examine all the options in the cause–effect spectrum. 'The highest cause may be (1) in *every* sense or aspect "uncaused", in no sense or aspect the effect of anything else; or it may be (2) in *some* aspects uncaused, and in others causally influenced . . . or . . . (3) in *no* sense or aspect uncaused. . . .'[23] Option two is the one that Hartshorne prefers. In the light of his doctrine of relations, the first is illogical and impossible, while the second is the necessary outcome of the way he conceives God to be related to the world. By another route, therefore, we have arrived at a concept of a God who is essentially dipolar: in some respects uncaused, or he would not be God; in others caused, and uniquely so, because of the range of influences to which his omniscience exposes him.

By combining the two dipolar descriptions, Hartshorne is in a position to present in summary form his concept of God, and he does this in the epilogues to two of his books.[24] It is above all an inclusive concept of God, in that it brings together most of the things that have been said about God throughout the metaphysical tradition, and that it conceives God as essentially

---

[21] Classically, in Berkeley, they are all the direct result of the divine agency. Here that doctrine is stood upon its head.
[22] *CSPM* 217, cf. 106.   [23] *MVG* 26.
[24] *MVG* 347–52 and *PSG* 499–514.

the one who includes the world within his reality. That is to say, there is both a linguistic and an ontological inclusiveness about the concept of God. Ontologically speaking, God the absolute-and-relative combine into a conception of God as 'Creator-and-the-Whole-of-what-he-has-created'.[25] If, on the other hand, we turn our attention to the language in which God is described, we find that Hartshorne's concept represents an attempt to make a more comprehensive use of the concepts that metaphysicians have developed in speaking about the world and God. It is in the light of his beliefs about language that Hartshorne can accuse the classical metaphysicians of being 'monopolar' in taking account in their theology of only one side of the pairs of concepts available to them. For the moment this can be put hypothetically. If one of a pair of linguistic (Hartshorne would say, *categorical*) contrasts, like cause or absoluteness, is predicated of God there is no reason *a priori* why the other should not also be predicated. If both sides of the contrasting pairs we have been examining—relative/ absolute and effect/cause—are predicated we obtain a fuller picture of God (or a picture of a fuller God!)[26] than one side alone can provide. Of the three types of 'perfection' that are possible only one, what can be termed panentheism as distinct from traditional theism and pantheism, 'has the advantage of synthesizing all the positive principles of the entire table. If there be a "higher synthesis" or golden mean with respect to the extremes, it seems this must be it'.[27] Only the neoclassical concept takes to itself our fundamental metaphysical language in all its meaning.

In other words, this is not for Hartshorne a hypothetical or experimental matter. His are not the assumptions of the classical negative theology which sets out deliberately to neglect one side of the categorical contrasts that he wishes to combine. Rather, he believes that a doctrine of God should include all the ultimate categories, and that it is a sign of its truth if it does. There is what he calls a 'Law of Polarity', which really is a law for thought, demanding that we take into account both aspects of a polar pair when we think metaphysically.[28]

---

[25] *MVG* 348.
[26] He has sometimes been unkindly described as 'the cocktail God'.
[27] *PSG* 512. [28] *PSG* 1–15.

Most schools of theism have neglected this law,[29] and, indeed, *Philosophers Speak of God* is a book devoted to the examination of different concepts of God to see whether the law has been kept; that is to say, to see whether the picture that is drawn of God by various philosophers is as rich as it might be, or whether it includes the kind of monopolar vices that have already been observed to infect the classical concept. But what are these polar categories, and how should they be predicated of God?

iii. *The Categories and God*

Hartshorne makes little or no attempt to list systematically the categories that are to be attributed to God;[30] it is almost as if it were taken to be self-evident that once the kind of possibilities that were outlined in §§ i and ii above have been discussed, and the neoclassical concept isolated as the only serious contender for consideration, the rest of the attributes would be seen to follow automatically. That this is to a large extent the case is shown by the fact that the attributes of Hartshorne's God are precisely those which an omniscient being must have if he is related to the world in the way in which this system holds. Our procedure then must be first to outline Hartshorne's way of describing God, the language, and what it means; and second to see the function of God in relation to the rest of reality. Chapter III presents an account of the beliefs about the nature of the world upon which the whole enterprise depends.

The concept of God is built up through the deployment of a cluster of terms that are logically interrelated and belong in complementary pairs. The two pairs of terms that control the meaning of all the others are absolute/relative and abstract/concrete. On the face of it, it is contradictory to say that God is both relative and absolute, and there are those who claim that neoclassical theology is for that reason internally inconsistent.[31] Indeed, Hartshorne would recognize the potential inconsistency: does he not teach precisely that the relative is internally, the absolute externally related, the one being that which knows, the other that which is known? Clearly it is contra-

---

[29] *PSG* 2 f.
[30] Though see *CSPM* 100 f. for a table of 'metaphysical contraries'.
[31] e.g. H. P. Owen, *The Christian Knowledge of God* (London, 1969), pp. 105 f.

dictory for something to be both absolute and relative in the same respect. But the claim of neoclassical theology is that God is relative and absolute in different aspects of his being.

And this brings us to the second of the controlling pairs of terms. God has both concrete and abstract aspects to his reality. In his concrete aspects he is relative; if he knows the world, then he is related to it. Moreover, if he knows the world as God, he knows all of it, and he knows it concretely—at any given moment.[32] But if he is related to all of it, then, *abstractly speaking*, he is absolutely related to it, and so in another aspect of his being he is absolute in relation to the world. He is then relative and absolute in different aspects[33] of his being, that is to say, depending upon how we are considering him. But it is not just a matter of aspect. A necessary inference from what has been said is that God is only absolute *because he is relative* to the whole of reality; in other words, his absoluteness *consists in* his all-embracing relativity. The most real thing about God is his relativity; this is ontologically and logically prior, and the absoluteness is a necessary implication of the relativity. Abstract qualities can only be understood in the light of the concrete, which describe what God *really is*.

This is an important inference, and will be shown to have crucial implications for the neoclassical concept of God. But as the inference, that God's absoluteness consists in his relativity, has not been explicitly made by Hartshorne,[34] its grounds and meaning must be examined. There are a number of passages where Hartshorne discusses the relation of the relative and the absolute. For example, in commenting on the work of Radhakrishnan, he objects to a passage that 'suggests that the absolute as such is *more* than the supreme as relative to the world. But the logical construction is rather that the absolute as such is an empty abstraction, a mere ingredient in the richness of actuality, worldly or divine.'[35] That is to say, God is first of all relative, and only absolute because he is relative. Similarly,

---

[32] This means exactly what it says.

[33] The term is Hartshorne's own: see e.g. *PSG* 15.

[34] But see *CSPM* 26 and 'Introduction' to *Philosophers of Process*, ed. D. Browning (New York, 1965), p. xix, where Hartshorne speaks of 'defining' one pole 'in terms of' the other; and *CSPM* 118 where he says that 'we can find' the one in the other.

[35] *PSG* 310.

using the letter R to stand for the relative pole of the divine reality and A for the absolute, he says '. . . R implies A as an abstractable aspect of its own meaning. . . . Thus A is required as self-identical aspect of what, in the respects in which it is not A, is R.'[36] Or again, '. . . the non-reflexive or non-relative is the necessary element of abstract identity required by the concrete, relative or changing'.[37] This is in stark contrast to the classical concept. While 'the absolute' provides a summary description of what this God is, for Hartshorne God's absoluteness is no more than his 'necessary element of abstract identity'.

When we move to other of the divine attributes, the same is found to hold. A corollary of God's being relative to the world is that he will know the world as contingent, and hence will have contingent elements or contents.[38] (Naturally, as it is the know*er* who is affected by the objects of knowledge, the contents of God's knowledge at any given time will be contingent or dependent upon the state of the world at the time.) Therefore, just as God *is* relative, so he is contingent, in his concrete reality; in fact, he is 'the supremely contingent being, in a certain sense the most contingent of all'.[39] And so God, in respect of his contents as a supreme knowing mind, is contingent. Contents may vary, and must do if the world is a contingent process. But, abstractly considered, God is not contingent but necessary, in fact the sole necessary being, for he *must* know infallibly all that is and was, and will know everything that will be, when it comes to take place. And so God's necessity consists in his contingency. He knows what he knows necessarily, and supreme contingency is seen to be necessary contingency.

A similar type of argument establishes the polarity of variety or multiplicity and integrity or simplicity. Because God knows and contains the whole complex world, he is complex; but as a single knowing consciousness, he is simple. His simplicity consists in the fact of his unique complexity, just as, to use an analogy from aesthetics that Hartshorne takes very seriously, the most beautiful unity can be claimed to be unity in variety. 'The most generally recognised principle of beauty, in art and in nature, is the principle of organic unity,

[36] *PSG* 508.   [37] *RSP* 115.   [38] *MVG* 132.
[39] 'The Philosophy of Creative Synthesis', *Journal of Philosophy* 55 (1958), 953.

or unity in variety.'[40] In interpreting this doctrine it must be borne in mind that concretely God is complex and only abstractly is he simple or a unity. Hartshorne emphasizes that although 'It does no harm to conceive the unchanging or abstract aspect of God as simple', the important thing to notice is that 'it is this concrete whole which possesses the value and hence deserves the name of God'.[41] Here it might appear that Hartshorne is in danger of contravening his own law of relations, and making the knowing subject, the agent unifying the complexity, into the abstract or known element. But this would be to misunderstand. As knowing subject, God is complex; and uniquely so, because of his unique clarity and scope of knowledge.[42] The simplicity is an abstraction not only from the content, but also from the successive occasions of the divine knowing. For all the divine attributes have to be understood as predicated of the God who is moving along with the world process. And this brings us naturally to another pair of attributes. This God is eternal not by virtue of being the creator of time, or by being in some way outside time or timeless; he is eternal only in abstraction from his involvement in time. He is eternal because he is necessarily temporal: 'in full possession in every present of all that is past to this present, and in this sense supertemporal or eternal . . .'[43] His eternity consists in his supreme temporality. Other corollaries are that God is infinite precisely because he is involved in all finitude; and that his being consists in becoming, and, more than that, that his being *is* becoming. For he 'is' only in abstraction from the becoming that takes place in him as the container[44] and unifying agent of the process as it rolls on its way.[45]

Here we have an instructive instance of neoclassical theology's reversal of the categories of the tradition. God is essentially not pure being but pure becoming. Only when this aspect of his reality has been established can we go on to speak

---

[40] *MVG* 212. [41] *MVG* 217 f. [42] *AD* 164.

[43] *PSG* 146. This doctrine has some strange consequences. 'Our God had no relevance for Abraham, for there was no such deity coexistent with Abraham.' Reply to 'Interrogation of Charles Hartshorne', *Philosophical Interrogations*, edd. S. and B. Rome, p. 353.

[44] It could perhaps be said that he is the personification of Newtonian absolute space/time, the container in which things happen.

[45] *PSG* 8, 'Introduction' to Browning, p. xix.

about 'being'. The classical mistake, here and elsewhere, was to reify the abstract;[46] neoclassicism puts the abstract in its proper place, subordinate to the concrete reality of God's becoming-in-relativity.

So far, then, we have seen how the pairs, relative/absolute, concrete/abstract, contingent/necessary, multiple/simple, temporal/eternal all imply each other in the one concept, and all provide descriptions of the two poles of the divine reality, with, however, the second pole logically and ontologically subordinate to the first. It should be becoming apparent that the conceptuality works against a background of an unusual view of God's relation to reality. Both sides of the attributes can only be predicated of a God who is necessarily involved in the cosmic process, and who, in a sense, *is* the process. (More of that later.) Thus, the placing of God in the time process makes intelligible the successive quality of the divine knowing, and the relation between time and eternity. Eternity just is infinite time, and this conception of God is designed to meet the difficulties involved in showing the relations with the temporal world of a God conceived to be timeless or eternal by virtue of his contrast to time.

Other attributes are understood in the same way. If God is related to the world in such a way that the world's contingent contents are all the time altering the reality of the divine experience, then God is essentially mutable. But because he is open to the reception of all that occurs, he is uniquely mutable, and so has an immutable element or pole. His capacity for being changed cannot change, and so he is immutably mutable. Abstractly, his character as being open to whatever happens is not open to change at all.[47] And if we shift the conception into time, there is a similar point to be made. The past also is immutable, as that which is fixed and gone, and also externally related to us, the new occasions of experience. God contains this past, and so the past serves to make up the immutable pole of his being.

The abstract pole is therefore both the logical outcome of an analysis of the concrete pole, as we have seen throughout this section, *and* the ontological outcome of God's movement

[46] *RSP* 110–25, especially 114 f.   [47] *MVG* 110.

through time. Therefore the term *abstract* has a double meaning in Hartshorne, as is also revealed in the analysis of another polar pair, potential/actual. Concretely, God is potential; abstractly, he is actual. This is best understood in the light of the rejection of the classical doctrine, as Hartshorne understands it, that God experiences all actuality and all potentiality as actualized in his immediate experience. Once God is conceived as being in the process, what is actual is seen to be the present and the past; any omniscient being will of course know or remember all of that. But the future is not yet actual, even for God, and is therefore *possible* (however much its possibilities may be restricted by the immediately preceding present). This avoids the contradictions involved in classical theology: 'How can there be a contradiction in the idea of a knowledge of all actuality and of all possibility?'[48]

Let us look very carefully at the implications of this potential/actual polarity. Concretely, God is potential. This means that in his being, at any given time, he provides all the possibilities on which the process will build; offers them, as it were, to the future. How does he do this? By virtue of the fact that he is, abstractly speaking, the totality of all actuality that has taken place until now. He is the infallible and all-embracing memory or container of the sum of past and present experience. To put it another way round: he is internally related to the past and the present. Indeed, if he experiences the present on the model Hartshorne has himself developed,[49] of the immediately preceding past, then in his concrete reality he faces backwards, to the past. He is, concretely speaking, that which *is now experiencing* all of the past, including the immediately disappearing present. He is therefore externally related to oncoming reality, that is, the future. New realities experience him *as the one who has remembered the past*. Like Moses in the cleft of the rock, they see only his disappearing back.

iv. *Abstract and Concrete in God*

At this stage a number of observations can be made. The first is that Hartshorne acknowledges that both sides of the categorical poles are in fact abstract descriptions of God. To say that God is mutable is to give as abstract a description as to say that he is

48 *MVG* 322.   49 See above, pp. 13f.

immutable. The difference lies in what we conceive God to be when we use the different abstract terms about him. There are then three things to say about God and the way he is described in neoclassical terminology:

   (i) that he is in fact related to everything that is actual at any given time;

  (ii) that to say (i) is to give an abstract description of his concrete reality; and

 (iii) that there is a further element, God's abstract pole, to be described, and the resulting descriptive language is an abstract description of God's abstract reality.

In the following passage Hartshorne makes the point the other way round, beginning with the abstract pole: '. . . besides the absolute element in deity there would be two other elements or aspects. These are: the relative element as such, that is, the generic quality of divine relativity; but also the specific divine relationships to specific actual things or world states.'[50] This brings into even sharper relief the fact that priority is on the side of the concrete pole: it is from what is believed to be the case concretely (e.g. that God is now related to all reality) that the dipolar description of him is abstracted. Hartshorne is explicit: 'The contrast of being–becoming, absolute–relative, necessary–contingent is contained as a whole in becoming, relativity, contingency' and not in the other pole of the contrast.[51] Or, as he says, 'becoming is reality itself, and being only an aspect of this reality'.[52] This provides yet further confirmation for the inference that God's absoluteness, being, etc., *consist in* his relativity, becoming, etc.

The second observation concerns the apparently polar categories of good and evil. If we are to assert that they both hold of God, does not this make nonsense of any claim that God is love? In any case, they appear to be in contradiction, in a way that relative and absolute are not. It hardly makes sense to say that God is good in his present reality but bad as containing the past, or that his goodness consists in his badness, or vice versa. It is clear that here we have an altogether different pair of terms. In the first place, evil is not a category,

[50] *RSP* 169 f., cf. *CSPM* 100.
[51] 'Whitehead and Berdyaev', *Journal of Relig on* 37 (1957) 76.
[52] 'The Philosophy of Creative Synthesis', *Journal of Philosophy* 55 (1958) 946.

for it is not universal. 'For example, the animals are incapable of it, because of their unconsciousness of principles.'[53] In the second place, there is a sense in which evil can be ascribed to God, though not in the doing so much as in the suffering of it. We must, therefore, distinguish between moral and aesthetic evil. When I perform a morally evil act, God suffers this, and for him it becomes aesthetic evil, something that hurts him but does not damage him in the sense that it damages me. God suffers pain when we abuse our moral freedom, and thus all evil is to him aesthetic evil.[54] However universal, then, is God's *experience* of evil, it is not a category, in the sense of being part of the essential structure of his being.

The third observation concerns two pairs of attributes that have not yet been given full consideration: cause and effect, and passivity and its polar opposite or opposites. Concretely, God as containing the world is the effect of the world process. This follows from the supreme divine relativity in exactly the same way as do the other concrete attributes. Everything that happens is experienced by God, and therefore makes him what he is. For he is the one who contains and therefore is the whole of the process to date. In what sense then can God be described as the supreme cause? The statements made about this are not always unambiguous. 'The meaning of causation is that, where there was previously only the potentiality of a certain value, there is now the actuality of this value.'[55] That is to say, we say that causality has operated where something once might have been but now is. The fact that this definition is taking causation in its weakest sense is brought out if we take a concrete example. 'God caused the walls of Jericho to fall down.' That is to say, 'The walls of Jericho were once in a state of possibly falling down, but now they are in ruins about our feet.' Hartshorne's definition is noteworthy for the fact that it lacks any reference to agency. Even if we take a less contentious example, one not involving anthropomorphic agency, it would appear to demand more than has there been conceded to it. 'The impact of the bullet caused the glass to

---

[53] *PSG* 15.
[54] 'Whitehead's idea of God', *The Philosophy of Alfred North Whitehead*, ed. P. Schillp (Evanston and Chicago, 1941), p. 522.
[55] *PSG* 221.

shatter.' Whatever difficulties may be raised in the light of Hume's critique, it is surely not enough to say that this means, that is, is the precise equivalent of, 'the glass once was shatterable, now is shattered'. We must at least ask what is meant by the addition of some such phrase as 'by the bullet'.

These examples are used to highlight the difficulty in which Hartshorne finds himself. He has to make sense of the claim that the supreme effect is also, in his other pole, the supreme cause. And his chief stumbling-block is, as we shall see, the ascription of agency, or something like it, to God. 'God as supreme (in the sense of universal) cause is what is universally required by other things and which itself requires only that the class of other things be not null.' Then he spots a possible objection: 'Perhaps this does imply that God, *qua* universal or supreme cause, is not concrete but abstract.' If Hartshorne is going to remain true to the relation of concrete and abstract in God that has obtained in every other pair of attributes, then of course that is what it implies. If God is essentially effect, then he can only be cause in abstraction from this. But rather than admit that this is so he puts up, in this particular passage, what can only be described as a smoke-screen. To justify this charge, the passage must be quoted at some length.

I have not said that God is only the supreme cause; therefore though this cause may be abstract, God in his total reality may yet be concrete. . . . In this concreteness he may indeed be effect as well as cause, which means that he may require other things than himself to be just what he concretely and in fact is. . . .

Taken concretely, deity would not be merely supreme cause but rather supreme power or agency, in the sense in which a man is a power or agency . . . God as an agent or power is not, perhaps, to be conceived as *a* cause of all things, nor yet as *the* cause of all things, but rather as a (or *the*) supreme chain of causation which at the same time is the supreme stream of effects.

After taking examples from human actions considered as causes and effects, Hartshorne completes the discussion of divine causality by saying that 'on the one hand, universal cause, pure cause, need not exhaust the sense in which God is cause, while, on the other hand, there is no absurdity in this idea of pure cause, *provided its concreteness is not asserted*'.[56] Whatever

[56] *PSG* 501 f. My italics in the final clause.

the difficulties and ambiguities of the passage, one thing is clear: the final clause represents the logical demands of the dipolar concept. If cause and effect in God are polar opposites, and if God as effect is concrete, then God as cause, however that be understood, must be abstract. It is difficult to see how a cause can be abstract, in any recognizable meaning of the word, but in an early work Hartshorne is quite explicit: '. . . on our view, God as efficient cause is past . . . while as effect he is present, and as eternal final cause he is abstract.'[57]

This division into efficient and final cause of the absolute pole complicates the matter, but it does at least serve to illustrate and clarify the double function performed by the term 'abstract' in Hartshorne's conceptuality. As efficient cause, God is past. That is to say, he causes things to happen in virtue of his pastness, his external relatedness to the realities that are future to him. Thus he is efficient cause not in an active sense, but as providing a fund of reality on which the future may draw. As resources for the future, he brings things about. As final cause, he is abstract in the sense of *logically* absolute. *The fact that* he is supreme effect exercises 'final' causality, injects a sense of purposiveness into things. That would seem to mean, at the very least, that the very fact that there is a God of the kind Hartshorne describes entails that there is meaning and direction in the universe. But at this stage, the important point to notice is that God appears in both senses of the word to exercise causality in respect of his abstract rather than his concrete pole.

This suggests that there is at the heart of this concept of God not so much a contradiction as a fatal flaw, in which it is comprehensively hoist with its own petard. It can best be elucidated, before we return to the discussion of causality in the next section, by moving to a related pair of attributes. A further implication of the relativity and mutability of God, derived from his capacity to experience all the world's suffering and misery, is that he be conceived as supremely passive in his concrete reality. But what is the polar opposite of passivity? There are two candidates for the position, impassibility and activity. A difficulty must immediately be apparent, for the two appear to be incompatible to say the least. If, then, the logic of the concept entails that they are but different names for the same attribute, then we face the problem of making intelligible the notion of this deity's activity. The problem is exactly parallel to that of conceiving God to be cause in so far as he is effect.

What is the polar opposite of God's supreme passivity? On the analogy of immutability being the abstract pole of the divine mutability, the natural term would be impassibility. Because God suffers everything that happens, nothing can happen that will upset his capacity to do so. His capacity to suffer cannot suffer. But the polar opposite that is most frequently used is *activity*. Hartshorne often says that God is passive as well as active (though if he is to be true to the priority of the concrete pole, he should say active as well as passive). For example, in one context he argues that God's existence should 'be construed with polar fairness, as involving an essential, not merely accidental passivity as well as activity . . .'[58] That he is himself uncomfortable here is suggested by another passage in which he confuses his own position by reversing the places of the two poles: 'contemporary theology ascribes to God, with full deliberateness, supreme sensitivity, that is passivity, not as contradictory of supreme activity, but as a necessary aspect of it.'[59] But this will not do. According to the logic of the position, it is passivity that is concrete and therefore ontologically prior, and activity that is an (abstract) aspect of it, not the reverse as Hartshorne here implies. It is an implication of the logic of Hartshorne's position that the concrete reality of God is passive, and supremely so.

This can only mean that the activity of God is abstract. The notion of abstract activity is a difficult one, but does become a little more intelligible when we remember that abstract for Hartshorne means also that which includes the past. Once again, we appear to emerge with a concept of a God who acts by facing backwards. But there are other problems as well. If it is true that polar opposites come in pairs, and if they are logically precluded from coming in, say, threes, as they appear to be in this system, and if, further, there are two possible ways of expressing the polar opposite of passivity

[58] *PSG* 84, cf. *CSPM* 277, *PSG* 482.   [59] *MVG* 273.

or passibility, then those two ways must be identical in their meaning. Impassibility and activity are two ways of describing the one pole, and they mean exactly the same. Therefore God's activity *is* his impassibility: he acts only in so far as he is impassible. This is precisely the kind of complaint that Hartshorne makes against the classical deity: how can a motionless deity create freely? And so, by turning the classical concept on its head, this philosopher has presented us with a kind of coincidence of opposites. Instead of the unmoved mover, he has achieved the conception of an equally ineffective deity: the moved unmover.

v. *How Does God Act?*

The conclusion of the previous section can be supported by other aspects of the logic of the dipolar God. We have seen that Hartshorne has divided God's (abstract) causality into efficient and final cause. This corresponds to the double meaning of abstract or absolute into past and logical external relatedness. As pure or final cause, God acts by virtue of his abstract pole *qua* totally independent and abstract; as efficient cause he acts by virtue of it as containing the whole past, as it happens to be at the moment in question. In the light of the doctrine of relations, it can be seen that, as the process proceeds, what is concrete now will be absolute or abstract (because 'drawn away' by the process rather than by an act of conception, and because, once past, it becomes immutable) in respect of the events which succeed it.[60] To return to the example used at the beginning of this exposition, the philosopher's perception of the woodpecker is a momentary event in which he is internally related to another entity. But once that moment is past, it becomes part of his experience, and so externally related to later events in his personal history in which he recalls the perception. And so, his past experience can act causally on him by influencing some aspects of his future behaviour.

God's memory is the source of causation by virtue of containing two classes of entity. First, he is cause ('pure cause') as the source of all the totally abstract, ideal possibilities on which any state of the world must draw. Clearly, as omniscient mind he will be aware of, and so the source of, all those things

60 *CSPM* 108 f.

that might happen or come to be in any world. This is similar to the doctrine, developed by combining belief in a single God with platonic thought, that God's mind is the receptacle of the 'forms' or 'ideas', the ideal possibilities for action and realization in matter. But second, God's causality is not only timeless, like that of the platonic forms. For what is possible now is different from what was possible in the universe ten million years ago. The divine memory contains far more now than it did then. And so God is efficient cause at any given time as containing the whole of universal experience up to that time. The doctrine is that the present state of reality affects but does not determine the next. Both sides of the doctrine are well summed up in this passage: 'We must . . . distinguish between "pure" or eternal possibilities, and spatio-temporally localized possibilities: what is possible in a given time and place. The pure possibilities are *wholly* rational. . . . But what is possible here and now depends upon what has previously happened, including the arbitrary decisions previously made.'[61] Here it must be emphasized that God is not conceived as acting upon the world from outside, in any sense of the word. He is not independent of the world except as containing the two types of reality that have been described. 'For the concrete character of God and the concrete unity of the cosmos are the same.'[62] And so it is God's abstract pole and such causality that it exercises that prevent this doctrine from collapsing into an unrelieved pantheism, and that only. An implication of this is that the weaker the sense in which God is said to 'act' on the world, the nearer to pantheism does neoclassical theism become.

The discussion of the causality of Hartshorne's God can be summed up in the statement that God is cause as he is known by us or by other entities in the world, as he is externally related to us: he is cause as he is in our immediate past. The question then arises, Does God actually *do* anything other than act as the recipient of the cosmic activity, and so exercise causality indirectly in this way? Does he in any sense so transform the data that he receives that better rather than worse possibilities may be realized in the future? According to some assertions,

[61] *AD* 185.
[62] 'Santayana's Doctrine of Essence', *The Philosophy of George Santayana*, ed. P. Schillp (Evanston and Chicago, 1941), p. 180.

apparently so. In discussing the problem of induction, Hartshorne says, for example, that 'an ideally clear mind . . . will obviously have the power and the will to limit the disorder among its presented contents'.[63] But how does it perform the relatively restricted task of 'limiting disorder'? In speaking of what he calls the 'radical control' by God of the cosmos, which, he says, is his 'internal environment', Hartshorne claims that 'It follows from the concept of the divine essence that the divine experience sums up with unique adequacy all the value of the entire actual world, and hence each thing can look to it for guidance and inspiration.'[64] But this gets us nowhere, first because the expression 'sums up' is far too vague to provide any solution to the problems raised by the logic of the concept, and second because it begs the question. For we are not at present concerned with whether or not we can look to God for guidance, but with whether God can and does actually do anything to, for example, make reality other than it is. If he does not, then are we to assume that everything in the universe is satisfactory as it is, and God merely that which validates the state of things? We can, of course, look to a map for guidance, but a map is passive. Or, to change the metaphor, we can ask the question that brings us to the heart of the problems raised by this concept of God, of whether God is any more than a memory.

At times Hartshorne claims that he is more than a cosmic memory, but at others seems to bow before the logic of the position that as cause God can (*logically* can) only be the essence of passivity. Evidence for the former position is never unequivocal, and comes in passages like that in *The Divine Relativity* entitled 'Causal Adequacy or Divine Power'.[65] This adequacy or power he holds to be 'power to do for the cosmos . . . all desirable things that could be done and need be done by one universal or cosmic agent', and it consists in setting 'conditions which are maximally favourable to desirable decisions on the part of local agents'.[66] Of course, we know this already, for conditions are set by the ideal possibilities in the mind of God and by the past in his memory. But is that all? Since, according

---

[63] 'Ideal Knowledge Defines Reality: What was True in Idealism', *Journal of Philosophy* 43 (1946) 582.
[64] *AD* 293 f.   [65] *DR* 134–42.   [66] *DR* 134 f.

to the logic of the position, *as Hartshorne himself realizes*, anything further could be achieved only by altering those data on which local agents base their decisions, that is, the data in their immediate past, 'The question then becomes, how can he alter . . . the object of our awareness?'[67] How indeed, as the past is by definition past, and therefore immutable. It is now suggested that God can achieve the necessary alteration by altering himself, because it is he that is the 'total object' of our awareness. 'Thus we return to Plato's self-moved mover of others.'[68] 'God changes us by changing himself in response to our previous responses to him, and to this divine response to our response we subsequently respond.'[69] But is it logically possible for God to alter himself? As pure cause and as cause containing the past, God has been shown to be immutable. Therefore, since the original ideals and the past cannot be changed, the only remaining possibility is that the contents of the divine knowledge are transformed as they enter the divine consciousness. God would then wipe out bad influences on future behaviour by in some way ensuring that they never enter the experience of succeeding entities; a kind of neoclassical version of the forgiveness of sins.

The obvious difficulty with this is that it appears to entail God's being active in the concrete pole of his reality, and thus the upsetting of the polar balance. Nevertheless, Hartshorne does pursue some such solution in *Man's Vision of God* (an early work, 1941) by suggesting that 'What God ignores he equally, and thereby, destroys or prevents from occurring.[70] But how can the omniscient, surrelative God ignore anything? It is clear that Hartshorne did not for long take this solution seriously, for twelve years later we find him criticizing Whitehead on this very point: 'As for the meaning of "transformation" we suggest that the data perceived are not altered but that an emergent synthesis is effected which as a whole or unity is more than the world taken collectively and, *in this sense only*, is a transformation of the world.'[71] In effect, if not in so many words, Hartshorne would seem to accept the logic of his position

[67] *DR* 139.   [68] Ibid.   [69] *CSPM* 277, cf. *DR* 142.
[70] *MVG* 265.
[71] *PSG* 284. My italics. A similar point is made by Hartshorne in 'Whitehead and Berdyaev: Is there Tragedy in God?', *Journal of Religion* 37 (1957) 82.

as it has been outlined in this chapter. A final quotation makes this clear. 'Passivity *is* activity so far as it is receptive to, or engaged in taking account of, the activity of others . . .'[72]

vi. *'Abstract Activity'*

The conclusion is inescapable: the only sense in which action can be ascribed to this God is an abstract one, with 'abstract' understood in the way in which it has been expounded. The emphasis must then necessarily be not on what God *does*, but on our experience of him. It is therefore scarcely surprising that a favourite term of Hartshorne with which to describe the divine activity is 'influence'. Now this is something that is susceptible of many different meanings: an army, for example, is influenced in its strategy both by the (active) personality of a strongminded general and by the (passive) nature of the terrain on which it is operating. Hartshorne's God is better understood by analogy with the latter types of influence. In the following passage, once again we find him discussing Whitehead.

When he says that God exerts providential influence upon the world, he means by influencing something identifiable in experience as he describes it. We are influenced by God because we 'prehend' him. . . . God's influence is supreme because he is the supreme actuality, supremely beautiful and attractive. . . . There is no 'power' anywhere . . . except the direct and indirect workings of attractiveness ('persuasion').[73]

It may be mentioned in passing that as a description of all aspects of the universe it is quite wrong, unless we are radically to change our understanding of the concept of 'power'. The lion does not persuade the antelope to enter its jaws, nor the judiciary the prisoner his cell, and they, whatever may be the liberal's ideal, are what the world terms powerful. But let us

---

[72] 'A Philosopher's Assessment of Christianity', *Religion and Culture: Essays in Honour of Paul Tillich*, ed. W. Leibrecht (London, 1959), p. 169, cf. *MVG* 273. For a similar point, see H. Parsons, 'Religious Naturalism and the Philosophy of Charles Hartshorne', *Process and Divinity: Philosophical Essays Presented to Charles Hartshorne*, edd. W. L. Reese and E. Freeman (La Salle, 1964), pp. 533–60, and especially pp. 554–6, where it is suggested that God's lack of 'decision and hence exclusion' with respect to the contents of his experience 'makes "love" meaningless as applied to God'.

[73] *PSG* 274 f.

confine our attention to the claim that this, according to Whitehead, is the way we should conceive God to operate, in contrast to the absolute monarch believed to be the model of the classical deity. Here Hartshorne adopts Whitehead's view for his own:

nothing is easier than to state a definitive characteristic of deity in terms of influencing. If A influences C and B does not influence C, then insofar A surpasses B in causal power. Hence the only way in which to construe causal unsurpassability is to state as minimum that, for any x, A influences x. It is not hard to show that God can meet this condition.[74]

In the previous sections we have, of course, seen precisely how he meets it.

God then acts by means of passive influence. How nearly this coincides with the way in which the classical deity is often conceived to operate can be brought out by a brief examination of the views of some of those who discuss or adopt Hartshorne's approach to theology. The Australian philosopher, A. Boyce Gibson,[75] for example, wishes to give Hartshorne credit for bringing into prominence a neglected strand in the philosophical understanding of God. He believes that it is possible to distinguish between the 'immobilist'[76] and the 'activist'[77] views of God in the western philosophical tradition, and that a balanced view of God must hold both of the strands in unison. However, the classical tradition has neglected the activist strand by following Aristotle. Gibson therefore accepts wholeheartedly Hartshorne's critique of this concept. 'In the first place, Aristotle's God is more like the Form of the Good than he is like Plato's God: a sort of magnet operating from an armchair.'[78] But once we introduce the notion of activity, and particularly creation, we are involved in the idea of change, and therefore in contradiction of the immobilist strand.[79] He proceeds to argue, with some reservations about the balance between the two strands,[80] that Hartshorne's philosophy

---

[74] *AD* 45 f.

[75] A. Boyce Gibson, 'The Two Strands in Natural Theology', *Process and Divinity*, pp. 471–92.

[76] Op. cit., p. 473.   [77] Op. cit., p. 475.

[78] Op. cit., p. 472, cf. p. 478. A memorable description.

[79] Op. cit., p. 477.   [80] Op. cit., p. 492.

achieves a combination: a general formula of outgoingness is supported by immobilist elements. So he sees the two poles of the neoclassical God. Unfortunately, Hartshorne's God is not outgoing at all, since all goes into him, and, paradoxically, Gibson's characterization of the immobilist God of the classical tradition very much fits its neoclassical successor: 'He can operate on the changing world only as a lure and not as a power . . .'[81] The question remains: Is the magnet operating from an armchair any more effective for travelling in the wake of the process, for being placed, we might say, in an evolving chair?[82]

Further discussion arises among those theologians who would like to appropriate Hartshorne's conceptuality for Christian theological use. Although it is hoped that the criticisms of Hartshorne's concept which have been made in this chapter will hold on grounds arising from the system alone—that is, as a purely immanent criticism—it is also true that not far below the surface is the concern for a conceptuality that will do justice to the historical activity of God, and particularly for those historical acts that can only be satisfactorily described as acts of initiative. Christian theology has always maintained and, I believe, must continue to maintain if it is to remain Christian, that certain historical events are decisive for its understanding of God in a way that others are not. If the neoclassical conceptuality is to be viable as a 'natural theology' or rational starting-point for faith, or if it is to be use in making sense of what Christians mean when they use the word God, then it must at least *leave open* the possibility of divine action in history. Without such action, its christology inevitably becomes Arian—or its modern equivalent, Jesus as a divinized man— and its anthropology Pelagian. All is thrown back on man rather than on God. It is useless to speak in this connection, as does D. A. Pailin, for example,[83] of God's 'active actuality', for those words suggest far more than they have been seen to mean

---

[81] Op. cit., p. 478.

[82] Cf. E. L. Mascall's comment on the father of neoclassical theism: '. . . it is noteworthy that in one place Whitehead quotes with general approval the famous passage from Aristotle about God moving the world as the object of its desire.' *He Who Is* (London, 1966), p. 157.

[83] D. A. Pailin, 'The Incarnation as a Continuing Reality', *Religious Studies* 6 (1970) 319 f.

in this philosophy: active actuality is the abstract pole of the passive experiencing universal memory.

There is one theologian who recognizes this, and accepts its implications with open eyes. In his paper, 'What Sense Does it Make to Say, "God Acts in History"?'[84] S. M. Ogden asks exactly the right question. But his possibilities for an answer are already circumscribed by what he has already said about the impossibility of modern man's finding mythological language about God meaningful. He believes that any specifiable act of God in history is, as such, mythological. He thus accepts some of the things Rudolf Bultmann has said about myth, but wishes to take the matter much further. Bultmann, he argues, has begun with the correct critique of mythology, but lapsed into mythology by insisting on continuing to speak of God's acts.[85] 'By saying that God acts to redeem mankind *only* in the history of Jesus Christ, he subjects God's action as the redeemer to the objectifying categories of space and time and thus mythologises it.'[86] Rather, all ascription of theological significance to individual historical events must be rejected as mythological. How then does God act in history? Ogden's solution is to use the theological conceptuality of Hartshorne and to say 'that the only God who redeems any history— *although he in fact redeems every history*—is the God whose redemptive action is decisively re-presented in the word that Jesus speaks and is'.[87] With Hartshorne, therefore, Ogden sees 'the primary meaning of God's action' as 'the act whereby, in each new present, he constitutes himself as God by participating fully and completely in the world of his creatures, thereby laying the ground for the next stage of the creative process'.[88] And so, he concludes, 'God's action in its fundamental sense, *is not an action in history at all.*'[89] Rather, it transcends history (rather as, one is tempted to add, the God of classical theism transcends history by being by definition outside of time and the historical process).

Despite this transcendence of history, the essential involvement of the dipolar God in time and space does leave open

[84] S. M. Ogden, *The Reality of God* (London, 1967), pp. 164–87.

[85] S. M. Ogden, *Christ Without Myth. A Study Based on the Theology of Rudolf Bultmann* (London, 1962).   [86] *The Reality of God*, p. 173.

[87] Ibid. Ogden's italics.   [88] Op. cit., p. 177.

[89] Op. cit., p. 179. My italics.

a sense in which Ogden can say that God does act in history. First, 'every creature is to some extent God's act.'[90] This is because all creatures have their basis in God's 'free decisions' and 'creative action'.[91] But Ogden does not specify further what he means by these highly personal and activistic terms. Second, 'Because man, at least in principle, can grasp the ultimate truth about his life, his words and deeds always carry within themselves, so to speak, the possibility of becoming an act of God.'[92] However, this still does not bring us any nearer understanding how God can act in history in such a way that some historical events are more appropriately described in theological language than others. What about Jesus? Ogden is very careful. 'To say with the Christian community, then, that *Jesus* is the decisive act of God is to say that in him, in his outer acts of symbolic word and deed, there is expressed *that* understanding of human existence which is, in fact, the ultimate truth about our life before God . . .'[93] There is a studied vagueness there, but what it would seem to be saying is that there is an ultimate truth about human life, available to every man, and in a sense timelessly true, and that Jesus happens to express it.

Whether or not this is a fair interpretation of Ogden, and whether or not what Ogden says is a satisfactory account of the act of God in Jesus, it is clear from Ogden's understanding of his assertion that God 'in fact redeems every history' that there is no need of any special act of God in history, because we are only interested in a self-understanding of man that *can* be obtained elsewhere.[94] No new knowledge of God and man can be given through a divine initiative, because everything is there already. This is what we should expect if the relation of passivity and activity in the reality of God is as it has been described, since anything amounting to an initiative on the part of God has been ruled out *a priori*. There is no doubt that for all his attempts to speak of God's freedom and creativeness, Ogden in fact understands fully the theological and logical implications of what he is saying. His most explicit admission

[90] *The Reality of God*, p. 180.   [91] Ibid.   [92] Op. cit., pp. 182 f.
[93] Op. cit., pp. 185 f.
[94] This is clearly Ogden's view in other parts of his writing. See the reference to a 'primordial revelation', which happens to be identical with the 'new' knowledge laid hold of in faith, *Christ Without Myth*, p. 166.

of the tendency of his theology comes in a review of a book by a fellow neoclassical theologian, who has claimed that it is possible for his God to initiate changes in the universe if he so chooses. Ogden comments: 'Given the unique relation by which Whitehead conceives God to be related to all other actual entities, such "initiative" would seem to be neither necessary nor possible . . .'[95] Though it is made about Whitehead's concept of God, this is precisely the point that this chapter is concerned to make about the concept of God developed in Hartshorne's metaphysical theology.

vii. *Further Implications of the Notion of Abstract Activity*

The seriousness with which objections of this kind to a concept of God are felt will in part depend upon what one expects God to do. As is often the case with Hartshorne, a comparison with Spinoza is illuminating. Like Hartshorne's, Spinoza's philosophy made the notion of historical activity on the part of God impossible. Theologies that found room for historical activity, purpose, or revelation he believed to be superstitious, because a clear understanding of reality would show that everything happened by the necessary outworkings of the divine logic and causality.[96] Yet despite this, his system was and is interesting in providing explanatory insights of great power. Simply to give intelligibility to the universe is to make a difference, both in satisfying men of the meaningfulness of their existence and in throwing light on aspects of the universe in which they live.

But it should be recognized that beyond this a system like Hartshorne's is peculiarly open to the use of Occam's razor, the philosophical principle that holds that entities should not be multiplied beyond necessity. Both Spinoza's and Hartshorne's Gods are, for slightly different reasons, easily made redundant. The peril of intellectual redundancy is well brought out by a contrast made by J. A. T. Robinson not between Spinoza and Hartshorne, but between another version of the classical deity, the deist, and the neoclassical God. The deist concept is criticized on the grounds that God 'did nothing

---

95 'A *Christian* Natural Theology?', *Process Philosophy and Christian Faith*, edd. D. Brown, R. James, and G. Reeves (Indianapolis and New York, 1971), pp. 113 f.
96 Spinoza, *Ethics*, i, note to Prop. xvii.

in particular . . . and did it very well'.[97] On the other hand, Hartshorne's God is commended because he is in everything: '. . . in the cancer as he is in the sunset . . .'[98] But is there any real difference between a God who does nothing in particular and one who does everything in general unless there is some particular activity—or type of activity—by which he can be identified in the first place? The fact that the two are so similar despite Robinson's contrasting them will be seen if the reader asks which description, that of doing nothing in particular or that of doing everything in general, better applies to the neoclassical God. Perhaps he will find that one of them accurately characterizes each pole of the dipolar reality. But, this apart, the danger is clear, and this is that God-talk according to the concept under review becomes little more than pleonastic talk about the world or man.

And there is a second, theological, difficulty to be faced by the proponents of the new concept of God. For Hartshorne, the contingent particulars in God are of little or no interest in themselves; that is, they are of no interest to him as a philosopher. 'As one way to know the "contingent contents of the divine" one might have to admit a rationally purified revelation.'[99] All he can do is grudgingly admit that it might be possible. The only really significant knowledge, and we have seen many reasons to believe that, despite this assertion of Hartshorne, it is the only knowledge we are likely to obtain, is the abstract. In other words, we have knowledge of a conceptual framework that holds true for God timelessly. In this, there can be no alteration, development, or process. To be God, God must always fit this framework which philosophy has prepared for him. The fact that God is temporal is as abstract and timeless as the fact that he is eternal, and so is the manner of his temporal eternity.

It is very important that this should be made clear in view of the claims that are made by some of the proponents of the new theism. It is missed, for example, in a study of Hartshorne by R. E. James,[1] who speaks as if Hartshorne has broken away

---

[97] J. A. T. Robinson, *Exploration into God* (London, 1967), p. 21.
[98] Op. cit., p. 109.   [99] *MVG* 67.
[1] Ralph E. James, *The Concrete God. A New Beginning for Theology—The Thought of Charles Hartshorne* (Indianapolis, Kansas City, and New York, 1967).

from the barrenness of abstract theology. He may well be correct in describing the critique of classical theology as 'the death of a classical abstraction'[2] or even in speaking of 'God as concrete reality'.[3] But it is scarcely an advance if he can tell us nothing more than that God is a concrete reality, or rather, to be just, that God's reality is concrete because the divine mind contains the whole of current reality as he perceives it. We are presented, then, not with a concrete God but with another abstraction, a neoclassical abstraction. This is because it is impossible for the dipolar God to present himself to us concretely, unless we can perform the impossible task of perceiving the whole of reality as it enters his consciousness. The only way to know God other than as an abstraction is to become God ourselves.

The further theological implications of the neoclassical abstraction have been spelled out by R. C. Neville.[4] He translates two of the terms into their theological equivalents, and shows what kind of meaning they then have. '. . . there is metaphysical necessity that God prehend everything perfectly (necessary redemption) and that everything prehend his influence (necessary creation). . . . Neoclassical metaphysics cannot escape necessitarianism.'[5] Of course it cannot, as everything is true by abstract conceptual necessity. What God is essentially, he is by logical necessity. Once again, we have the coincidence of opposites. The very philosopher who accused the classical deity of necessitarianism must face the same charge. There are differences, but if the description of the logic of the neoclassical concept is correct, then Neville too is correct, and for the following reasons. The neoclassical metaphysic attempts to uphold the freedom of the creature in the face of what it holds to be the necessitarianism of the traditional God. But this freedom is only achieved at the expense of the freedom of God. God is in metaphysical chains both because he is the essence of passivity in his concrete aspect, and because everything that he is in his abstract aspect he is by timeless logical necessity. Whether he is approached from the angle of his reality or of his logic, the outcome is the same.

[2] James, op. cit., pp. 83–106, the title of ch. VI.
[3] Op. cit., pp. 107–26, the title of ch. VII.
[4] 'Neoclassical Metaphysics', *International Philosophical Quarterly* 9 (1969), 605–24.
[5] Art. cit., p. 618.

viii. *The Neoclassical Concept of God*

In this chapter the neoclassical concept of God has been argued to be best understood in terms of those attributes that are logically appropriate to God if he is supremely relative, or surrelative as it has sometimes been expressed. The word 'logically' is important, for the chapter has been an inquiry into what supreme relativity entails, or compels us to say about the God so conceived. From the inquiry there has emerged what can best be described as a cluster of concepts, each of them logically related to each other—or, more strongly, logically *bound up* with each other—so as to form a kind of system of axioms, in which each of the attributes follows from any other when understood in the light of the system as a whole. The analogy with Spinoza's system is once again marked.[6]

There is another way of viewing the concept which is, in its way, equally illuminating. This is by means of a contrast with certain other aspects of the classical concept than those that have been at the centre of interest. That concept, as has been suggested,[7] is largely derived by a process of negating certain characteristics of the natural world believed to be inappropriate to the cause of all things. *Largely* so derived, for there are other things to be said. If the uncaused cause is the negation of certain aspects of being-an-effect, he is also the elevation to infinity of other aspects—goodness, for example. And so a complete exposition of the classical concept of God will contain both negative attributes and attributes of *eminence*. It must here be said, that whether or not Hartshorne's critique of the concept as a whole is just, this aspect of its logic is unimpeachable. Attributed to deity are all those qualities that are appropriately attributed to a God conceived as cause of all that is.

In this respect Hartshorne is not always fair to his Aristotelian predecessors. He describes their method so: '. . . one decides in each case which member of the pair (of ultimate contraries) is good or admirable and then attributes it (in some supremely excellent or transcendent form) to deity while wholly denying the contrasting term.'[8] Sometimes, he appears

---

[6] Spinoza, *Ethics, passim*, but especially Part I.
[7] Introduction, p. 2 above.   [8] *PSG* 2.

to accuse them of arbitrariness. 'Whereas the way of eminence, if consistently executed, treats the categories *impartially*, the way of negation plays favourites among the categories.'⁹ But it is not so much the classical theists as their system that is under attack. The very principle of obtaining a concept of God by negation has been shown to be a failure. Therefore the philosopher must try another method, and that consists in attributing all qualities that appear universally in non-divine reality to God in an appropriate degree, that is, to an infinite or supreme degree. Hartshorne's God is therefore one in whom the principle of eminence reigns to the exclusion of all else, and particularly to the exclusion of the negative way. God is conceived negatively in only one respect: he is *un*surpassable. But that negation is not the same as previous negations: '. . . what it negates is not properties in God, but only the possibility of better properties in another individual.'¹⁰

The question now to be asked is why this particular version of the way of eminence is believed to be appropriate to God, and why the attributes based on, for example, the notion of causality are to be replaced by this particular cluster of concepts, and not by another (or by nothing at all). In neoclassical metaphysics we are offered one particular suggestion of how to solve the problem of correct speech about God. But what is it that authorizes this speech rather than some other? Traditionally speech about God has been claimed to derive from at least two sources. What is often known as the analogy of faith refers to that descriptive language about God which is held to be given or authorized by him in some special act or acts. Clearly that is out of the question here. Contrasted to it are those analogies that are in different ways believed to be derivable by the use of reason, both because they subsist in the very nature of reality, and because reason is believed to be capable of deriving them. The neoclassical method is the second, or rationalist, one. Its method is therefore the same as that of classical theology. But its deployment of its method is different, because of its concentration on the way of eminence. Its use of this way is based on the belief that certain features are common to all reality, and are thus worthy of the title 'category'; God will then necessarily be the being who exemplifies the categories

---

⁹ *DR* 78.   ¹⁰ *AD* 231 f.

eminently. 'Whatever is good in the creation is, in superior or eminent fashion, "analogically not, univocally", the property of God.'[11] Hartshorne here does himself less than justice, for if he were to attribute 'whatever is good' to God, he would himself appear to be 'playing favourites among the categories'. What he would appear to mean is that what is *real* is attributed to God in eminent degree. It may also be the case—as will appeal later—that this whole process is only possible with the assistance of the assumption that what is real is also by that very fact good. For if what is evil is real, it may be that God is evil in eminent degree.

In saying this, we are already moving from the concept of God proper to the view of reality as a whole on which it is based. In this chapter the discussion has been of the kind of God that emerges when the principle of eminence is put into practice in the light of a certain view of reality, parts of which have necessarily emerged in passing. Now is the time to look more closely at this underlying metaphysic. Therefore in the next chapter the question will be discussed of what the universe must be like that a God of this kind should be seen as its crown. That is to say, the question of analogy will emerge into the full light of day. What is there about the world as he sees and reasons about it that makes Hartshorne feel that he is justified in describing different aspects of it by the use of basically the same language? And how does the eminent, supremely relative, dipolar God fit into a world so conceived?

[11] *DR* 77.

III

A MONISM AND ANALOGY OF BECOMING

i. *The Concept of Experience*

H ARTSHORNE believes that an analysis of our general experience will provide him with the conception of reality that he seeks. Inevitably the neoclassical conception of experience is different from that of an empiricist or naturalist.[1] The concern is not with particular empirically testable events or objects but rather with what Ogden has called the 'constant structure' of our experience.[2] That is to say, the neoclassical metaphysician wants to discover what is true of all experience: what it is that makes it to be experience at all. To put it yet another way, Hartshorne wishes to find those elements of experience that remain real whatever may be the particular state of affairs that obtains at the time, and so embarks upon a *metaphysical* analysis of the *notion* of experience. ' "Experiential" is not the same as "empirical": the latter connotes "compatible with some, but *not all*, conceivable experiences": the former, "confirmed or manifested at least by some, perhaps by all, conceivable experiences".'[3] Thus the analysis of experience is, in effect, the establishing of *a priori* truths, to find what is true before we have any experiences at all. There are then three ways in which the analysis may be described. It is metaphysical in that it seeks to establish what *underlies* the actual; it is concerned with experience, for it wishes to establish what experience *really is*; and it is an *a priori* endeavour in that it wishes to establish what is true

---

[1] See H. Parsons, 'Religious Naturalism and the Philosophy of Charles Hartshorne, *Process and Divinity*, edd. W. L. Reese and E. Freeman (La Salle, Illinois, 1964), pp. 533–60.

[2] S. M. Ogden, *The Reality of God* (London, 1967), pp. 116 f. Despite the language, the ideal seems to be a platonic one—to find the unchanging in the changing.

[3] *AD* 64.

independently of sense experience. Metaphysics is defined by Hartshorne as '*a priori* but experiential, though non-inductive'.[4] His approach to it is subtly different from the metaphysical programmes of the past. Speculative philosophers in the classical tradition have usually set out to establish the existence of concrete realities, often including God, by their reasoning. But since the publication of Kant's *Critique of Pure Reason* it has been widely held to be logically improper to move from the realm of logic to that of real existence. Hartshorne's attempt to avoid such logical impropriety is shown in the fact that he claims not to be attempting to establish the existence of concrete realities whose existence makes a difference to observed reality. Rather he is in search of the universal conditions that enclose the realities of our experience. 'Metaphysics we may now define as the search for necessary and categorical truth—necessary in that, unlike empirical truths or facts, it excludes no positive possibility . . . and categorical in that . . . it applies positively to any actuality.'[5]

In this chapter, then, we shall be expounding what it is, according to Hartshorne, for a being to be a being. Despite the fact that he makes no claim to be establishing the reality of any concrete entity, the following exposition will be clearer if it is realized that in another respect he is traditional and pre-Kantian as a metaphysician, in that he does believe, as will become increasingly apparent, that our concepts do contain the clues of a proper understanding of reality. Therefore, philosophical analysis can be for him revelatory of what the world really is.

ii. *Metaphysical Monism*

There is a further assumption on which Hartshorne's whole metaphysical quest depends. He believes that it should be—indeed, is—possible to understand all reality with the aid of a single, all-embracing conceptuality. He is in this sense a monist. All there is can be subsumed under one single descriptive category.[6] In a sense it is, for him, nonsense to believe that it could be otherwise, for example, that there could be two

---

[4] 'Anthropomorphic Tendencies in Positivism', *Philosophy of Science* 8 (1941) 198, cf. *CSPM* 19–42 for an extended discussion of the topic.   [5] *LP* 285.
[6] *LP* 191 f. It is also possible for Hartshorne to speak of pluralism but only one which has 'a common logic for all becoming . . .', *CSPM* 195.

ultimate realities, or that there could be a fundamental ontological distinction between God and the world. Some kind of
monism is axiomatic for Hartshorne, and is revealed in a
number of statements that he makes. (It is, incidentally, of
a piece with his claim to have provided an exhaustive classification of the possible concepts of God. Once a possible dualism is admitted, possibilities for conceiving the relation between
God and the world multiply.) The axiomatic monism is present
in the following remark: '. . . if things were simply "outside"
God, there would be a greater reality than God, God and the
world.'[7] Again, if one were to try to conceive of God as in
some sense independent of the world, 'then God-and-what-is-
other-than-God must be a total reality greater (more inclusive)
than God'.[8] Both statements abound with unproven assumptions. In particular, one would ask why the totality of God
and what is not God must make a more *inclusive* reality than
the two considered separately. What is the necessity that they
should be included, and in what? Why *must* there be one concept (of ours) that covers everything there can be under its
wing? Perhaps reality is such that we have to describe parts
of it in different terminology. But questions of this kind do not
occur to Hartshorne, because monism is required if there is
to be a metaphysical quest of the kind he envisages. 'For there
are metaphysical principles at all only if all existence does have
common features, expressible in common terms, or in one
language.'[9] As to this, the same point can be made as at
the close of the previous section, that however post-Kantian
Hartshorne may strive to be, there is little doubt that he is a
metaphysical philosopher in the classical mould, with his antecedents in philosophers like Parmenides and Spinoza.

iii. *Asymmetry of Time and Social Process*

Two terms in particular are used to express what Hartshorne
finds to be common to all reality: 'process' and 'creativity',

---

[7] *AD* 109.

[8] *PSG* 505, cf. *PSG* 19, *DR* 79, and *CSPM* 48. The argument has something
in common with Plato's argument against the duplication of forms, *Republic* 597 c.
Another parallel would seem to be that in that passage, as in Hartshorne's system,
the term 'God' appears to stand for little more than a semi-redundant unifying
principle.

[9] 'Metaphysics for Positivists', *Philosophy of Science* 2 (1935) 295, cf. *CSPM* 8 f.

both taken from Whitehead. In a discussion of 'Whitehead's Metaphysics'[10] Hartshorne asks what we should make of Whitehead's idea of creativity. Is it, as some argue, a God beyond God? Rather, it, or the principle of process, should be regarded as ' "an analogical concept" functioning in Whitehead's system somewhat as "being" functions in Aristotelian theology.'[11] Whatever is real is in some sense an instantiation of creativity or process, just as once all that existed was said to do so because of its participation in 'being' or 'substance'. In place of an ontology of being there is posited in this new system an ontology (gignomenology?) of becoming or event.

What is the connection between this basic ontological judgement and the kind of logico-metaphysical construction that Hartshorne seeks from his analysis of experience? In an article, 'Anthropomorphic Tendencies in Positivism', he gives an illustration of how the system is constructed. Of two metaphysical propositions, both of which are formally analytic, only the first has experiential meaning. (i) The relatively indeterminate future is relatively indeterminate. (ii) The absolutely determinate future is absolutely determinate. Both of those, he claims, are analytic in the sense that they are true simply in virtue of the terms they contain. But the first also throws light upon the character of the world in which we live, and is therefore more than a linguistic tautology. The reason for its experiential metaphysical viability is that 'the partial indefiniteness of the future . . . is that by which we identify the future as such'. Metaphysical judgements of this kind are therefore 'a priori, though not formally analytic'.[12] They are not formally analytic, because it is possible to dispute the necessity of their being true, but only if full consideration is not given to the real (metaphysical) meaning of the terms involved. Thus, according to this argument, what is on the face of it a question of fact (albeit possibly an irresolvable one), namely the question of whether the future is or is not determined by the

---

[10] V. Lowe et al., *Whitehead and the Modern World* (Boston, Mass., 1950), pp. 25–41.

[11] Op. cit., p. 40. In *CSPM* 128 f. Hartshorne argues that in metaphysics he is not dealing with 'just a metaphor'. He wants to claim far more than that his system is the generalization of a pictorial way of viewing reality, as the following exposition will show.

[12] 'Anthropomorphic Tendencies in Positivism', art. cit., p. 199.

past, is solved on at least partially linguistic grounds, that is, from the alleged meaning of the word 'future'.

Whatever the merits of this kind of argument, it enables Hartshorne to develop the notion that the universe as a whole is in process. For in the argument he has established to his own satisfaction a decisive difference between past and future. The past is by its very nature determinate, or, in another Hartshornian term, absolute.[13] The future, on the other hand, is at least to some degree indeterminate, as we have just seen. There is therefore an asymmetrical relation between past and future. '. . . such is the logical structure of time, that it gives determinations a unique asymmetrical order of involvement'.[14] What is most noticeable is the confident transition from the order of logic to that of ontology. *Time* has the logical structure, apparently because our words for time do. There is, in a later work, a different and less linguistic form of argument, where asymmetry is held to be necessary for pragmatic reasons. 'The belief in a wholly determinate future is not translateable into action . . .'[15] As human action is of such a kind that it assumes some kind of openness in the future, then that is what there has to be. As in the other argument, it can be seen that experiential factors bulk large.

In whatever way it is established, this conception of the asymmetrical relation between past and future performs a crucial function. In the first place, it provides the ontological grounding for the conception of omniscience required by the system. In a monist scheme God's omniscience must be the kind of knowledge that the ruling notion of process allows. 'We could then say that omniscience is all the knowledge that is possible, which by definition is perfect knowledge, but that since some of the truths about the future could not be known at present, omniscience does not know them.'[16] At most, 'sufficient knowledge about the future to constitute a providential plan' can be granted.[17]

In the second place, the conception makes possible the application of the notion of process or creativity both to the

---

[13] See above, Ch. I, § i.

[14] *MVG* 131. Hartshorne has all but the first two words of that citation in italics. Cf. also *CSPM* 179.

[15] *CSPM* 93 f. (1970).   [16] *MVG* 140.   [17] Ibid.

universe as a whole and to its constituent parts. First, the universe as a whole must be seen to be a process that is open to development as it passes through time. Meaningful process is a logical requirement of the fundamental insight about the nature of time. Commenting on the thought of Schelling, Hartshorne speaks of the general situation: '. . . one should not seek a ground or cause of process . . . concrete reality is process or becoming, with an abstract aspect of being. . . . Becoming goes on to realise ever more value, but not as if there were the alternative of resting content with actual value.'[18] The future is open in the sense that it is metaphysically necessary that there should be produced good (or value, as he would prefer to say) in excess of that which is contained already in the past. 'What is not to be decided, even by God, is that progress . . . there shall be, for this is the "necessary goodness" and perfection of power of God, which lie beyond the "accidents of will".'[19] Only the rate of progress has to be decided.[20] And so the asymmetry of time is now linked with a metaphysical optimism, a doctrine that an open future is also necessarily a better future. Once again the quantitative conception of perfection is lurking in the background. If the totality grows ever greater, and if there were not 'a *net increment* of value accruing to God at each moment' it is doubtful, Hartshorne believes, whether life could go on.[21]

Here can be made explicit the connection between what has just been said about the nature of the universe and the doctrine of relations. In Chapter I, § i, it was shown that for neoclassical metaphysics the past is externally related to the knowing subject. In Chapter II, §§ ii and iii, it was shown that the neoclassical conception is of a God who partakes in the temporal process as its perceiver. God, as memory, is therefore the unifying factor in the universe, and his reality provides a reason for the necessity of progress as well as process: '. . . if process enriches the determinateness of existence, then since

---

[18] *PSG* 242 f.

[19] 'Whitehead's Idea of God', *The Philosophy of Alfred North Whitehead*, ed. P. Schillp (Evanston and Chicago, 1941), p. 554.

[20] Ibid.

[21] *DR* 46, Hartshorne's italics. Hartshorne never treats seriously the possibility that things may be getting worse. See *RSP* 118 f., where the possibility is at least mentioned.

esthetic value varies with such determinateness, process can add to the total value of existence.'[22] God is the being who guarantees that the past is always there, and that, as time proceeds, there will be an addition to it of new experiences which both build upon it and add their own contribution to the sum total of reality. It is in this sense that the notion becomes intelligible that at any given moment the process as a whole in its presentness is the subject which knows and experiences (in Whiteheadian terminology, prehends) the object which is the whole of the cosmic past.

But the notion of the cosmic moment, poised between past and future in the asymmetry of time, brings with it serious difficulties. If all is as Hartshorne says, then there must be, for God, a position in time from which, at any given time, all the past is 'visible' as past and all the future anticipated as indeterminate futurity. The difficulty becomes apparent when it is realized that such a conception requires that time be an absolute, a given, so that it is possible for the divine observer to delimit absolutely the past from the future. However, Einstein's theory of relativity would appear to make this impossible, for it and its supporting data 'reveal that under certain conditions there is no unique physical meaning of "simultaneous",' and that a God of the kind envisaged by neoclassical theory would seem to have 'a special agreement with certain creaturely observers and their space-time system and disagreements with all the others. . . .'[23] The question J. Wilcox asks on the strength of this consideration is pertinent: 'Is temporalistic omniscience merely a ghost of Newtonian time, a smile which remains when the cat has vanished?'[24] Hartshorne himself has long been aware of the problem, at least since 1941.[25] But he has provided no satisfactory solution, as is shown in the passages claimed by two of his supporters to represent a 'rebuttal' of criticisms,[26] but in fact representing little more than special pleading or pious hope. The former is revealed by the following passage. 'The assumption of a divine

[22] DR 97.
[23] J. Wilcox, 'A Question from Physics for Certain Theists', *Journal of Religion* 41 (1961) 293–5.
[24] Art. cit., pp. 296 f.   [25] 'Whitehead's Idea of God', p. 545.
[26] G. Reeves and D. Brown, 'The Development of Process Theology', *Process Philosophy and Christian Thought* (Indianapolis and New York, 1971) pp. 40 f.

simultaneity need not mean that some actual perspective on the world is "right" as against others. For the actual perspective might be "eclectic", agreeing (approximately) as to some items with one standpoint, as to others with another, and the incidence of agreement might be constantly shifting.'[27] But this will not do, for it is impossible to see how Hartshorne's God could perform these contortions without making his knowledge *in principle* different from other knowledge in precisely the way the system wishes to avoid. As Ogden has said,

The crucial insight of the neoclassical theism Hartshorne has pioneered in developing is that God is to be conceived *in strict analogy* with the human self or person. The force of the word 'strict' is that God, as Whitehead says, is *not* to be treated as *an exception* to metaphysical principles, but rather is to be understood as exemplifying them.[28]

The point about Wilcox's question is to ask whether the analogy to human knowing can be carried through in view of the radical critique by Einstein of the notion of absolute time, without making God an exception to the metaphysical principles that obtain elsewhere. So far as the accusation of pious hope is concerned, a brief quotation will suffice: '. . . there seems no way to divide the universe as a whole into past and future. Yet if neoclassical theism is right, it seems there must, for God at least, be a way. . . . Somehow relativity as an observational truth must be compatible with divine unsurpassability.'[29]

So much, then, for the application of the fundamental insight about the nature of time to the cosmic process as a whole. Second, it must be applied to individual entities as well, if the metaphysical monism is to be consistently carried through. Because process is believed to be characteristic of all reality (as distinct from reality as a whole), it must now be shown in its application to the individual units that make up the cosmos. What is true of the universe as a whole is true also of every part of it. Reality is made up of subjects, which exist momentarily before passing into objectivity. Hartshorne

---

[27] Reeves and Brown, art. cit., p. 41, citing Hartshorne, Reply to 'Interrogation of Charles Hartshorne', *Philosophical Interrogations*, edd. S. and B. Rome (New York, 1964), pp. 324 f.
[28] S. M. Ogden, op. cit., p. 175. My italics.   [29] *NTOT* 93.

calls this doctrine 'panpsychism',[30] the doctrine that the universe is made up of minds or subjects. As subjects these entities are, of course, internally related to whatever comes within the sphere of their experiencing. This entails that everything there is is, *qua* subject, necessarily related to something else. When these relations are seen in their totality, the conclusion is drawn that reality is a system that forms an interrelated whole. And so it is described not only as process, but as *social* process.[31] Hartshorne lists four characteristics of reality that derive from this fundamental belief. 'The social theory of existence denies that any individual unit of reality . . . is absolutely without feeling or free creative action.'[32] It is, then, 'pan-psychistic, pan-indeterministic (or pan-creationistic), pan-relativistic, and pan-temporalistic, in the sense that every concrete being has psychic, free or creative, relative, and temporal aspects'.[33] And it must be re-emphasized that by 'concrete being' neoclassical metaphysics means an event, taking place in the process that is reality.

In this section it has been shown how Hartshorne moves from an analysis of the inner meaning of our words for time to the doctrine that free temporal becoming is a universal characteristic of the universe in which we live. Mind, creativity, relativity, and temporality are attributable to all reality and to each reality. The four categories are logically related, as a system of axioms, and summed up in the notion of process. Further, they are related to each other in the same way as the attributes of God, because these themselves are either eminent instances of the four categories, or corollaries of them. Now we shall see how the four are shown to hold true at all the different levels of reality, from the very lowest up to God.

iv. *The Metaphysical Categories: (i) The Sub-human Analogy*

How, then, is it possible to describe those entities that are 'lower' than man, and apparently not personal, in terms of

---

[30] 'Panpsychism', *A History of Philosophical Systems*, ed. V. Ferm (London, 1950), pp. 442–52.

[31] Hence the title of Hartshorne's book, *Reality as Social Process*, itself echoing one of Whitehead's, *Process and Reality*.

[32] *RSP* 134.

[33] *RSP* 135, cf. *BH* 125, where Hartshorne speaks of 'freedom as a cosmic variable'.

process, with its four associated ideas? Hartshorne's favourite term with which to make the transition in thought is 'organism', which he defines as 'a whole whose parts serve as "organs" or instrument to purposes or end-values inherent in the whole'.[34] There is a sense in which everything is an organism, like an organism, or made up of organisms. The term is applied in the light of what Hartshorne calls 'the principle of continuity, the supreme law of rationality'—what has here been described as his axiomatic monism—which 'implies that every individual in nature is in some degree akin to man, either as inferior or as superior to him . . .'[35] The ubiquitous word 'experience' recurs here too: 'I do not know how matter can be interpreted save by analogy with experience as such . . .'[36] Of course experience is understood in terms of the system, but the point to be noted especially here is the movement from the assumption of monism to the application of language. Because reality *must be* analogous in its different levels, then its different parts can be justifiably *described* by different uses of the same predicates. Or, conversely, the analogous use of language is ontologically grounded in an analogy subsisting in the very nature of reality. The predicates are applied at the different levels by a process Hartshorne describes as 'stretching'.[37] How, then, are things 'below' and 'above' man in the order of things shown to be organic?

The first difficulty to be faced is the presence in the universe of wholes that are either not organisms, or cannot obviously be said to have anything in their make-up that is analogous to mind. In the first category come mountains, stones, bodies of water, clouds, etc.[38] If we are to understand how these fit into the system we must take account of the distinction, which Hartshorne attributes to Leibniz, between individuals and aggregates.[39] The problematic entities are aggregates because they are made up of parts that can themselves be considered to be organisms, but not in such a way that the collection of organisms thus assembled has any more unity than its assembled parts.[40] To count as an organism, the entity must

---

[34] *LP* 191.   [35] *BH* 50 f. cf. 192.
[36] 'Interrogation of Charles Hartshorne', *Philosophical Interrogations*, edd. S. and B. Rome, p. 333.
[37] Art. cit., pp. 384 ff.   [38] *LP* 192, *MVG* 205 and 177.
[39] *MVG* 205.   [40] *BH* 111 f., *LP* 192.

display some unified organic or social behaviour. The second difficult group is the vegetable, which apparently functions as an organism, but yet displays no sign of relation, freedom, etc., in its relations with other entities or as a whole. According to Hartshorne, this is because a plant is only a '*quasi*-organic colony of true organisms, the cells, and not, like the vertebrate animal, itself an organism'.[41] Similarly, although there are intermediate cases where there is some room for doubt, there is a criterion, for 'Novelty is essential to action and to time as such, and any unity which does not exhibit it is secondary or derivative from its parts'.[42] This may appear to be a *petitio principii* and, further, to involve the stretching of language to such an extent that entities which are known as organisms according to ordinary linguistic usage are claimed not to be such in order that those which are not normally thought to be organic may be shown to be so. But at this stage we are less concerned with the justification of the analogy than with its exposition. If the neoclassical system is to be viable, reality must be shown to be social or organic at every significant level. Here it is being argued that at certain levels, that is, in the case of aggregations of matter and of certain combinations of cells, actual reality is perhaps not what we see on the surface; and it is claimed that there is some justification for this in the discoveries of modern science.[43] Less of a problem to Hartshorne is the so-called group-mind, at least when it is applied to human groups: '. . . there are no good indications that human groups are organisms which could think and feel as individuals.'[44]

We come now to an account of the different levels of reality to which the term 'process' with all its connotations can be said to apply. The lowest level is that of the sub-atomic particle. 'Electrons and protons are, for all that anyone knows, simply the lowest actual levels of social existence.'[45] The difficulty here lies in deciding whether the idea of organism can be applied to the electron, and it is a difficulty that would recur if there should be some more primitive level of existence, below that of the sub-atomic particle. For the lowest level (if there be such) is

---

41 *LP* 193, cf. *BH* 112.   42 *MVG* 206.
43 See *MVG* 176 f., 204–7 and *LP* 192 f.
44 *LP* 193. See *RSP* 53–68 and *CSPM* 141.   45 *DR* 29.

bound to be without parts, while an organism is necessarily, on most understandings of the word, made up of parts. Here the difficulty is escaped by saying in effect, though not explicitly, that the electron is only analogically an organism. The entities that contribute to the whole

> need not be internal to the whole in the sense of spatially smaller and included parts, as electrons are smaller than and within an atom.... To render an electron or other particle an organism it is only necessary that neighbouring electrons or other particles should contribute directly to each other's values, that is, should directly feel each other.... With the simplest organisms it is the community of neighbouring entities that constitutes the plurality contributing to each entity.... Where there are no smaller entities as parts, there will be no sharp distinction between internal and external.[46]

That the particle should be analogically organic appears to be at least conceivable, for it is made quite clear that mind is ascribed in only a very limited degree.

> The way to bring the most beauty into our picture of the world is to regard atoms and other inferior individuals as very simple, low-grade types of minds, or sub-minds, with their own to us more or less unimaginable feelings. Then we have immense but positive contrasts between the various levels and kinds of mind or feeling.[47]

But however qualified the claim, Hartshorne does sometimes make startling claims about the possible extent of the mental constituent of electron behaviour. Thus, in an admittedly early work, he alleges that there is no absurdity in speaking in terms of sentience; that an electron can be said, apparently on the authority of J. B. S. Haldane, to pursue an end; and that it is possible to use in this connection terms like 'memory' and 'psychology'.[48]

Other types of organism that have the requisite social qualities are atoms,[49] molecules,[50] and the cell. 'Each of the cells of a tree has more functional unity than the whole tree. As Whitehead put it, "a tree is a democracy".'[51] In what sense can a cell be understood as a social organism? 'We have only to

[46] *LP* 195.   [47] *MVG* 214.
[48] *BH* 119, 190, and 251 respectively (1937, republished 1968).
[49] *BH* 111 f., *RSP* 36, and *CSPM* 11.   [50] *BH* 111, *GSPM* 142.
[51] *RSP* 35.

suppose that these cells possess humble forms of feeling or desire to reach the position that the human mind influences and is influenced by them through immediate . . . sharing of feeling . . .'[52] Cells are such that in an entity with a higher centre of unity they become part of that higher being's social existence; in an entity without it, it is their individual social existences that jointly determine the character of the entity. (Hence Whitehead's use of the term 'democracy'.)

That cells literally enjoy health and suffer from injury is a supposition that conflicts with no facts, while there are facts it helps to explain.[53] It is cells, genes and things of that order of magnitude which, as it were, 'know' (feel) something of what they are up to, not embryos (except when and as they turn into animals with functioning nervous systems.)[54]

In all these instances the paradigm case of experience, human knowledge (understood as that which relates us to the world in feeling), is attributed by analogy to 'lower' beings in the world. In so far as this is so, it is a kind of anthropomorphism,[55] though perhaps *anthropopathism* would be a more satisfactory term pointing as it does to the analogy of feeling between the two levels of being. Whether the attribution of feeling qualities to electrons and the rest is justifiable must depend in part on whether such anthropomorphic stretching of language is meaningful. Clearly, if it is not meaningful it cannot be true, or, at any rate, cannot be known to be true. Of the four categories, temporality and perhaps relativity present little difficulty, certainly where the latter means affecting and being affected by other entities in its temporal succession. But when that relativity is construed in terms of mind and creativity, difficulties multiply. For along with them Hartshorne uses terms like 'act'[56] and 'freedom'.[57] The difficulty of judging the intelligibility of the analogy in this case is compounded by the fact that the two terms are problematic enough in their paradigm meaning, that is, when used of the human agent.

---

[52] *MVG* 188.   [53] *LP* 192.   [54] *LP* 213.
[55] The word is used in a neutral rather than pejorative sense. Hartshorne defends himself against the charge of (illegitimate) anthropomorphism in *BH* 119, but is quite happy to say in *CSPM* 129 that man must provide the model in metaphysical construction.
[56] *BH* 190.   [57] *LP* 126.

For they are terms which have special application to the notion of the human as a moral, responsible agent.[58] The intelligibility of the analogy hangs upon whether it is legitimate to describe as 'freedom' the element of randomness in the behaviour of sub-atomic particles. The situation is made easier for Hartshorne in that he tends to base his conception of human freedom too on randomness.

> Moral freedom, we have held, is a special, high-level case of the creative leap inherent in all process, the case in which the leap is influenced by consciousness of ethical principles. The leap itself always involves 'chance'—meaning simply that the causal conditions do not require just the particular act which takes place. . . . Moral freedom is chance plus something; no-one . . . identifies the two.[59]

However, if Hartshorne's undefined 'something' is the determinative factor in moral freedom, the two uses of 'freedom'—moral and cosmic or metaphysical—run the risk of being so far apart that there is no longer analogy, but equivocation. If, on the other hand, the element of chance is determinative, then the account of moral freedom is implausible. Suppose, for example, I have just exercised my moral freedom by resisting a temptation that in the past has proved irresistible. It is hardly credible to say that in this case chance has supervened to ensure that in this case I have resisted the universal causal laws that have formerly operated in a similar situation. At least, it may be credible, but not if I want to continue to believe that the act was the result of human moral freedom.[60] Thus if Hartshorne wants to establish that electrons, cells, molecules, and the like exercise something analogous to human creativity, then he has to do far more just to establish that the analogy is meaningful, let alone credible on other grounds.

[58] Cf. *CSPM* 116: 'If each atom must at every moment have something like will . . .'

[59] *LP* 169, cf. *BH* 125. Incidentally, the definition of 'chance' is highly questionable.

[60] The situation is not made any clearer by Hartshorne's failure to explain just what he means by 'something'. For a criticism of the attempt to establish human freedom by appeal to cosmic indeterminism, see J. R. Lucas, *The Freedom of the Will* (London, 1970), pp. 51–64.

v. *The Metaphysical Categories: (ii) The Divine Analogy*

The monism of becoming has its problems also in the extension upwards, so to speak, of the categories. At this stage there is a double analogy at work, and this can be accounted for by the fact that we are concerned with a more complex level of existence. The first analogy can be called the *social* analogy, and is an extension of the one with which we have been concerned in the previous section. The social relatedness of the electrons, etc., is minimal, and so therefore is their freedom and influence. The relatedness of the human is likewise limited, both in area and in time, though to a lesser degree. In the case of God there is no limit, for his omniscience relates him to everything that is actual. The second analogy is one that arises naturally from the conception of God as the supreme knower, and is therefore logically complementary to the social analogy. It is that of the *mind-body*. God is the mind who has the whole universe for his body. '. . . we shall never understand a God of love unless we conceive him as the all-sensitive mind of the world-body.'[61] This analogy can be seen to be the answer to two related questions: (i) What gives unity to the cosmic process? and (ii) How is God to be conceived as analogous to man, who, as a knowing and related entity is more than the unity of his parts (i.e. cells) and expresses this organic unity as a body controlled by a mind? Thus, once again, the analogy is 'anthropomorphic', in the sense that it applies human attributes to God in the appropriate 'stretched' sense. And Hartshorne can both admit an element of anthropomorphism, and deny it if it implies lack of proper superiority of God over man.[62]

As an aid in constructing his analogy, Hartshorne draws upon the idea of the world-soul as he finds it in Plato's *Timaeus*,[63] and presents a full exposition of the idea in the chapter entitled 'The Theological Analogies and the Cosmic Organism'.[64] We have already seen that a 'body . . . is really a "world" of

---

[61] *BH* 208, cf. *CSPM* 220.

[62] For the former, see 'A Critique of Peirce's Idea of God', *Philosophical Review* 50 (1941) 521, where he speaks of a 'critical' anthropomorphism; for the latter, see *BH* 119 where in answer to a charge of anthropomorphism he argues that 'it is precisely in its psychic makeup that a being can be *infinitely* other than man.'

[63] *PSG* 38–57.   [64] *MVG* 174–211.

individuals, and a mind, if the body is one having a mind . . . is to that body something like an indwelling God'.[65] The whole universe can be seen on this understanding to have an individuality of its own without infringing the freedom of its parts to express their own appropriate creativity. In other words, the social analogy avoids the danger that the mind of the universe might exercise so overwhelming a control over its body that there would be no room left for the freedom of the individuals within it, while the mind–body analogy ensures that God's knowledge of all that takes place in the universe will be direct and immediate. In the relation of our mind to our body 'and here alone we are Godlike in directness of power over individuals other than our own ego'.[66] But it is still an *analogy* for in many respects we are highly deficient in our awareness of what goes on in our cell systems. 'God's immediacy is perhaps not more immediate than ours, but it is certainly more vivid and distinct.'[67] In the combination of the two analogies, the difficulties attaching to either of them when used alone are avoided.[68] And it is possible at this stage of the exposition to link this conception with the description of God as supremely relative in the opening sections of chapter two. The mind–body analogy is the necessary development and completion of the conception of the eminent relativity of God. To know is to contain. To know everything is to be the mind that contains the whole of experienced reality, and that means that God, as containing the whole of reality *is* the whole of reality and something more. Just as in certain theories of the human person we are our bodies and something more, that more being the mind that gives unity to the whole, so it is with God. We come then to a kind of modified pantheism, or panentheism as Hartshorne calls it.[69] Concretely speaking, God is the universe, conceived as a multiplicity of experiencing selves, for those selves take place within him, as a body. But abstractly considered, he is more than they. Two quotations will bring out the meaning of this conception. 'God is the self-identical individuality of the world somewhat as a man is the self-identical individuality of his ever changing system of atoms.'[70]

---

[65] *MVG* 177.   [66] *MVG* 179.   [67] *MVG* 184.   [68] *MVG* 187.
[69] 'Panentheism', *Encyclopedia of Religion*, ed. V. Ferm (London, 1956).
[70] *MVG* 230 f.

Clearly, the analogy between man and God is here very close. 'He is distinguished from his parts wholly by being more than they, but this more is not simply outside the parts, yet a factor of them, as a man is more than any of his cells; it is a factor of all of them.'[71] But however close the analogy, there remain essential differences, which are, as we have seen, related to the all-embracing immediacy of the omniscient experience.

However, the analogy requires further clarification in the light of the central neoclassical doctrine that the basic unity of reality is the event. The terms body and mind may obscure the character of the analogy because they are associated in our common-sense language with notions of substantial existence, and in particular with the notion that they are realities that have a continuing existence independently of what happens to them. According to neoclassical metaphysics, they *are* what happens to them. The primary point of likeness in the analogy of becoming between God and other entities is that the reality of each entity consists in the fact that it is a temporal series of events. The unity of any particular continuing entity in the flux of becoming consists in the fact that there is abstractable from a particular series a unity higher than the total of events that make up the series. (If there can be no such abstraction, we are back in the situation of the 'democracy', where, of course, the entity is understood exhaustively in terms of the separate event-sequences it contains.) That is why the unity of God is an abstraction. The rule holds true of the lowest level of reality as of the highest. 'Atomic events do not literally occur to a moving entity called an atom; rather by an atom we simply mean a sequence of events having a certain persistent atomic character, the same atomic number, say, and a certain continuity, or near continuity, through space-time.'[72]

What is true of the atom is true, at their own level, of persons. 'Things or persons can then only be certain stabilities or coherences in the flux of events. The stabilities are in the events, not the events in the stabilities.'[73] Thus W. A. Mozart is the name we give to the series of events that took place between 1756 and 1791: the events of breathing, eating, loving,

---

[71] *MVG* 285.   [72] *LP* 218.

[73] *LP* 219, cf. *CSPM* 105: 'as ordinary language, with profound justice, has it, the man is "in a state".'

playing the piano, composing, along with all the other 'personal' and cell events that belonged to this particular sector of the space-time system. The events were his reality; he was not a substance to which the events happened.[74] It is then true to say that there is a new 'self' at each moment, 'partly inclusive of the old experiences, not an old self with partly new experiences'.[75] Further, we can on this basis say that whether we are dealing with God, a person, or an atom, the process is the same. We have first to see it in its concrete reality as a series of events, and only then can we arrive at the abstract pole, which expresses the unity and 'character' of the series, by abstracting it conceptually from all the other events in the total cosmic process.

But an analogy requires also an exposition of the differences between God and that with which he is compared. Some of the differences have already emerged from the discussion, but it is now possible to pinpoint the chief one. God, as the universe and yet more than the universe, is the latter by virtue of his abstract pole. And his abstract pole is an abstraction from the event-sequence that is the whole of reality. God is therefore the unity or the character of the universe. Just as the event-sequence we name W. A. Mozart is an abstraction from the events that make up a finite part of the process, both in space and time, so God's abstract, timelessly conceived reality or pole is an abstraction from the whole (meaning, of course, all the events that have happened so far). Once this has been established, it is possible to move on to two other important differences between God and finite entities. They can best be understood under two heads, in connection with the body-mind and the social analogies respectively. It must, however, be stressed that this is a division employed in the cause of intellectual clarity, and in no sense implies a separate kind of relation between God and the world. 'Body-mind' and 'social' are used here to express two aspects of the one relation of God to the rest of reality already set forth in the statement that God is the character or abstract identity of the universe. That this is so will be realized if it is borne in mind that everything

[74] See C. Gunton, 'Process Theology's Concept of God: An Outline and Assessment', *Expository Times* 84. 10 (July 1973) 293.
[75] *LP* 219.

down to the most basic entity in existence is an event series that is analogous to body–mind, and can also be understood in terms of its relatedness to previous events taking place in its sector of the system. Perhaps it is not too much of a simplification to say that the one description concentrates on the reality of the entity in itself; the other stresses its reality as related to entities outside its momentary existence.

(i) The points of difference in the case of the body–mind analogy are twofold. First, as has already been mentioned, God's knowledge of his contents will be whole and perfect, not fragmentary and partial as is ours. Second, because there in only one mind for the whole of the universe, God's whole environment is internal, whereas most of ours is external (and so mediate and indirect). For example, my knowledge of the apple tree in the garden is mediate in that it reaches me from the outside world via my senses. God's knowledge of everything is direct as is my knowledge of my toothache or the thoughts which pass through my mind as I consider the appropriate words with which to expound the philosophy of Hartshorne. The interesting development here is that in my case as distinct from God's, the body–mind analogy spills over automatically into the social analogy. For my perception of the apple tree immediately relates me to entities outside of my own mind, whereas the idea of an event taking place outside the mind of God is a logical impossibility. This brings God marked advantages. 'To have an external environment is to depend upon factors not under immediate control . . . But the universe as a whole, if it is an organism at all, must immediately control all its parts. . . .'[76]

Whether Hartshorne is correct to describe God's relation to his environment as one of control must be open to question. If the argument of Chapter II is correct, that the supreme passivity of the neoclassical God entails the impossibility of his initiating action by an act of will, it would appear also that the possession of a totally internal environment is no guarantee of the control of that environment. God on this understanding is, as has now been repeated regularly, the one who experiences. In that case, the example of the toothache may be the appropriate model on which to understand his experience.

[76] *MVG* 181.

The human person is not in control of his toothache. He can take action to remove it or diminish its painfulness. But this would seem to be impossible for God, who can but wait upon the next instalment of experience brought to him by the autonomous process. The whole implication of the difference between the finite experience and the divine is that I can take action about the pain by cutting myself off from that part of the cosmic process that I find unbearable. God cannot do this, for he is logically bound to experience as his internal environment the totality of the process.

Discussion of the analogy between the divine body-mind and the lower reaches of the universal scale of being serves only to repeat the problem. We have seen how, in the case of the lowest levels of reality, there is only analogically an instance of organism because the particle cannot be said to have parts.[77] It is therefore most marked in its differences from the supreme organism.

As we have seen, the particle has no special internal organs, because its neighbours serve it as organs. The universe, conversely, has no neighbours as organs, because everything is its internal organ. Everything contributes equally directly to the cosmic value. This means that the world-mind will have no special brain, but that rather every individual is to that mind as a sort of brain-cell.[78]

But who is in control, the brain-cell or God? All the evidence suggests that it is the former, with whatever clarity God may be said to perceive immediately what each of them is up to. It is beyond doubt that here we arrive at another reversal of the classical conception of God. The part played by God in traditional theism now passes to man. He is the one who is free to make the world what it is, while God is the one privileged to watch him making a success of it.

(ii) The social analogy. To say, as has just been said, that God's environment is totally internal is the other side of the coin that depicts him as supremely relative. Therefore there is a sense in which Chapter II is itself an exposition of the concept of God that holds him to be the supreme instance of what holds everywhere else, being in becoming. The final section of that chapter pointed out that Hartshorne's is a theology of eminence,

---

[77] See above, § iv.   [78] *LP* 197.

in contrast to the classical use of the principle of negation. In this system the principle of eminence holds that God be the supreme instance of the notion of process, creativity, or relativity, by whatever name it be known. Whereas other realities instantiate the categories according to their place on the hierarchy of becoming—that is to say, more or less imperfectly —God instantiates them perfectly, supremely, and unsurpassably. This categorical supremacy, as Hartshorne terms it, has implications that have not yet been spelled out, particularly in relation to the way in which our language can be said to describe God successfully. The remaining section of this chapter will therefore spell out some of the implications of the analogy as a system of speaking about God in terms usually reserved for finite entities, and will close with an illustration of Hartshorne's illegitimate use of the language structure he has erected.

vi. *What it Means to Describe God as Supremely Relative*

If the world is as Hartshorne has described it, then we have a system of language in which we can successfully stretch human language in order to describe God in a way that is both accurate and comprehensible. In particular, the claim is that the problem of religious language as it besets classical theism is on this system overcome. This is not the place for a rehearsal of classical theism's problems, but it can be said that they arise chiefly from the doctrine that God can only be known through his effects[79] and that therefore our language about God can primarily be only of the way in which he does not exist.[80] Any positive, affirmative analogies can then only be predicated secondarily against the background of the essential negations. And so the first claim made on behalf of the neoclassical concept is that it allows positive, affirmative statements about the nature of God to be read off directly from the primary assertions that are made about him on the basis of the system of reality that he crowns.[81] 'If God can be conceived as the infinite degree . . . of whatever variables are applicable in finite degree to man, and man as the finite degree of whatever variables are infinitely applicable

[79] Aquinas, *Summa Theologica* 1a.2.2.

[80] Op. cit. 1a.2.3.

[81] See also S. M. Ogden, op. cit., pp. 149–54 and J. B. Cobb, Jnr., *Living Options in Protestant Theology* (Philadelphia, 1962), pp. 55 f. and *A Christian Natural Theology* (London, 1966), p. 220.

to God . . . then the problem is solved both logically and aesthetically.'[82]

At this stage in Hartshorne's understanding of the situation, the process involves taking language that applies in the first instance to man, and then applying it to God. The categories have a different meaning when applied at the two different levels. Therefore he says that the eminent predication of the categories to God is made 'analogically not univocally'.[83] But the standard use of the language is that in which it is used to describe the human level of reality, and something beyond this ordinary use is done when the language is stretched to fit God. How does he understand this use of analogy to be justified? It is possible because there is a crucial difference between God and other realities, and it is this which compels us to speak analogically.

. . . God is the *one individual conceivable a priori*. It is in this sense that concepts applied to him are analogical rather than simply univocal, in comparison to their other applications. For in all other cases, individual otherness is a mere specificity under more general characteristics. . . . But in the case of deity, the most general conceptions without anything more specific, suffice to 'individuate' . . .[84]

And so, as often within this metaphysical system, we are brought round to aspects that have previously been introduced from a different direction. Here it is shown that our analogical language about God, as this system understands him, is based on his reality as the whole of the cosmic process and more. The *more* is precisely what licenses the fact that there is language at all: the universe has to be conceived in abstraction from the events that make up its concrete reality. But the special, eminent, use of the language is made possible by the fact that it is an abstraction from the whole and not just part of the process as happens with everything else. Because there is no reference to particulars, only God can be conceived *a priori* and can be described in the most general terms. God *is* relativity, becoming, etc. Other entities are merely instances of it. Thus in this first discussion of the use of language to describe God we have seen that the process is one that goes upward from man to God, but that its justification lies in the fact that God is as he is described.

---

[82] *MVG* 220.   [83] *DR* 77.   [84] *DR* 31.

In later works the emphasis is different, in that less is made of the fact that language that really belongs in the human sphere is stretched upwards. Here we come to the second major implication for language of the neoclassical analogy, and it concerns Hartshorne's realization that the language of relativity etc. belongs first in the divine sphere, and only secondarily in the lower orders. The standard use of the categories is the theological one. 'Concerning the question of literalness in theological concepts, I wish . . . to urge Barth's procedure (when taken to task for treating God in terms of personality).'[85] It is not we but rather God who is literally a subject, by which he means that only God literally possesses or includes the objects of his perception. Similarly, God's is the 'standard finitude'.[86] Only God is really finite, because of the fact that he is the sum of all finite happenings. Therefore, when we are speaking of the meaning of our language, we come to realize that relativity etc. means what it means in the case of God. All other senses are derivative from the only real instance.

We now move to an instance of where Hartshorne has used his system of analogy to make an illegitimate transition to another area of discourse. We have seen that, by analogy with the rest of the universe, God is to be described as supremely relative. One corollary of this is that he is supremely aware. But it is not, without further discussion, legitimate to move from this to the fact that God loves everything of which he is aware.

When Charles Wesley . . . wrote: 'Father, thou art all compassion . . .' he was not distinguishing God by denying relativity or passivity to him. Yet he was distinguishing God metaphysically. For all things limit their compassion at some point. . . . Love, *defined as social awareness*, taken literally, is God. . . . God is socially aware— period.[87]

Rarely can love have been defined so passively. Further, there is no necessity that a being who perceives everything should also love everything. Of course, he will be impartial, but only because he has no choice. We can, for example, conceive of a computer that is programmed to scan impartially the whole of a particular system. It will be related to everything in that

[85] 'Tillich's Doctrine of God', *The Theology of Paul Tillich*, edd. C. Kegley and R. Bretall (London, 1952), p. 179.
[86] Ibid., cf. *CSPM* 149.   [87] *DR* 36. My italics.

system, but can hardly be said to love it. The point against Hartshorne is not that he may not have other reasons for characterizing God as love, but that he cannot say that God's supreme relativity entails (logically) that God be in some sense personal love. Yet that is what he does. 'What is a person if not a being qualified and conditioned by social relations, relations to other persons? And what is God if not the supreme case of personality?'[88] The doctrine that God is love does not then arise directly from the metaphysical system. The truth is that the transition from relativity to love is made easier by the assumption of certain metaphysical doctrines, that have been mentioned before, but whose function now becomes clearer.

One of the central conclusions of Chapter II was that God operates causally by being in the immediate past of entities as they come to be. If God, as containing the sum total of past experience is to bring about good in this way, then the contents of the divine memory must be, on average, more good than bad. If it were not so, the influence of God on the present would be in the direction of decline rather than progress. For if more entities started life under bad influence, the likelihood would be that at the next moment, too, the same would hold, and the universe be set for decline. But Hartshorne cannot treat this as a serious possibility, because of another axiom of the system. This derives from the basic metaphysical intuition that reality is process or a series of events. However, the term event is not evaluatively neutral. An event, as such, is the coming into being of something that is valuable. It *may* exercise its freedom for evil ends, but the over-all picture is that this cannot be so. And so in principle it can be said that in general the event will have a beneficent relationship to its world, and can therefore be said to love it. Something that is related to all reality will, *a fortiori*, be describable in terms of love.

There we have the basic rationale of the illegitimate transition from relativity to love. It remains illicit unless the axioms of the system are accepted. But those very axioms owe far more to the classical tradition than to novel philosophical insights. '. . . all things are good insofar as they exist',[89] as Aquinas learned from Aristotle.[90] Hartshorne himself appeals to Plato

---

[88] *DR* 25.   [89] Aquinas, op. cit. 1a.6.4.
[90] Op. cit. 1a.2.3 (the Fourth Way).

rather than Aristotle: '. . . the Platonic principle that the Good, the principle of intrinsic value, which is the central conception in practical or ethical matters, is also the key to the intellectual realm, is logically as well as emotionally pre-eminent.'[91] The difference comes when the metaphysical optimism is transferred from the static world of Plato, Aristotle, and Aquinas to the becoming of neoclassical metaphysics. For it produces the notion of necessary progress, and the sentimental conception of God that accompanies it.

To summarize: Hartshorne bases his concept of God on the metaphysical insight that certain categories or characteristics are attributable both to the whole of reality and to all of its component parts. Each entity, from the elementary particle to God, can be described in the same set of terms, those that belong logically with the notion of relativity, creativity, or becoming. God is the being whose reality consists in the becoming of the whole universe, though he is more than this as well. The description of his being as a being in becoming, and the analogical system by which this is done, are described by means of a logical construction that takes place according to certain rules and not, as is sometimes (and certainly wrongly) alleged to be the case with the classical analogy, in an arbitrary manner. What are the rules to be observed when developing or assessing a system of analogy?

If the idea of God is to have a rational place among our ideas, four conditions must be satisfied. (1) There must be rules or principles valid for all individuals, not excluding God, rules definitive of individuality purely in general . . . (2) There must be rules valid for all individuals *except* God . . . (3) There must be a criterion for the distinction between the two sets of rules. (4) There must be reasons why the distinction needs to be made.[92]

What these rules are, and how they are applied, has been the subject of the previous two chapters. The chief contention of the chapters has not been that there are any major faults in the development of the system. Internally, it is coherent and tightly knit. What can be questioned is, first, the axiomatic

---

[91] 'Four Principles of Method', *Monist* 43 (1933) 54, cf. *CSPM* 285 f.
[92] *NTOT* 37.

optimism that appears to be an essential foundation of the system; second, the expansion of the language from relativity to personal categories like love when the logic of the concept does not seem to require it; and third, the inability of the neoclassical God to be anything other than a receiver of impressions. The strength of the third question in particular is suggested by the fact that the lines of inquiry in both this and the previous chapter point clearly to the same conclusion, that it is difficult to conceive of this God being able to take initiatives on behalf of any or all of his creatures, precisely because they are not his creatures. On the contrary, he is theirs.

None the less, there are further important things to be said about the neoclassical conception of God and its background. In the next chapter we must go deeper into the rational grounds for such a conception. This will involve a further exposition of Hartshorne's understanding of the metaphysical quest, and a look at a final central question. We have seen how our language about God applies to him, in contrast to the way language applies to other realities. We have yet to see why it should be applied at all. In a sense, of course, if the world is as Hartshorne has claimed that it is, it is a nonsensical question. One can hardly have a hierarchy of this kind without necessarily supposing that it has a crown in a single, divine being. But the proofs of the existence of God are important for Hartshorne, and so part of the final chapter will be concerned with an exposition of the use that he makes of them.

IV

FROM ANALOGY TO PROOF

i. *Analogy* and *Analogous Predication*

IN describing the neoclassical concept of God and its meta-physical basis, it has seemed preferable to avoid much of the technical terminology that has been developed in connection with the classical doctrine of analogy, because that terminology is chiefly illuminating in clarifying the complexities of an analogy based on a causal conception of reality. In this con-nection, the remark of B. Mondin is very important. 'Tillich's symbolism is based on the principle of correlation; Aquinas's analogy is based on the principle of the similarity between cause and effect; Barth's *analogia fidei* is based on the principle of the *sola fides*.'[1] The remark enables us to make two observa-tions. First, it is clear that before one can use language about God according to any of these outlooks, it is first necessary to believe either that the universe is so structured or that God behaves in such a way that descriptive language is possible at all. Second, the principle can be extended to apply to what has been seen to be the case with the theology of Hartshorne. Hartshorne's doctrine of analogy is based on the principle of the common character of relativity of all parts of the cosmic system.

To elucidate the situation, it would be well to devise a simple technical vocabulary, so that at least one important distinction can be made. For the situation we have reached requires expression under two heads. *Ontologically*, it has been shown that for Hartshorne there are certain features of reality common to everything that exists; in terms of the relation between God and the world this entails that there is an analogy between God and all other existents. This situation authorizes a certain use of *language*: thus the terms relation, creativity, etc., are

[1] B. Mondin, *The Principle of Analogy in Protestant and Catholic Theology* (2nd edn., The Hague, 1968), p. 155. See Chs. III and IV for the metaphysical doctrines underlying Aquinas's use of analogy.

able to be used in related senses both of God and of entities that are not God. Put in another way, it could be said that Hartshorne's use of language for God is based on *the fact that* God is in certain respects like other entities in the universe. For the purposes of this discussion we can therefore distinguish between the (or an) *Analogy* (ontological, or what is believed to be true about the world) and the *analogical predication* (the system of language) that is developed on its basis.

In the construction of a straightforward system of analogical predication such as the one we have been considering, four terms are involved. First, consider a non-theistic case, a situation where it is proposed to consider the linguistic propriety of attributing intelligence to dogs. The four terms will then be:

A. Man   B. Intelligence
C. Dog   D.   ?

Whether the attribution of intelligence is justified can be decided from an examination of linguistic and behavioural evidence relating to the three known terms, and will therefore involve both linguistic and empirical study. Such an examination could be made in deciding the appropriateness of the application to electrons, cells, etc., of the metaphysical categories derived from an analysis of human experience. But when we wish to predicate qualities of God by this means, the problems are greater. The situation can be shown with the help of another simple diagram:

A. Man   B. Social relatedness
C.   ?   D.   ?

In the absence of compelling reasons for belief in God, we cannot be certain if there is an entity to which any kind of language can be ascribed. And unless we know in advance what kind of language would be appropriate to God were he to exist, then we have no idea where to look to see if there is such a being. It appears that in the absence of information to fill in blanks C or D we are in the position of a mathematician who cannot solve an equation because there is one unknown too many.[2] We can neither know whether the predication of

---

[2] This is a version of the point made by David Hume in different ways throughout the *Dialogues Concerning Natural Religion*. See especially his arguments concerning the nature of arguing from analogy in Part II.

analogous terms is possible at all nor, if it were possible, what kind of language would be appropriate. Each of the subjects of this study believes that rational theology is possible, and that it is possible to use language that is both meaningful and accurate to a degree of a real God. But they solve the equation in different directions. Barth claims some knowledge of a real God, who has laid himself open to knowledge, and therefore to the use of language. He therefore moves from C to D, with the assistance of A and B. With Hartshorne the situation is somewhat different.

What he is arguing, in effect, is that he knows, on the basis of his metaphysical insight and construction, what kind of language is appropriate to God, and in what sense. It is a final step, and little more than a rounding off of the system, to establish the real existence of the kind of God that the metaphysical world-view requires. As a student of Hartshorne's work, R. E. James, has observed, 'Hartshorne's concrete God is certainly presupposed when the proof is discussed, but this does not making speaking (or proving) superfluous; *it makes it possible!*'[3] If, then, the neoclassical proofs, and particularly the ontological argument, are given less attention than the space they occupy in the work of Hartshorne may appear to demand, this is for two reasons. The first is that of chief interest for this study is the relation between concept and proof, rather than proof in itself. And second, as has already been suggested, the metaphysic under consideration is of such a kind that proof is almost superfluous. Here an illuminating parallel is provided by the thought of Spinoza. If Spinoza uses a proof of the existence of God, it is an ontological argument somewhat after the manner of Descartes, and yet in explicit formulation it takes up no major part of his chief theological work, the *Ethics*. There is, however, a sense in which his whole system *is* a version of the ontological argument. If reality is as Spinoza argues it to be, then 'God' must exist. As he holds that it is and must be as he describes it, then God does exist. Spinoza is a paradigm case of what is meant by a rationalist philosopher, in that he believed that it was through reason, and that alone, that a man comes to understand the universe in which he lives. Charles Hartshorne

---

[3] R. E. James, *The Concrete God. A New Beginning for Theology—the Thought of Charles Hartshorne* (Indianapolis, 1967), p. 105. My italics.

is a rationalist through and through. If we examine his assumptions about the relation between language and reality we shall find that the terms rationalist and idealist are well fitted to describe the type of philosophy he represents.

ii. *Hartshorne as an Idealist*

The term 'idealist' can be used in (at least) two related but different senses.

(i) In the first sense Hartshorne not only accepts that he is an idealist, but also preaches the necessity of an idealist view of the world if it is to be intelligible. Speaking of his philosophical predecessor A. N. Whitehead, he says that the latter is a thoroughgoing idealist 'if this means the doctrine that subjectivity is the principle of all beings'.[4] The world consists before all else of subjects, entities whose reality is essentially mindlike or mental. That this is manifestly Hartshorne's teaching too emerged in the discussion of analogy in Chapter III above. And as in that analogy the two chief centres of interest are God and what is not God in the appropriate measure of creativity accorded to them, so here we find the theme of idealism developed in terms of both the lower world and God. In the former the theory is that all beings are in their different ways subjects; that is the panpsychism already mentioned. To be a subject is their primary reality. But when they cease to be subjects, they become, as part of the divine memory, objects in their turn. And so Hartshorne can link his idealism with something that is sometimes opposed to it, perceptual realism. For the subjects do not in any way create what they perceive. They perceive in their subjectivity what is really there in the everlasting divine memory, and therefore they perceive what is objectively real. Hence Hartshorne can speak of his metaphysics as representing 'A Synthesis of Idealism and Realism'.[5] None the less, it is the idealism that is primary, and particularly as an explanation of the way the world is, for it is 'the doctrine that psychological categories alone explain the universe . . .'[6] So much for the world apart from God. In the divine case, the

---

[4] 'Whitehead's Metaphysics', V. Lowe *et al.*, *Whitehead and the Modern World* (New York, 1950), p. 29.
[5] The title of *RSP* 69–84.
[6] 'Contingency and the New Era in Metaphysics', *Journal of Philosophy* 29 (1932) 466.

divine mind performs an appropriate explanatory function and, beyond that, also provides what is in effect an argument for the existence of God. Hartshorne believes that the universe remains opaque unless it is seen to find its reality as subsisting in the mind of God. That is to say, we can *define* what is real as 'whatever is content of knowledge ideally clear and certain'.[7] This is meant to entail precisely what it says: 'that the phrase "all things" simply means whatever the ideal knower knows.'[8] But why should we wish to speak in this way? We have to because we do in fact assume the reality of the past, and must assume it. 'We have to live and think *as though* the past were indestructively real, for otherwise "fact" would have no definite meaning. "God" merely makes this necessary idea more intelligible, that is all.'[9] Common sense makes idealists of us all. The past must exist, and so must the God whose primary function is to perceive and immortalize it and us.

Once again, a comparison with a great philosopher in Hartshorne's past may help to throw light on this aspect of the scene. It is likely that this 'psychological' understanding of the universe owes something to the idealism of Bishop Berkeley. Berkeley had too much common sense and was too good a theologian to dabble in panpsychism; quite the reverse, in fact. It was his very refusal to attribute agency to inanimate 'ideas' that led him to reject theories of causation that appeared to do so. All ideas or phenomena were attributed rather to the direct agency of a real personal mind, God's or a man's. In this respect, as in some other of his doctrines, Hartshorne can be seen to stand a classical philosopher on his head. The real agency passes from God to the contents of God's mind, and the deity becomes a receptive rather than an active, willing omniscience. But Berkeley and Hartshorne do stand together in believing that non-personal reality is subordinate to the personal. Reality is what it is because of its mental component, and the non-mental is dependent on and secondary to the mental. Both are idealists in the sense that God provides the final reason for things being as they are; they differ in the functions they attribute to him, one making him a guarantor of the reality of the present, the other of the reality of the past.

[7] 'Ideal Knowledge Defines Reality', *Journal of Philosophy* 43 (1946) 573.
[8] Art cit., p. 574.   [9] *AD* 107.

(ii) The second sense in which the term 'idealism' is used is that in which its proponents appeal not so much to the structure of reality as being dominated by mental characteristics as to the *contents* of the conceiving mind. According to this conception, the mind is able to comprehend reality with the help of its structure of concepts. Here, incidentally, idealism is not contrasted with realism, as it often is in the case of philosophers like Berkeley, but equated with it, as a form of conceptual realism. The concepts of the mind, however obtained, are believed, when properly understood, to perform the function of providing a clue to the metaphysical understanding of reality. In this sense, idealism goes back at least as far as Plato, for whom the 'forms' or 'ideas' are anything but the conventional constructions of those who use them. It is by contemplation of the ideas that a man comes to understand the very structure of the universe. What is not being suggested here is that Hartshorne is a Platonic realist. But it is true that he shares something of the views of Plato, and of later rationalists like Descartes and Spinoza, of the relation between concepts (and the language in which they are expressed) and the extramental world. There is a real link between the two, such that the language can throw light upon the nature of the world. Some such view of the relation between language and reality provides the necessary underpinning for the neoclassical system of analogy, and possibly for any system of analogy developed with the use of human reason, as in the case of St. Thomas Aquinas.

iii. *Hartshorne as a Rationalist*

This aspect of Hartshorne's thought is best brought out by an exposition of his rationalism, for it is clear that in this area the terms idealism and rationalism describe different aspects of the same phenomenon. A rationalist is one who believes that the human mind has innate to it the capacity to understand and describe the world as it really is. This capacity has at least two prior conditions. First, the world must in some way be open to the inquiries of the mind. It must itself have a rational structure. Second, the language the philosopher uses must in some way be suitable to bear the load that is carried by it. Language must be at least potentially capable of describing the world. It is not then surprising that many philosophers in this tradition have subscribed to a theory of innate ideas as, classically, have Plato and Descartes.

But what of Hartshorne himself? That the first condition is fulfilled in his system of thought is clear from the doctrine outlined in Chapter III. If the doctrine is true, it is also true that reality is open to being understood by the inquiring mind as creative at all of its levels. The same goes for the second condition. Terms such as relativity, creativity, becoming and temporality are argued to be the correct ways in which our language must, even if at times it has to be 'stretched', characterize the world about which it speaks. It would then appear that Hartshorne is a rationalist, and indeed he accepts the description. In one article he even describes himself as being, in certain respects, 'ultra-rationalist'.[10] And while he does not make a point of developing a doctrine of innate ideas, many of the things that he says are heavily suggestive of a belief that the mind is already equipped to decide by reason alone what is and what is not true: 'if we had perfect command of our ideas we should see logical absurdity in any description that is really impossible'.[11] That is, he is not merely claiming that what cannot, under any circumstances, be true is a matter of principle rather than experiment or observation but also that the clear mind is able to come to a decision about the matter of principle.

Hartshorne's belief in the innate rational capacity of the mind has two important implications. The first is that for him language in general performs a revelatory function. We have already seen the importance for him of the argument from ideal knowledge. In one formulation of it Hartshorne makes this assumption about the nature of language explicit. He says, '. . . by "the past", one appears to mean, not merely what we remember . . . but what unlimited or cosmic memory can nevermore forget. "The moving finger writes . . . nor all thy piety nor wit shall lure it back to cancel half a line." Deny such theistic implications *of language*, and paradox immediately

[10] 'Is God's Existence a State of Affairs?', *Faith and the Philosophers*, ed. J. Hick (London, 1964), p. 32.

[11] 'Real Possibility', *Journal of Philosophy* 60 (1963) 594. He also believes that 'experience is, without residuum, illustrative of rational, i.e. logical, structure . . .'—'Four Principles of Method', *Monist* 43 (1933) 43.

appears.'[12] If the implications of our thought about the past are theistic, so much more is our language about God. We shall have more to say about this when the proofs are expounded, but it is worth citing a passage where Hartshorne, claiming that it is a mistake to make an 'absolute disjunction between thought and experience', argues that 'if we have a meaning for our thought about God, we also have experience of him . . .'[13] 'If we have a meaning:' of course, the complaint of Hartshorne against the classical theists is that this is precisely what they did not have, because of the radical incoherence of their concept. His claim is that *correct* thought about God by its very nature brings God into the experience of the thinker.

The revelatory function of language in this system is most marked in relation to the categories, those terms that are predicated analogously of all levels of reality. If the predication is successful, it is so for the very simple reason that the categories do in fact describe what is really there. They are written indelibly into the very structure of the universe, and are therefore far from being useful and possibly dispensable constructs of the human mind. Further, there is a sense in which they are themselves divine: '. . . if a vision of God is the hidden source of all metaphysics . . . then we need not suppose that "our categories" are just human affairs. . . .'[14] Rationalistic man is thus in a sense divine man, for between his mind and the more than human structure of the universe there is enough in common for him to know by his own efforts the secrets of the cosmos.

The second implication of Hartshorne's rationalism is that it brings together what generations of modern philosophers have progressively put asunder. The distinction between the worlds of logic, or language, and ontology, or reality, has tended to be drawn ever more sharply, certainly in the empiricist tradition, since Spinoza so uniquely blended the two in the seventeenth century. For Spinoza, to solve a problem about the interrelatedness of certain basic ideas like substance, attribute, and mode *was* to solve the riddle about the nature of reality. Hartshorne follows Spinoza in this respect, and rejects any

---

[12] *LP* 152. My italics.   [13] *MVG* 311.
[14] 'Tillich's Doctrine of God', *The Theology of Paul Tillich*, edd. C. Kegley and R. Bretall (New York, 1952), pp. 190 f.

sharp distinction between idea and reality. 'Metaphysical questions are indeed logical questions, questions essentially about ideas; but since *an idea about nothing is not an idea*, unless the idea of "nothing" itself, to say that logical questions are "merely" logical, and therefore "not about existence", is an antimetaphysical dogma, not a self-evident truth.'[15] There are many examples of Hartshorne's solving of apparently factual— if also metaphysical—questions by appealing to the meanings of words. His means of arriving at the conception of the asymmetrical nature of time by appeal to the meaning of the word 'future' is a case in point.[16] And the related question of determinism can be decided with the same ease of *a priori* discussion. 'Thus to say "every possible entity is also necessary", is to destroy the contrast between possible, actual and necessary as distinctive aspects of reality.'[17] This may well be so; but, on the face of it, it would appear that a question of fact, albeit metaphysical fact, requires deeper consideration than it is given here. It may be necessary to destroy the contrast Hartshorne mentions because we are compelled to do so by our experience of the world; in other words, the world may compel us to change the meaning of our language even at as deep a level as this. For it is conceivable that we may discover that the world is determined in all that happens, and that the future follows from the past with the iron necessity of a mathematical theorem.

But the whole point of Hartshorne's rationalism is that this could not be so unless the rationalism he has propounded is shown as a whole to be false. As it is, there are certain concepts, the categories, which are written into the world in which we live. And they require, in particular, that we conceive of God in a certain way, that is, as dipolar. The classical theists were wrong precisely because they neglected certain of the categories in favour of others. They did not realize that they were breaking one of the laws of reason. The law of polarity holds that

ultimate contraries are correlatives, mutually interdependent, so that *nothing real* can be described by the wholly one-sided assertion of simplicity, being, actuality, and the like, each in a 'pure' form, devoid and independent of complexity, becoming, potentiality

[15] *AD* 24 f. My italics.   [16] Above, Ch. III, § iii pp. 59 f.   [17] *CSPM* 89.

and related contraries. This principle of polarity . . . may be traced back through Hegel to Heracleitus and Plato . . .[18]

Thus we return to the topic of Chapter II. We can now see that there is another motive beyond the description of God as dipolar. That motive is provided by reason, whose view of the structure of reality requires that it be so.

There is one brief qualification to be made to the discussion of Hartshorne's rationalism. It does not qualify the rationalism, but rather any impression that may have been given that Hartshorne has a 'Platonic' view of universals, in that he believes in the existence of an unchanging world of forms that the mind can recall or discern. Clearly, on his views, any reality must instantiate the categories if it is to be real at all, and to that extent there is a world of forms. But the categories operate in a world in process, and therefore other universals than the categories have room for change as the instances of process change. This leads Hartshorne to what he calls an Aristotelian view of universals, 'that they are not ultimately and absolutely separable from concrete instances . . .'[19] Moreover, 'It is instances which alone give universals any foothold in reality . . .'[20] But the basic rationalism is in no way qualified, as can be seen when it is realized that the 'instances' which give universals their foothold are not any instances but *necessarily* instances of creative process. There can be no reality that is not an instance of creative becoming.

iv. *The Neoclassical Proofs*

It is now clear how and why Hartshorne can fill in one of the two unknowns that would baffle the exponent of theological analogy. Because Hartshorne is a rationalist, he can be certain of the kind of language that is appropriate to the supreme being in his metaphysical system. That this language must apply to a being is scarcely in doubt. But the system must be rounded off by the development of proofs of the existence of God that are appropriate to it. Clearly, appropriate in a rationalistic system are proofs that centre on the appeal to ideas or concepts rather than to sense experience or existential *Angst*. If the categories

[18] *PSG* 2. My italics.   [19] *AD* 56, cf. *RSP* 72.
[20] 'Metaphysics and the Modality of Existential Judgments', *The Relevance of Whitehead*, ed. I. Leclerc (London, 1961), p. 110.

are indeed more than human affairs, it is to them that we should look as a source of revelation. So that we shall find that even where Hartshorne does deal with those proofs that have sometimes been treated empirically he is only concerned with the conceptual side. His characteristic argument is of course the ontological, in its rationalistic use rather than the one to which Karl Barth puts it.

In fact Hartshorne expounds six proofs in all, describing them as the aesthetic, ethical, epistemological (or idealistic), design, cosmological, and ontological. The first three, he says, are 'normative', the rest 'classical'.[21] All of them are for him dependent upon the ontological, because they are all conceptual or linguistic in character. '*All* arguments for the necessary being are essentially of one type, and all must in some sense be *a priori*.'[22] Indeed, there is a sense in which they are all versions of a single proof: 'All the arguments are phases of one "global" argument, that the properly formulated theistically religious view of life and reality is the most intelligible, self-consistent, and satisfactory one that can be conceived.'[23] This is because the proofs, like the analogy and the concept of God derive their origins and their power to convince from the more than human categories. 'All proofs for God depend upon conceptions which derive their meaning from God himself. They are merely ways of making clear that we already and once and for all believe in God, though not always with clearness and consistency.'[24] How then is there room for arguments other than the ontological? The answer lies in the fact that there are conceptual versions of the other arguments also. The argument from design, for example, 'is not observational. For, if the reasoning is correct, the alternative to God's existence is not an existing chaos, but, rather, nothing conceivable. The argument is that the very concept of reality . . . implicitly involves order and an orderer.'[25] The final sentence of that passage is in itself illustration of the point already twice made, that after the work of metaphysical construction the work of proof is virtually redundant. Of course 'the very concept of

---

[21] *PSG* 25, *CSPM* 275–97.

[22] 'The Philosophy of Creative Synthesis', *Journal of Philosophy* 55 (1958), 952.

[23] *CSPM* 276. The second phrase is in italics in Hartshorne. See *NTOT* 45 ff. for a similar statement of the position.

[24] *MVG* 274.

[25] *NTOT* 53.

reality' involves an orderer if by reality is meant what neo-classical philosophy means by it. Similarly, in making a slightly different point, Hartshorne can say that 'All the proofs, properly stated, proceed from ideas; but not all from the idea of God itself. And all show that we must either admit some basic idea to be absurd, or take it to be necessarily true, and admit also that this truth entails the necessary existence of the Greatest being.'[26] That is to say, all Hartshorne's philosophical speculation has been concerned to show what must necessarily be true about the universe. If he is correct not only is he necessarily correct, but also the existence of God follows by irrefutable logic from what has been said.

In the passages that have been cited, Hartshorne is presenting a classical pre-Kantian view of the function and power of the proofs of the existence of God. Since the time of Hume and Kant it has become widely accepted that it is logically illegitimate to attempt to establish the existence of a concrete reality by logical means. The transition from idea to reality is an impossible one, a μετάβασις εἰς ἄλλο γένος. One of the distinctive marks of Hartshorne's rationalism is that he accepts and attempts to avoid the prohibition. Indeed, he can sometimes give the impression of displaying 'unquestioning acceptance of the empiricist theory of meaning . . .'[27] While this is a false impression, it is nevertheless true that he does claim that in his proofs of the existence of God he is not attempting to establish the existence by logical means of a concrete reality. The claim is based on his conception of metaphysics and the nature of metaphysical statements. Metaphysical statements are those statements whose truth is compatible with the truth of any statement concerning the empirical world. A statement that for example, a particular piece of space is occupied by a waste-paper basket is incompatible with one that that same space contains an electric fire. That is the way things are in the empirical world. But it is not so with metaphysics, which is what it is precisely because metaphysical truth is compatible with the truth of either or neither of the statements used above. Put otherwise, metaphysical statements are expressions

[26] *AD* 135.
[27] G. N. A. Vesey, 'Foreword', *Talk of God* (Royal Institute of Philosophy Lectures II, London, 1969) p. xx, cf. p. xvii.

of necessary truth, while empirical statements are concerned with empirical and therefore contingent matters. Indeed, the very necessity of metaphysical statements lies in the fact that their 'affirmation cuts off no conceivable state of affairs'.[28]

Hartshorne employs another discovery of modern logic when he says further that every metaphysical statement is related logically to every other metaphysical statement. A perfect example of this from his own system would be the interrelation of all the attributes of God as they were expounded in Chapter II. There it was seen that everything that was said about God was derived by a process of logical analysis from the fundamental insight that God was supremely relative. The reason for the logical interrelatedness of all metaphysical statements is the fact that all necessary statements are entailed by any and every other statement.

A necessary proposition is one whose truth is included in that of any other proposition whatever. For, were this not so, it must be possible for the other proposition to be true while the necessary proposition was false. But the hypothesis is that the proposition cannot be false under any circumstances, since what it affirms is necessary. In this sense, then . . . a necessary proposition is entailed by any proposition.[29]

The logical interrelatedness of the body of necessary truth follows from this quite simply. For if a necessary proposition is entailed by any proposition, then *a fortiori* it is entailed by any necessary proposition, and every necessary proposition entails every other necessary proposition. Put in terms of logic, we might say that the body of necessary truth is that which makes speech possible, as its necessary assumptions or presuppositions. But we have to remember that for Hartshorne there is no such thing as a truth that is merely logical. Logic has ontological implications. Therefore necessary truth is what must be true if anything at all is *to be*; and the metaphysician's task is to set out that tight circle of propositions that define what being is.

Given, then, the conception of metaphysics as the development of a system of necessary truths that are both compatible

---

[28] 'Metaphysical Statements as Nonrestrictive and Existential', *Review of Metaphysics* 12 (1958) 36.
[29] *AD* 41.

with and entailed by any empirical states of affairs,[30] how is Hartshorne able to argue that a proof of the existence of God avoids the Kantian difficulties? Among the necessary truths with which the metaphysician deals is the necessary—*logically* necessary—existence of God; but, it is claimed, it is his existence in the *abstract* form outlined in Chapter II. (After all, how could it be otherwise? Knowledge of the concrete reality of God would require knowledge of all the free events which make up the universe at the moment in which the knowledge was sought.) *If* reality is as it is claimed to be in the doctrine outlined in Chapter III—though of course for Hartshorne there is no *if* involved; it must be so—then the abstract framework of the divine experience can only be the concept of a supremely relative, dipolar deity. Moreover, as being part of the framework of interrelated necessary truths it is entailed by any proposition. That is to say, understand the implications of any statement at all and you will see that a God of the kind neoclassical metaphysics has described must exist. That is the extent of the rationalism of this philosopher. 'The idea of God is the integrated total of all predictions that can be made *a priori.*'[31] And perhaps more important for bringing out the assumptions of the metaphysics:

Given a supersyntactical or phenomenological reference for the categories, the rest is *a matter of deduction* from definitions which attempt to state the interrelations of categories exhibited in the phenomena. Metaphysical judgments from that point on are *formally 'analytic'*. The phenomenological enquiry, however, seems formally 'synthetic'. But it is not *contingent or a posteriori* in the sense of consisting of judgments whose contradictories are (*a*) empirically meaningful and (*b*) formally consistent.[32]

The formulation is technical but the gist clear. Hartshorne rejects out of hand Kant's doctrine that the categories of metaphysical construction can tell us nothing of the world outside our minds. Statements that appear to be merely truths of language or logic ('formally analytic') are not so, for they really tell us about the world. But they do not tell us such things about the world as are open to empirical testing, for

---

[30] Or *statements* of empirical states of affairs. Once again, there is no difficulty felt in making the transition from logic to the world.

[31] *BH* 256.   [32] *BH* 271. My italics.

they cannot be false. Kant's class of synthetic *a priori* also had to be true, but they were true only of the phenomena of sense experience as these were given to the mind. Hartshorne is therefore going back beyond Kant to the classical rationalists whose work he claimed to have shown to rest upon impossible assumptions.

Before, however, we come to the grounds for Hartshorne's attempt to revive traditional *a priori* metaphysics, a little more must be said about the nature of the proofs as part of a single system of necessary truth. They are even more closely related to each other than the other truths, if that be possible. For they are all elaborations of the same concept and therefore variations on a single theme.

Any one argument for God is either fallacious or proves God to be necessary. No number of arguments can add to necessity. And necessary truths mutually imply one another, are really aspects of one and the same necessity, namely, God. The only value of a multiplicity of arguments is that it diminishes the probability that we have overlooked fallacies in the reasoning . . .[33]

Like all metaphysics, the arguments represent attempts at linguistic clarification, and no more. 'Grubbing among facts is neither here nor there. Self-understanding is the issue: someone is confused, either the theist, or the non-theist.'[34] Clearly by 'self-understanding' is meant the understanding of one's innate conceptual equipment rather than anything psychological. As Hartshorne remarks elsewhere, '. . . atheism is bad grammar'.[35] Thus a question of fact—for surely the existence of God, at least in one sense of the term, is a question of fact, even though it is not a sense of fact which the radical empiricist or positivist would allow—is claimed to be in effect one of meaning.

On the face of it, this might appear to be a very modern approach to philosophy, as it is widely believed that modern philosophy is largely or even wholly concerned with questions of meaning. Hartshorne sometimes even reinforces the impression. 'Here contemporary philosophers might well agree . . . metaphysical blunders are due to the misuse of words.'[36] The chief difficulty for Hartshorne lies in the fact that most of

[33] *MVG* 251 f. 　　　　[34] *NTOT* 88. 　　　　[35] *CSPM* 131.
[36] *CSPM* 94.

these same philosophers would regard his whole system as based upon a misuse of words. For, rightly or wrongly, they believe that the attempt to change our understanding of the universe by philosophical speculation, or to change the meaning of the words by which we describe the universe, is to attempt to do more than the philosopher can do, which is merely to elucidate the meaning of language as it is actually used. Speaking of Spinoza, but in words that would apply to Hartshorne, Stuart Hampshire gives one reason for this belief: '. . . to many twentieth century philosophers the construction of metaphysical systems of any kind has come to seem finally useless and impossible. . . .'[37] Another related point that Hampshire makes about Spinoza brings out both the contrast between Hartshorne and much modern philosophy and, more positively, his concept of what it is to elucidate the meaning of our concepts. Hampshire observes that for the rationalist the criterion of truth cannot be what it is for the empiricist—for example, correspondence of our words with extralinguistic reality—but rather the coherence of all the concepts in the system. 'A case might even be made for saying that it is *the* central logical doctrine on which all deductive metaphysics or *a priori* "theories" of the Universe are based; it can be argued that, without some form of this logical doctrine being assumed or accepted, no such philosophical "explanations" or "theories" would be attempted.'[38] That this applies to Hartshorne is clear from his deprecatory reference to 'grubbing among facts'. Further, he says quite explicitly that metaphysics is not to do with relating 'ideas to observed facts' but 'only to other ideas'.[39] And so it can be seen that Hartshorne too is in quest of coherence, as is shown by the statement that in one of the central areas of metaphysical inquiry it is 'merely a question of clarity or coherence'.[40]

What now emerges is that even though Hartshorne believes that he can evade the traditional criticisms of rational proofs of the existence of God there is a sense in which he remains as committed a rationalist as any of his predecessors. Therefore

[37] S. Hampshire, *Spinoza* (London, 1962), p. 211.   [38] Op. cit., p. 101.
[39] *CSPM* 131.
[40] 'Is God's Existence a State of Affairs?', *Faith and the Philosophers*, ed. J. H. Hick (London, 1964), p. 32.

an enormous weight has to hang on the one aspect of his thought by which he hopes to evade the pitfalls of this approach to truth. He claims that he can avoid empiricist critiques by means of the doctrine that the arguments for the existence of God are concerned with abstractions only. Their validity cannot be impugned because they only attempt to establish God's abstract essence and not his concrete reality, from which the essence is abstracted. That is to say, Hartshorne accepts only part of the empiricist case. He accepts that metaphysical processes of thought cannot establish the existence of any single concrete reality. But that is not to say that they are not in any way concerned with the existence of concrete realities. They can and must establish what kinds of reality can exist, without attempting to restrict the possible existence of any particular being within the framework of meaning that has been laid out. That is left to the concrete, free decisions of the beings that determine the reality of the universe from time to time.

What examples are there of metaphysical, and therefore necessarily true, statements that have existential import? Hartshorne takes in illustration the statement, 'something exists.' Because it is falsifiable in no conceivable circumstances, he argues, it is necessarily true.[41] His conclusion, of course, does not follow, any more than the argument with which he backs it up: ' "There might be nothing" cannot, by any conceivable experience, be given a clear and consistent meaning . . .'[42] The weakness lies in the words, 'by any conceivable experience'. Clearly, if there were nothing, there would be no experience to give the statement meaning. But conceivability is not the same as imaginability, although Hartshorne has confused the two. To take the famous example of the table in Bishop Berkeley's study, to conceive that the table might be there even though no perceiver were present to ensure its reality is not the same as imagining a table in the study, and so falling into Berkeley's trap by having a mental image of the table. In just the same way it is possible to conceive the possibility that there might be nothing without making the absurd supposition that 'nothing' has to be experienced by something or somebody

[41] 'Metaphysical Statements as Nonrestrictive and Existential', *Review of Metaphysics* 12 (1958), 36.
[42] *CSPM* 58.

before it can be verified. Similarly, 'something exists' could be falsified in the same way that a belief in life after death would be falsified on the believer's failure to survive. It could not be falsified by him, but would be falsified in the sense of proving false. Thus if the whole of the universe falls into a black hole that is correctly described as 'nothingness'—as is at least conceivable, for the possibility is discussed—the statement 'something exists' will be false. It cannot therefore be necessarily true.

None the less, for the sake of the exposition of Hartshorne's position, let it be supposed that he has established his point, and that 'something exists' is admitted to be necessarily true, and therefore a metaphysical statement that is of existential import. '. . . if the proposition, "something exists" is necessary, then we must give up the reigning dogma that a statement is rendered contingent by the mere fact that it asserts existence.'[43] The question now is whether the Kantian critique can be avoided in another direction, by establishing that 'something exists' is also an abstraction. Hartshorne believes that it is the most abstract existential statement of all, because of its extreme generality. It is both entailed by any other statement of existence and itself entails no other statement of existence. And so being utterly general, it is also correctly described as abstract. Hartshorne puts it thus:

Contingency is found wherever one goes from the abstract toward the concrete. 'Something exists' does not entail 'Animals exist,' this does not entail 'Foxes exist,' and this does not entail 'Fox with torn left ear exists.' Any step toward concrete particularity is logically a non-necessary one. But, likewise, any step from the particular to the specific of which it is a particularisation, or from the specific to the generic of which it is a specialisation, is logically necessary. Thus when we reach the most abstract and universal conceptions, we arrive at entities which are entailed by any statements whatever, and this is precisely what necessary means.[44]

We now come to a crucial point. Having seen how Hartshorne argues for the abstract necessity of 'something exists' we have to turn to statements of the existence of God. Necessity can for now be left on one side, as that will follow or fail to follow from the neoclassical proofs. But how can the existence

43 'Metaphysical Statements', p. 37.   44 LP 97.

of God be seen to be abstract? The argument stands or falls with the neoclassical conception of reality, and in clarification two doctrines that have already been mentioned in other contexts must be recalled. First,

the most concrete particular entities are not enduring individuals but momentary events or states. The existence of an individual is the actuality of a certain sort of event-sequence. The sequence can be defined without specifying all the particular events, for we identify a person without committing ourselves to all his adventures past and future.[45]

Thus the character of any event-sequence is *abstracted* from the primary reality that it is.[46] In the case of all sequences but one the character but not the existence is an abstraction. In the case of God, because he is by definition an abstraction from the whole of the cosmic event-sequence both character and existence are pure abstractions. In establishing the existence of God, therefore, we do not establish any particular concrete reality, for the existence must be *whatever* particular events make up the universe at any given time. Second, God, as we saw in Chapter II, is both abstract and necessary in different poles of his being. *Purely as existing* he is abstract. In other words the statement of the existence of God has the same kind of abstract character as the statement that 'something exists' because like that it is both utterly general and an implication of any other statement. If, as the classical theists claimed, we were still trying to establish by reason the existence of a God whose concrete reality consists in being necessary in all aspects, then we would indeed be in contravention of the rule that concrete reality may not be established from abstract idea. But we are not, for the concrete reality is not for us to establish: that is left to the free entities that make up the universe. We merely take the step from idea to abstract necessity, and specifically the necessity that the reality of God is 'necessarily somehow actualised'.[47]

But is 'necessarily somehow actualised' completely abstract, in the sense that 'something exists' is said to be so? Certainly, in the sense that the existence of God does not, in itself, entail any particular contents for the divine experience, and is

---

[45] *AD* 284.   [46] *AD* 51.   [47] *AD*, heading of Part I.

entirely nonrestrictive with respect to any concrete occurrence. 'The mere existence of God . . . cannot make an empirical difference. However, it implies that there are divine actualities which do make differences. . . .'[48] Whether it fulfils other criteria of abstractness will be seen after the proofs themselves have been expounded.

v. *Hartshorne's Cosmological Argument*

While the ontological argument is the crown of Hartshorne's attempts to prove the existence of God as he is conceived in neoclassical metaphysics, it is worth while to examine briefly another of his arguments, both to illustrate the essentially conceptual nature of an argument which in some philosophers takes a more empirical direction and to expound further the implications of the view that time is absolute. The conceptual nature of the argument is shown by the statement that the cosmological argument 'would perhaps show that any language adequate to formulate the universal categories, or to discuss the most general cosmological questions, would also make "perfection exists" L-true'.[49] The objection to any version of the argument that is coloured by merely empirical considerations is that 'God, if he exists, is the ground not only of this actual world but of any possible world, so that the imaginary worlds with which we have compared the real one either are impossible, and hence not really imaginable, or else they involve God no less than the real world, and the comparative merits of the latter are irrelevant.'[50] That is to say, the cosmological argument purports to show that any world that is really conceivable requires for its adequate conception the existence of God as its ground.

Hartshorne's only extended version of the argument[51] consists of a number of analyses of different characteristics of the cosmos as it is conceived in neoclassical metaphysics. Thus, the relativity of all existence entails that all existence be characterized by change.[52] This change involves entities going into and out of existence, and this in itself requires that there be

---

[48] *LP* 109 f.
[49] i.e. true by virtue of the meaning of the terms used, *LP* 56. The 'also' is used because all the arguments take their shape from the ontological argument. Cf. *CSPM* 278.
[50] *MVG* 253, cf. *CSPM* 258.   [51] *MVG* 251–98   [52] *MVG* 256.

something that is prior to (ontologically prior to) this universal flux, for 'generation consists in . . . a change in something
which exists before the generation'.[53] Classically, of course, this
kind of argument led to the postulation of an entity that was
changeless. But in this metaphysics there can be no such entity.
What is established on this view of the world is that there must
be an entity that is eternally changing.

For a generated subject can appear as a new state only of a subject
not at that moment generated, and if this pre-existent subject were
itself generated earlier, then it could itself only constitute a state of
a still earlier subject, which must still endure, and thus there must
be at least one subject to whom no beginning or end can be
assigned.[54]

The peculiarly neoclassical shape of the argument is revealed
not only by the type of being established, but also by the use of
the appeal to the impossibility of an infinite regress of subjects
of change. Where Aquinas uses it to reach a being who is
outside the finite world, Hartshorne uses it for a being who is
totally involved in all finitude. And, as he develops its theme,
Hartshorne shows that it serves to establish a being who is
properly conceived as the mind of the cosmos. 'What then is
the sufficient subject of all change? . . . Surely the most flexible
positively known thing is mind in so far as it is sensitive . . .
and able to harmonise all this variety of experience into one
tolerable aesthetic whole . . .'[55]

But, as we have seen, the notion of process involves not only
temporal change, but also the notion of 'events "following" each
other' in space-time and a revised conception of cause. By
taking each of these notions, Hartshorne is able to produce
variations on the cosmological theme. Of the first, he argues
that it requires completion by the notion of omniscience;[56]
and of the second that if there is causality, then it can only be
satisfactorily conceived in the light of a universal causality.[57]
These observations do not add much to our understanding
of the argument as Hartshorne develops it. That they do is
illustrate once more the interrelation and logical interlocking
of the different concepts in the neoclassical system. Just as all

the categories belong in a conceptual cluster that expands the meaning of the words 'process' and 'relativity', so here the different aspects of that same cluster make possible variations on the theme of a cosmological argument.

As we have seen, the cosmological argument depends upon and presupposes the neoclassical belief that change, time, and causality are fundamental and eternal realities, and it moves to a conclusion that a satisfactory explanation of those realities is found only in God. The doctrine that space-time has persisted and will persist eternally follows logically from the notion of process. If all reality is temporal, it is clearly meaningless to speak of an order of reality in which there is no time, or in which 'time' has undergone some kind of radical transformation (for example, eschatologically), or in which the divine eternity means a different kind of time. Once again, the antecedents of Hartshorne's cosmology in certain aspects of the Newtonian theory of space and time may well be observed here. What is also to be noted is the fact that there can, on this understanding, be no doctrine of *creatio ex nihilo*, and not only for the reason that according to neoclassical metaphysics the only creation in any meaningful sense of the word is that carried out by the world and experienced by God. If *creatio ex nihilo* requires the belief in the beginning of time, it is impossible, for 'the idea of a beginning of time is self-contradictory, as Aristotle pointed out'.[58] But that Hartshorne's rejection of the idea is based more on metaphysical presuppositions than on pure logic is shown by the way in which he defends his position. 'A first or last moment is nonsense, for a moment is only a boundary between past and future. . . . If process cannot begin or end, then that there is process is no accident but a necessity.'[59] Of course, if the word moment is understood univocally, and in terms of neoclassical metaphysics only, then Hartshorne's case is irrefutable. But it is begging the whole question about the conceivability of the idea of a first moment in time if the questioner does not ask the question in abstraction from the metaphysic whose necessary truth is at stake. Compare what can happen when an attempt is made to stretch the meaning of the terms in the light of a new apprehension of fact.

[58] *MVG* 233.   [59] *PSG* 60.

As for the ancient puzzle of time and eternity, Dr. Whitrow gives a convincing logical demonstration that it simply makes no sense to say time stretches eternally backwards. We are to understand that time and the universe 'began' . . . at the same 'time', somewhere about ten thousand million years ago. (There is, clearly enough, no time without phenomena.)[60]

Hartshorne, then, appears to be taking the position that his metaphysical position is immune from attack by philosophers of science even on the grounds of observations of fact. This tallies exactly with his defence against attacks from the theory of relativity, and applies also to criticisms made on theological grounds. 'Hartshorne's negative position follows from a view of the self which cannot accommodate immortality in any stronger sense, *whatever the demands of religious belief.*'[61] The point made here is about personal immortality rather than the nature of the cosmos, but the relevance is direct. Resurrection, for example, at the last day or in some alleged order of time and space different from this one, is ruled out *a priori*. Neoclassical metaphysics becomes a religious system in itself, laying down conditions that must be observed by any other theology or religion that wishes to make use of its insights.

What is most astonishing of all is Hartshorne's cavalier treatment of a problem that Kant believed to be beyond rational (i.e. by means of *a priori* reasoning) solution. In later works, he does at least refer to it as a problem, but even then dismisses it with a shrug of the metaphysical shoulders. 'This brings us face to face with Kant's first antinomy about the infinity or finitude of the past. I incline to the infinite horn of the dilemma, though I confess myself puzzled in the matter.'[62] That must rate as an understatement of major proportions, for as we have seen the metaphysician cannot 'incline' to anything, for all his conclusions are either necessarily true or nonsensical. It is very likely that Hartshorne here falls into the latter category. He knows that he is in danger of this. 'A first moment in time would be an ontological lie through and through, a joke of existence upon itself. True, the alternative is the—to us unimaginable—infinite regress of past events, but all attempts to

[60] Philip Toynbee, review of *The Voices of Time*, ed. J. T. Fraser, *Observer*, 18 Feb. 1968.
[61] Julian Hartt, 'The Logic of Perfection', *Review of Metaphysics* 16 (1963) 751. My italics.   [62] *CSPM* 235, cf. 125 f.

show this idea to be self-contradictory seem to have failed.'[63] Hartshorne's first difficulty is that he appears to hold in other contexts that what is unimaginable ('cannot, by any conceivable experience, be given a clear and consistent meaning'[64]) cannot be true. He could evade this difficulty by supposing that God's experience could give the idea a clear and consistent meaning, but then there comes a more serious question. Can the idea of infinite time be made intelligible on his own terms? The chief difficulty is that Hartshorne's conception of time is of an absolute 'given' that is increasing by units that at least for God are distinguishable as units. There is a total that is added to with every moment of cosmic experience. But can one add to infinity? It might be claimed that one could, for the total would still be infinity. But suppose we look at it another way. Imagine that we are standing at time t on the cosmic timescale. Then yesterday's breakfast began at—say, using large units for convenience—$t-100$, and a year ago was $t-36500$. At each of these three positions in time, and at any other we choose to imagine, there is a *totality* of moments in the divine experience (to be succeeded next moment by a new totality) which is also infinite, and this holds however far back in time we go. This would at least appear to be absurd, for how can one even conceive of an infinite totality? Is not infinity by definition a symbol for that which is not and cannot be a totality? In this area of his thought at any rate Hartshorne appears to have attempted a transition from the world of idea to that of reality, and by metaphysical reasoning to have postulated what is, according to that very reasoning, an impossibility.

vi. *Hartshorne and 'Anselm'*

It is when we come to Anselm that the persistent comparison-in-contrast or likeness-in-difference that will be argued to obtain between much of Hartshorne's and Barth's theology begins to show itself. On both sides there is an adaptation of Anselm's so-called ontological argument at the very heart of the work. Yet their use of the argument divides them, along the lines of a distinction suggested by J. Moltmann between proofs from the 'name' and the 'concept' of God.[65] It is the

[63] *MVG* 234.   [64] *CSPM* 58; see above, p. 88.
[65] J. Moltmann, *Theology of Hope* (E.T. by J. Leitch, London, 1965), pp. 272 f.

difference between the concept of a God who reveals his 'name' on particular, concrete, occasions, and the God who is believed to be inferable from man's universal (metaphysical and linguistic) experience.

We have seen that Hartshorne seeks to avoid the illicit step from idea to actuality by claiming merely to establish God's abstract existence by means of the proofs. We must therefore bear in mind a threefold conceptuality when thinking of the kind of God for which the argument is claimed to be valid. The three terms are essence, existence, and actuality. The first of these is the conception of God with which the proof is concerned, the statement of what God really is according to the neoclassical view; the second is that which the proof wishes to establish, the instantiation in reality of a being such as the essence describes; the third is unknown, at least so far as a conceptual argument is concerned, for it differs from moment to moment. The argument is therefore devised for a conception of God as dipolar, that is, one whose essence can be distinguished from its actuality (as the classical God's cannot).

'Existence' is merely a relation of exemplification which actuality . . . has to essence. Thus I exist if my identifying personality traits . . . are somehow embodied in actual events, no matter which. Upon the legitimacy of applying an analogous, but even more radical, distinction to the idea of God depends the possibility of an ontological proof. . . . Philosophers should . . . give due heed to the manifest difference between *existence*, the mere abstract truth *that* an abstraction is somehow embodied, and the *actuality*, the how, of the embodiment.[66]

Armed, then, with this distinction between abstract existence and concrete actuality, an approach can be made to Hartshorne's ontological argument. There are three asumptions on which the argument depends. The first concerns what Hartshorne calls the 'role of faith', by which he appears to mean man's general capacity to ask religious questions. It is this that 'furnishes the question, and this question turns out to be self-answering, a logical not a factual question'.[67] This

[66] *AD* 131.
[67] 'What did Anselm Discover?', *Union Seminary Quarterly Review* 17 (1962) 221, cf. 'What the Ontological Proof Does Not Do', *Review of Metaphysics* 17 (1964) 608 f.

is of a piece with the rationalist doctrine already expounded that belief in God is a question of meaning. Thus in this very context Hartshorne repeats the claim that 'error must be confusion'.[68] The role of faith then is to furnish basic questions by a kind of intuition, and it is this faculty which comes into play also in the second assumption that must be made, and this is that 'the acceptance or rejection of either the minor premise (that deity is conceivable) or the Anselmian Principle (existential contingency is a defect, because necessary existence is conceivable and better) will, for each individual, involve . . . an element of intuitive judgment'.[69] If the mind is not prepared to accept that it is better to exist necessarily than to exist contingently even this jewel in the rationalist's crown will go unregarded. The third assumption is the concept of God that has been described in Chapters II and III. That is to say, the assumptions brought to this version of the proof consist of the whole axiomatic of neoclassical metaphysics, which is to receive its final seal of approval by means of the proof. *But there is no claim that the proof will give a new foothold that is outside and independent of the system of axioms.*

A large part of Hartshorne's work has been concerned with the neoclassical reformulation of the ontological argument.[70] However, much of the material is concerned with its defence, and as that must stand or fall with the whole system, the chief steps in the argument itself can be outlined fairly briefly. The first major step consists in an assertion of the modal character of the argument. Hartshorne wants to establish a sharp distinction between the ideas of contingent and necessary existence. The distinction centres on the notion of the competitiveness and general ontological inferiority of contingent existents. He lists ten of the characteristics of contingent existence to bring out his point. Four of them will suffice to illustrate it.

An individual which exists contingently is of such a nature that it:

(1) By existing prevents some other things (otherwise possible) from existing;

[68] 'What did Anselm Discover?', p. 221.   [69] *AD* 59.
[70] *LP, AD, MVG*, Ch. IX, as well as numerous articles and allusions in the course of the discussion of other topics.

(2) Depends causally for its existence upon some, but not all, other individuals . . .

(8) Has, or can be conceived to have, a beginning at some time and an ending at some time . . .

(10) Is 'good' for some legitimate purposes only.[71]

The ideas of competitiveness, dependence, and limitedness in time or value are part of the meaning of what it is to be (existentially) contingent. They are part of the definition of an entity that does not exist necessarily or eternally, and therefore for a contingent entity 'existence' cannot be a predicate, though 'contingent existence' is a predicate.

In the ontological argument, however, our concern is not with the contingent but with its categorical contrast, the necessary, the abstract, and the non-competitive. Here must be recalled Hartshorne's understanding of necessary propositions as those propositions that are entailed by any other proposition. In the ontological argument we are not concerned with the status of propositions so much as with that of entities. But as Hartshorne's understanding of metaphysics is such that there is no real distinction for him between logic and ontology the connection is clear: the existence of necessary, non-competitive *entities*—albeit entities that he would wish to describe as *abstract*—can be established by the means of necessary *statements*. In the case of God, the argument seeks to establish that his existence is in a different mode altogether, and that this entails that in this special case existence (because it is by definition perfect) is either necessary (Hartshorne's claim) or meaningless (the positivist's). 'Since nothing is strictly impossible unless it is inherently contradictory or meaningless . . . the choice is not between theism and atheism, but only between theism and positivism.'[72] Thus the ontological argument hinges upon the doctrine that there are two modes of existence *because* there are two modes of statement asserting existence: '. . . *modality of existence* is always a property of and is always deducible from the definition of a thing.'[73] Take any entity you like, and you will be able to tell from its definition, or more precisely from the meaning of its name or identifying description, whether it is contingent or necessary. If Gaunilo had, for

---

[71] *LP* 74 f.   [72] *LP* 70.   [73] 'What did Anselm Discover?', p. 215.

example, considered the fact that any island, perfect or otherwise, is by definition contingent as God is not, he would have
realized the inappropriateness of his counter to Anselm's
proof of the existence of God. Thus, while 'existence' may not
be a predicate,[74] as the traditional objection to the ontological
argument holds, both 'contingent existence' and 'necessary
existence' may be. Further, necessary existence is superior (as
lacking the limitations of contingent existence) while contingent
existence is obviously inconceivable in the case of God. Therefore, in this case, though not in the case of contingent entities,
it is possible to argue that God can be shown to exist by means
of metaphysical reasoning. That is appropriate for an entity
belonging to the world of abstract logic, but not for others,
whose reality is established by empirical means. 'Like contingency, necessity must be a property knowable *a priori*, the
difference being that whereas from the modality "necessity of
existence" existence is deducible, from the modality "contingency" it is not.'[75] It must be emphasized that Hartshorne
is not saying, If God exists, he exists necessarily. Rather, the
argument can be put hypothetically, but as follows. '*If* "God"
stands for something conceivable, it stands for something
actual.'[76]

At this stage it has been shown how Hartshorne answers
three traditional objections to the ontological argument. To
Gaunilo's contention that any sort of being could be equally
well established by such an argument, he replies with the
distinction between the two different modalities of existence.[77]
To Kantian objections that existence is not a predicate, he
replies that necessary existence is a predicate, though existence
may not be. To objections that it is impossible to move in
thought from the ideal to the real, he replies, in effect, that he
does not leave the realm of the ideal. To the last of these
points we shall return, but now we turn to Hartshorne's
assault on a fourth objection to the ontological argument, the
claim that 'God' does not stand for anything conceivable,
because the term can be given no consistent meaning. The

[74] It has not yet been proved that it cannot under any circumstances be so.
See Jonathan Barnes, *The Ontological Argument* (London, 1972), pp. 39–66.
[75] *AD* 156.   [76] *MVG* 312.
[77] See also N. Malcolm, 'Anselm's Ontological Arguments', *Philosophical
Review* 69 (1960) 42–52.

contention is a characteristically modern one, perhaps most clearly illustrated in J. N. Findlay's claim that for that very reason the ontological argument proves that God does not exist.[78] Hartshorne's reply to this is that if he has developed a consistent concept of God and if necessary existence is one of the defining characteristics of this God, then the argument holds and God is shown to exist. The latter point will not detain us long. Clearly, the neoclassical God is necessary both to the metaphysical world-view as a whole and in himself. Here we come full circle from the beginning of the exposition of the concept of God in chapter two. There it was shown that the concept of God arises from an analysis of 'perfection' as that is understood on neoclassical assumptions. The classical conception had been shown to fail largely because it was internally inconsistent. Here is a metaphysical system devoted to showing that a certain analysis of our language as it applies to reality requires that there be one being who is perfect, eternal, and necessary.

But necessary in what sense? Here lies the key to the consistency of the concept, for more than anything else it was the Achilles' heel of the classical concept. Neoclassical theism is consistent where classical theism was not because it is dipolar. Only one pole of the divine reality, the abstract, is necessary, the other is contingent, and therefore the problems arising from the relations of a wholly necessary God and a contingent world are absent. The situation is saved by the neoclassical doctrine of *modal coincidence*. God's reality, that is to say, coincides by means of its dipolar structure with the structure of the world to which it is related. 'Item for item, everything actual is accounted for in his actual knowing, as everything possible in his potential knowing. Thus we may define perfection as *modal coincidence*, and we may interpret this under the analogy of infallible knowledge.'[79] A certain definition of perfection is argued to be consistent both internally and externally, so to speak. Internally, in terms of its logic, the relation of the necessary and the contingent is characterized by the fact that one is the abstraction of the other. (God's is a

[78] J. N. Findlay, 'Can God's Existence be Disproved?', *New Essays in Philosophical Theology* (edd. A. Flew and A. MacIntyre, London, 1963 edn.), pp. 47–56, especially p. 55.   [79] *LP* 38.

necessary contingency.) Externally, in terms of the relation between God (the necessary existent) and the world (contingent happenings), a conception that does not involve contradiction is made possible by virtually identifying the contingency of God with that of the world. God in his concrete actuality is understood as containing (and so in a sense *being*) the entire (contingent) world, past and present: we can know that this is so, but not what this is that is so.[80] We can also know that his knowledge will in fact be adequate to whatever the future may bring. And so by means of the doctrine of the world-soul, moving along with the process and instantiating the categories eminently, Hartshorne claims to have established a doctrine of God free from the contradictions of former conceptions and to have shown him to exist necessarily.

vii. *The Neoclassical Dilemma*

The upshot of the discussion so far is that a criticism of the ontological argument in Hartshorne will be a criticism of the metaphysic as a whole. Like everything else in the neoclassical system, they belong together logically. What I do not want to dispute here is Hartshorne's great contribution to discussion of the ontological argument in his clarification of the notion of modalities of existence. If God is to be understood as in principle superior to the rest of reality, he must exist in a different way from the entities we understand as contingent, whether or not along with Hartshorne and his classical predecessors we conceive reality in terms of different levels of becoming or being. The difficulty lies rather in Hartshorne's understanding of the modality of the divine reality, and specifically in the equation of the necessity of God's existence with necessary logical truth. It is here that Hartshorne's attempt to be both empiricist and rationalist brings him into the greatest difficulty. For it would seem that by trying both to have an ontological argument of a rationalist type and to escape Kant's prohibition he is introducing an ambiguity into the idea of necessary truth.

This ambiguity is merely an instance of an ambiguity that runs through the whole of Hartshorne's philosophy, and in particular derives from the use of the word 'abstract' in two

[80] Cf. above, Ch. II, §§ iv ff.

quite different meanings. (1) The statement that God is both relative and absolute is, as Hartshorne himself says,[81] an abstract description of God's dipolar reality. It is a *logical* abstraction, by which he describes what is timelessly true about God. (2) But if God is dipolar, one pole being concrete, the other abstract, are we not speaking not so much about language, as we are in (1), as about God himself? It is a different area of discourse altogether, for the abstract pole of the divine reality is something that is claimed to *be there*; it is an ontological reality, and therefore not logically but *ontologically* abstract. Similarly, it was shown above[82] that the past is abstract, as being the object of knowledge. But the heart of Hartshorne's position is that the past really exists, because it is held in the memory of God. That is some abstraction, and unless with Hartshorne we are prepared to identify the logical and the ontological in so thoroughgoing a manner, the ambiguity must constitute a fundamental weakness in his system.

The question that stands over the system can be stated in the form of a dilemma. Either Hartshorne must, on the one hand, accept the full implications of his rationalist position and claim that the abstractions—including the abstract existence of God which is the object of the ontological proof—are more than just abstractions because they have a foothold in extralinguistic reality, as indeed some of the things that he says suggest.[83] In that case is he dealing with abstractions at all, and not rather with crypto-concrete conceptions? If that were the case, he need not bother at all with the objections concerning the transition from the ideal to the real, because in fact his argument for the existence of God represents rather a move from the real to the real, or at the very least from ideas that are a direct reflection of the real to that real they reflect. The ideas then are more than abstractions because they are held to have a subsistence in reality apart from our conception of them.

Or, on the other hand, Hartshorne would seem bound to accept a more nominalist view of abstractions if he is going to

[81] See above, Ch. II, § iv.
[82] See above, Ch. I, § i, where for all Hartshorne's uses of 'absolute' or externally related' the word 'abstract' could equally well be read.
[83] See above, §§ ii and iii.

avoid empiricist criticisms by claiming that in metaphysics he is concerned with *mere* abstractions. For on the realist account of the categories, abstractions are not merely abstractions at all, but far more substantial parts of the universe. But if he were to opt for the nominalist horn of the dilemma, he would find himself running up against the doctrine that necessary truths are merely a matter of linguistic convention and that abstractions are no more than that. In that case it would be difficult for him to maintain the equation of the logical and the ontological, and specifically the credibility of the move from logical to existential necessity. For there is a distinction in thought between logical necessity and that necessity which believers would ascribe to God, whether they would use the term 'factual'[84] or 'theological'[85] or 'existential' of that necessity. Ironically, it is to Hartshorne with his doctrine of the two modalities that we owe the clarification of what can be meant by the necessary existence of God. But the question still remains as to whether we can go so easily from language to God; certainly we cannot in the absence of some such rationalist theory of the relation between thought and reality as the one presupposed by the neoclassical proofs of Charles Hartshorne.

The question of the relation between God and our language about him is one that will be with us throughout this study, and some comments by J. N. Findlay, in partial recantation of the views recently mentioned, on Hartshorne's attempted rehabilitation of the ontological argument will aid the transition to the second main section of the comparison. Having mentioned what he takes to be the chief contribution Hartshorne has made, he proceeds to make some suggestions of his own.

If there is to be a valid ontological argument, it must proceed, not from concept or character to existence, but in the reverse direction, from existence to concept or character. One must be clear, in the first place, that there must be something, and it must then follow that only what is of a certain character can necessarily be.[86]

[84] J. Hick, 'God as Necessary Being', *Journal of Philosophy* 57 (1960) 725–34.

[85] J. J. C. Smart, 'The Existence of God', *New Essays in Philosophical Theology*, p. 40.

[86] J. N. Findlay, 'Reflections on Necessary Existence', *Process and Divinity* (edd. W. L. Reese and E. Freeman, La Salle, Illinois, 1964), p. 522.

This is something that Karl Barth is seeking to do in the steps of Anselm, but it involves a very different understanding of Anselm, a very different concept of God and a very different analogical predication. This time the move is not from analogy to proof, but from proof to analogy.

PART TWO

BARTH'S TRINITARIAN THEOLOGY

V

THE BECOMING OF GOD IN BARTH'S THEOLOGY

i. *Anselm: the Object of Theology*

THE importance of Barth's book on Anselm is now generally accepted. One student of Barth has rightly seen that, 'This is perhaps Barth's greatest work, his most important contribution to theological literature.'[1] Without it we should lack vital information on why Barth considers theology to be a rational pursuit and on what he conceives to give it its rationality. He himself calls the book 'a vital key, if not the vital key, to an understanding of that whole process of thought that has impressed me more and more in my *Church Dogmatics* as the only one proper to theology'.[2] From the book on Anselm we can learn something about two closely related topics: the way in which Barth justifies speaking of God and what he regards himself as doing when he proceeds to use descriptive language about God. But why should he be interested in the ontological argument, since that is often believed to be the most rationalistic of the arguments for the existence of God? A short answer would be that the term 'ontological' should not be used of Anselm's argument at all: 'it is in a different book altogether from the well-known teaching of Descartes and Leibniz . . .'[3]—and, we might add, from that of Hartshorne.

To understand it, Anselm's argument should be examined in the context of the whole of his theology, and so Barth first asks what Anselm was seeking to do as a theologian. He claims that Anselm's primary aim was *intelligere*, understanding, and that this is reflected in the original title of the *Proslogion* (of which the argument is a part), *Fides Quaerens Intellectum*.[4] 'Anselm

---

[1] T. H. L. Parker, *Karl Barth* (Grand Rapids, Michigan, 1970), p. 70.
[2] Preface to the second edition (1958), *FQI* 11.   [3] *FQI* 171.
[4] *FQI* 16.

wants "proof" and "joy" because he wants *intelligere* and he wants *intelligere* because he believes.'[5] Anselm's intention is not to lead men to faith by means of the proof but to expound the faith, because faith is such that it desires knowledge. '*Credo ut intelligam* means: it is my very faith itself that summons me to knowledge.'[6] Here we see emerging a theme always associated with the name of Barth, and one that would appear to bring him into total conflict with the assumptions of the thought expounded in the previous chapters. But while there may be a danger of making too facile a comparison, there is one that should be made. It is not simply that Barth accepts 'authority'—that of the creeds and the Bible, for example—and then proceeds to theologize as if there were no problems about this authority, while proponents of an alleged natural knowledge of God operate as men free to hold dialogue with the world of human culture. Rather, there is a fundamental difference in what is held to be authoritative. It should have been made apparent in the exposition of his position that Hartshorne has made a radical commitment to a particular way of understanding the world before he begins to speak about it. The belief that the whole of reality is to be understood in terms of process is not an empirically derived doctrine, but one held on the basis of a metaphysical intuition of the way things must be, and then justified by appeal to a certain understanding of human reason and its relation to extra-linguistic reality, itself held on 'faith'. Indeed, it could be said without exaggeration that Hartshorne's basic 'creed' is wholly present in the very first of his writings. It springs from the earth fully armed, and henceforth requires nothing but elaboration, elucidation, and expansion. Its authority is the most rigid and unchanging imaginable: the authority of the mutual logical implication of a limited number of key concepts. By contrast, Barth's 'given' is not innate intellectual equipment so much as the gift of God in Christ. This, too, he finds in Anselm. 'Faith is related to the "Word of Christ" and is not faith if it is not conceived, that is acknowledged and affirmed by the Word of Christ. And the Word of Christ is identical with the "Word of those who preach Christ"; that means it is legitimately represented by particular human

5 *FQI* 16 f.   6 *FQI* 18.

words.'[7] The final phrase is the key one. Theology as a *legitimate rational* pursuit is made possible by the incarnation. Here we glimpse a theme that is to emerge as a major burden of the *Church Dogmatics*: certain things provide the starting-point for the theologian. They are given as the physical universe is given to the natural scientist. It is not that the theologian's problems have ceased. The problem with which we are here concerned, the existence of God, remains, but it is not dealt with in the same way. In one sense it may be given; but it remains a matter for investigation, discussion, and hence proof. 'Anselm always has the solution of his problems already behind him (through faith in the impartial good sense of the decisions of ecclesiastical authority), while, as it were, they are still ahead.'[8] But why can he have faith in 'the impartial good sense of the decisions of ecclesiastical authority'? For his predecessors, as for Anselm, there is an 'objective *Credo* which compels Christian humility before the *ratio veritatis* that is the pre-supposition of all human knowledge of heavenly things and that belongs to the actual revelation of God. And this *Credo* makes the science of theology possible and gives it a basis.'[9] Theological science is for Anselm science of the *Credo*: '*Intelligere* comes about by reflection on the *Credo* that has already been spoken and affirmed.'[10]

The Credo performs here somewhat the same function that the notion of the superstructure of necessary truth, lying as yet latent in the rational mind, performs for the neoclassical theorist. This analogy between the two can be taken a fair way, though it has its limits. The neoclassical superstructure, once discovered, forms a tight logical circle, for example in the relation between descriptive category and the proofs of the existence of God. The notion that reality can be so described rests upon the belief that there is a fundamental community of being between the language and the world. Truth lies in the coherence of a set of axioms. Might the same be said about the relation of proof and concept in Barth? R. S. Hartman has argued that Anselm's proof, understood very much as Barth expounds it, does open the way to a system of axioms of which

---

7 *FQI* 22.   8 *FQI* 25 f.
9 *FQI* 26.   10 *FQI* 27.

it is itself a part.[11] If this were what Barth was doing with Anselm, the analogy with Hartshorne would be very close indeed. But, as we shall see, this is not a satisfactory model for understanding Barth's method where, although the relation between proof and analogy is a close one, it is more open in its application and development than the almost geometrical scheme of both Hartshorne and Hartman would allow. The essential difference lies in the fact that the object of theology—Barth's equivalent for Anselm's *Credo*—is not conceived to be conceptual. There is no latent set of innate ideas, but the language that is used has to be made to fit the object of theology as he makes himself known. Although there is no essential community of being between language and object, the language can fit the object because he empowers it to do so.

Theology is not a deductive science, but it is a science because it is about something that is real, and because its task is to ask 'to what extent is reality as the Christian believes it to be?'[12] This is something that Barth takes directly from Anselm. The theologian believes something to be so, and proceeds to investigate the truth of that belief. He cannot pretend, after the manner of some conceptions of natural theology, not to have the belief, for that would be the height of irrationality. What, therefore, appears to some of Barth's critics to be 'irrationalism', to others will be seen to be rooted in the character of the Christian gospel: that the theologian stands under grace, and is a theologian only because of what he has been given. In a sense, all derives from Barth's understanding of God. As Jüngel puts it, the being of God has for Barth a prevenient character.[13] Reason, to be rational, must operate within the sphere of this prevenience.

ii. *Anselm: the Manner of Theology*

It is from this viewpoint that Barth discusses, in 'The Manner of Theology',[14] the relation that Anselm believes to hold between the object of faith and the theologian. He distinguishes three meanings of *ratio* in Anselm. First, there is a *ratio* which is

[11] R. S. Hartman, 'Prolegomena to a Meta-Anselmian Axiomatic', *Review of Metaphysics* 14 (1961) 637–75.   [12] *FQI* 27.
[13] E. Jüngel, *Gottes Sein ist im Werden* (Tübingen, 1967 edn.), p. 9.
[14] *FQI* 40–59.

peculiar to man, his capacity to reason: 'the primary capacity of dealing with experience, of formulating conceptions and judgments . . .'[15] Second, there is 'the *ratio* that is to be known, the *ratio* that belongs to the object of faith itself'.[16] By this Barth appears to mean what might be called conceptual rationality: 'the object of theology' referring not so much to God as to the *Credo* about which the theologian reflects. But there is in Anselm a third understanding of *ratio*, the '*ratio veritatis*. Strictly understood, the *ratio veritatis* is identical with the *ratio summae naturae*, that is with the divine Word consubstantial with the Father. It is the *ratio* of God.'[17] The three types of *ratio* form a definite hierarchy, in what can be called subjective, objective, and absolute rationality,[18] and is a hierarchy in the sense that the lower are, in theology, dependent upon the higher. The correctness of human reasoning will depend upon its apprehension of the truth of its object, and not vice versa. Necessity can therefore be ascribed to statements of—say—the existence of God if we already have grounds for believing in his ontological necessity; there can be no move in the opposite direction as appears to happen in conceptual versions of the ontological argument, like the version outlined in Chapter IV above. For Barth the problem of theological *language* cannot be discussed prior to the question of the *being* of God. God comes first; our language can only rationally follow after his prevenience.

We have now arrived by a slightly different route at the same understanding of the theologian's task as in the previous section: not to establish the object of his reflection, for its nature is such that it can be established only by itself, but to reflect upon that object, and thus to make intelligible its nature, and hence its rationality and necessity. The aim of theology is undoubtedly proof, not in the sense that it is usually understood in philosophical theology, but as something that can perhaps be called intellectual conviction.

In his study of Anselm, Barth is concerned in particular with the 'proof' of that article of faith which concerns the existence of God. For the proof, one thing is presupposed, or given: a name of God. It is a name that, on Barth's interpretation, Anselm

---

[15] *FQI* 44 f.   [16] *FQI* 44.   [17] *FQI* 45.
[18] R. S. Hartman, art. cit., pp. 650–2.

believes to have been given him by God.[19] 'In *Prosl. 2–4* Anselm
wants to prove the existence of God. He proves it by assuming
a Name of God the meaning of which implies that the statement "God exists" is necessary. . . .'[20] This 'name' of God, as
That than which no greater can be conceived, is concerned to say one
thing only about the object under consideration, and that is
negative: 'nothing greater than it can be imagined; nothing
can be imagined that in any respect whatsoever could or would
outdo it . . .'[21] It is, as Hartshorne would say, unsurpassable.
Further: 'we are dealing here with a concept of strict noetic
content which Anselm describes here as a concept of God.'[22]
There is much in common with Hartshorne here. Both agree
that the formulation is a purely conceptual one, and they agree
about what the concept does not mean: 'it does not say—God
is the highest man has in fact conceived, beyond which he can
conceive nothing higher. Nor does it say—God is the highest
that man could conceive.'[23] The two even agree that it is to a
large extent a question of understanding that is at stake. Yet
while Hartshorne sees this as essentially a question of *meaning*,
or even of *self*-understanding,[24] Barth believes that the fool's
error is to misunderstand not himself or his concepts but the
nature of his situation before God. 'The *insipiens* thinks and
speaks as one who is not saved by the grace of God. That is the
reason for his perversity, and why he can say, *Deus non est.*'[25]
Because Barth does not share Hartshorne's rationalism and his
beliefs about the revelatory quality of language, it is not enough
for him to give intelligible meaning to a concept. The concept
for him must be filled out with meaning by the object it aims
to describe.

It [the formula] contains nothing in the way of statements about the
existence or about the nature of the object described. Thus nothing
of that sort is to be derived from it on subsequent analysis. If it is
to be of any use in proving the existence and nature of God then a
second assumption, to be clearly distinguished from this first one,
is necessary—the prior 'givenness' (credible on other grounds)
of the thought of the Existence and of the Nature of God which

---

[19] *FQI* 77.   [20] *FQI* 73.   [21] *FQI* 75.   [22] Ibid.   [23] *FQI* 74.
[24] *NTOT* 88.
[25] *FQI* 160. But there is undoubtedly an intellectual component: 'nullus in-
telligens id quod Deus est, potest cogitare quia Deus non est', *FQI* 78.

with his help is to be raised to knowledge and proof. *Aliquid quo nihil maius cogitari possit* is therefore on no account the condensed formula of a doctrine of God that is capable of later expansion but it is a genuine description . . . one Name of God, selected from among the various revealed Names of God for this occasion and for this particular purpose, in such a way that to reach a knowledge of God the revelation of this same God from some other source is clearly assumed.[26]

Whatever the merits of this as an interpretation of Anselm, it throws a flood of light on Barth's conception of the manner of theology. Perhaps this can best be understood with the help of a contrast with Hartshorne's theological method. There, it was seen, there is a logical relation between the proofs of the existence of God and the concept of God: that is to say, in neoclassical thought as Hartshorne understands it proof and concept form a logically related system of axioms. Once the transcendent relativity, temporality, etc., of God are established, everything else follows analytically. On the face of it, the process Barth has described has much in common with this. What else are these 'other assumptions' but other axioms of a system, drawn upon to back each other up? Similarly, it may be possible to see the doctrine of God in the *Church Dogmatics* as the 'meta-Anselmian axiomatic' suggested by Hartman. By presupposing all the other articles of the creed in order to discuss one of them, the theologian does something very similar to what a geometrician does in constructing a system of axioms.

On the assumption that it is true to say: God exists, God is the highest Being, is a Being in Three Persons; became man, etc.— Anselm discusses the question of how far it is true and in asking and allowing himself to be asked about this 'how far' in respect of particular articles of faith, in his answers he takes as his starting point the assumption that all the other articles are true.[27]

And yet such an interpretation needs to be modified significantly if it is to do justice to Barth's view of Anselm and to his own theological programme. The geometrician, like the rationalist philosopher of old and Hartshorne his modern

---

[26] *FQI* 75.   [27] *FQI* 61 f.

successor, is concerned to produce a system of timelessly true necessary truths. The circle is entirely closed. Barth will not accept that this is Anselm's view of theology: 'there is no general doctrine of necessary thoughts standing behind the thesis of *Prosl.* 3.'[28] And his own conception of theology repudiates the analogy of the circle for something more open, or rather, it would be more accurate to say, uses the analogy of the circle in an altogether different way.

> . . . the unfolding and presentation of the content of the Word of God must take place fundamentally in such a way that the Word of God is understood as the centre and foundation of dogmatics and of Church proclamation, like a circle whose periphery forms the starting point for a limited number of lines which in dogmatics are to be drawn to a certain distance in all directions.[29]

As the later exposition will show, theological language is, to use the modern jargon, open-textured for Barth in a way that it cannot be for Hartshorne. Barth draws out the corollaries of this understanding of theology in a way that sets him apart from the rationalist: there can be no system of *a priori* principles,[30] there is no system of axioms, but rather the 'distinction and independence of the four *Loci*' is not necessarily to be deplored[31]—each line, though going outwards from the same circle, is of independent interest and rationality—and the impact of the gospel is blunted if it is made into timeless truth, rather than a concrete word in the present.[32] All these denials are made in defence of the central positive doctrine: 'Essentially dogmatic method consists in this openness to receive new truth, and only in this.'[33] Once again, Barth's view of what he is doing can be seen to arise from his understanding of the nature of God. Because God is always going before, no words are ever adequate to the object, and there must therefore always be a search for new and better ways of putting the truth. How far Barth has succeeded in his own work in his aim of leaving dogmatics open to the reception of new truth has been a constant theme of his commentators, and will have to be discussed in the light of what he says in his doctrine of God.

---

[28] *FQI* 139.   [29] *CD* I/2 869.   [30] I/2 483, 861 f.   [31] I/2, 877 f.
[32] IV/3, 813–16.   [33] I/2 867.

iii. *Barth: Applications of Anselm's Insights*

There are three areas in particular where it will be seen that Barth makes use of and develops in the *Church Dogmatics* insights that he has argued to be central to Anselm's conception of theology.

1. Barth's conception of revelation is his equivalent of the proof of God from God as he finds it in Anselm. An exposition of Barth's arguments in his development of the doctrine of the Trinity will reveal that his phrase 'God reveals himself as the Lord' performs for him the same function that 'that than which no greater can be conceived' performed for Anselm: it provides him with reasons for using the word *God* in rational discourse. 'Lordship is present in revelation because its reality and truth are so fully self-grounded, because it does not need any other actualisation or validation than that of its actual occurrence . . .'[34] More than this, Barth wants to say that the phrase is a correct interpretation of revelation as this is pointed to by scripture. In fact there is a sense in which scripture only is what it is because of the revelation to which it witnesses, because it is the instrument by which God proves his existence and authenticates his lordship. Scripture is not in itself revelation.

2. Barth's situation is very similar to the theologian's as he described it in the view of Anselm, except that here the emphasis on the creeds and the good sense of ecclesiastical decision—though that is never completely absent from Barth— is replaced by a more biblical centre. 'If in order to clarify how Church proclamation is to be measured by Holy Scripture we first enquire into the prior concept of revelation, already in this enquiry we must keep to Holy Scripture as the witness of revelation.'[35] This, the first sentence of the exposition of the doctrine of the Trinity, is an uncompromising assertion of Barth's view of the situation. The theologian is in a situation of being confronted with certain claims that the Bible makes for itself, or rather for what is prior to it, the God who makes it what it is. It is the problems that are set by the Bible that provide him with his material. The converse of this is that neither autonomous anthropological doctrine nor some *a priori*

---

[34] I/1 306.   [35] I/1 295.

theological scheme can be brought to the Bible as a means of clarifying what it has to say. So far as the concept of God is concerned, the Bible not only gives answers—though in what sense it gives answers is not at present under discussion—but must be allowed to set the questions as well.

3. Dogmatics is a rational procedure. First of all, this is so in a way that is scarcely controversial. 'All dogmatic formulations are rational, and every dogmatic procedure is rational to the degree that in it use is made of general concepts, i.e. of the human *ratio*.'[36] Slightly more controversial is the meaning this has for Barth: that philosophical concepts have to be borrowed and used by the theologian. '. . . linguistically theologians have always depended upon some philosophy and linguistically they always will.'[37] Barth's conception of the use of reason in theology, in which it is necessary to distinguish between the rational and rationalistic uses of formulae,[38] is far more subtle than many superficial critics have supposed. For him, the fact that the Word became man does as much for human language about God as is sometimes claimed to subsist in it *naturaliter* by rationalists like Hartshorne: '. . . if we are not to dispute the grace and finally the incarnation of the Word of God, we cannot finally contest the use of philosophy in scriptural exegesis.'[39]

However, the second way in which Barth understands the rationality of theology is more controversial. Traditionally the name of rational theology has often been limited to the establishing, by the use of reason, the existence and sometimes also the character and attributes of the object of theology.[40] But for Barth this is unnecessary, if not positively misleading, because God has given himself in his revelation in such a way that we can speak rationally of him on the basis of this very revelation. Rational theology is the description of what is in fact the case, and he is fond of citing the statement of Hilary: 'Intelligentia dictorum ex causis est assumenda dicendi, quia non sermoni res, sed rei sermo subjectus est.'[41] Language must conform to its object, and not the reverse. Theology begins from the circle drawn round the theologian by God's subjecting himself to human thought and reasoning.

---

[36] I/1 296.   [37] I/1 378.   [38] I/1 296 f.   [39] I/2 729 f.
[40] e.g. in Aquinas, *Summa Theologica* 1a. 1–26.   [41] e.g. CD I/1 354.

Above all for Barth Christian theology is rational because it is concerned to say what is true. 'The Creed of Christian faith rests upon knowledge. And where the Creed is uttered and confessed knowledge should be, is meant to be, created. Christian faith is not irrational, not anti-rational, not supra-rational, but rational in the proper sense.'[42]

iv. *The Triune Becoming* (1)

In beginning the doctrine of God with a treatment of the doctrine of the Trinity, Barth differs from all of his predecessors but two,[43] and in doing so sets the scene for a radical change of direction in theological thinking.[44] He proceeds in the way he does because he believes that it is the only proper way to answer the questions that Scripture forces upon him. The exposition is therefore 'Anselmian' from the start: it is because the God of the Bible validates himself, so to speak, through the events to which Scripture bears witness, that we must take seriously both the Bible's claim to uniqueness and the questions it compels us to consider. When the Bible makes us ask about the identity of the God who reveals himself, we find that further questions follow inevitably. This is where it all begins.

The question of the self-revealing God which thus forces itself upon us as the first question cannot, if we follow the witness of Scripture, be separated in any way from the second question: How does it come about, how is it actual, that this God reveals Himself? Nor can it be separated from the third question: What is the result? How does this event affect the man to whom it happens?[45]

Not only do the questions, if correctly put, lead into one another, but the answers are bound up inextricably together: 'if the first question is intelligently put, when it is answered the second and third questions will be answered as well, and only when answers to the second and third questions are received

---

[42] Barth, *Dogmatics in Outline*, E.T. by G. T. Thomson (London, 1949), pp. 22 f., cf. *CD* IV/2 312–14. See also II/1 204–54, 'The veracity of man's knowledge of God', and T. F. Torrance, *Theological Science* (London, 1969), and *God and Rationality* (London, 1971).

[43] The exceptions are Peter Lombard and Bonaventura, *CD* I/1 300.

[44] In this and the following sections I am in part dependent upon E. Jüngel, *Gottes Sein ist im Werden*, especially pp. 27–37, and R. W. Jenson, *God After God: the God of the Past and the God of the Future, Seen in the Work of Karl Barth* (Indianapolis and New York, 1969), especially pp. 95–122.

[45] *CD* I/1 295 f.

is an answer to the first question really received.'[46] The explanation of this situation lies in the basically straightforward starting-point for theological thought. '*God* reveals Himself. He reveals Himself *through Himself*. He reveals *Himself*.'[47] Already, in a simple description of what happens we are 'close to the problem of the doctrine of the Trinity' because 'the God who reveals Himself in the Bible must also be known in His revealing and His being revealed if He is to be known'.[48] Rational inquiry will lead us inexorably from what happens in Jesus Christ to the description of God in his triune reality.

In this adaptation of Anselm, then, Barth is claiming that there is a threefoldness about the way in which the God of the Bible authenticates his reality, and that he does it in such a way that we are led to think of him as threefold in himself.[49] What is distinctive about Barth's formulation is that the threefoldness is a threefoldness of event, of something that really happens and can properly be described as *God*. 'Revelation in the Bible is not a minus; it is not an other over against God. It is the same, the repetition of God (*Wiederholung Gottes*).'[50] Moreover, it has a threefold personal centre and unity: 'Thus it is God Himself, it is the same God in unimpaired unity, who according to the biblical understanding of revelation is the revealing God and the event of revelation and its effect upon man.[51] It is because the one God is all of these, because the answer to all three of the opening questions is the same—*God*—and because there is no way of finding a synthesis in a fourth reality without straying from the biblical witness that the doctrine of the Trinity has to be formulated. It is, therefore, an answer to the question of how all three can be equated and yet differentiated; of how there can be both unity and variety in one and the same God.[52]

The key concept of the exposition so far is that of the *Wiederholung Gottes*, for it is this that prepares the way for the notion of God as 'God who happens'.[53] The following stages would seem to be crucial to the development of the argument.

    1. Barth begins by saying what he means by revelation,

---

[46] I/1 297.   [47] I/1 296.   [48] I/1 298.
[49] If the threefoldness is not there, the doctrine of the Trinity is impossible, as Professor Wiles has argued. See M. F. Wiles, 'Some Reflections on the Origins of the Doctrine of the Trinity', *Journal of Theological Studies* n.s. 8 (1957) 92–106.
[50] *CD* I/1 299.   [51] Ibid.   [52] *CD* I/1 299 f.
[53] This is the title of Part III of R. W. Jenson, *God After God*, pp. 95–135.

which is, he says, *Dei loquentis persona*.[54] This is a phrase that is
easier to explain than to translate satisfactorily, and great care
is needed if we are to grasp Barth's point, especially as the word
revelation is often discussed as though it were monolithically
univocal in meaning. Barth is referring to revelation as something that happens; not to subjective experiences but to events
that *are* God, and specifically the events that come to expression
in the story of the life, death and resurrection of Jesus Christ.
Because this revelation is where God happens among men,
it is impossible to distinguish between God's word and himself,
between what God *does* and what he *is*. There is no other reality
lying behind it: it *is* God himself. '. . . God's revelation has its
reality and truth wholly and in every respect—both ontically
and noetically—within itself.'[55] 'The reality of God in His
revelation cannot be bracketed by an "only", as though
somewhere behind His revelation there stood another reality
of God . . .'[56] This 'realism of revelation' provides the ontological grounding for Barth's understanding of revelation, and
therefore for his doctrine of God. It is based upon an insight of
blinding simplicity: if Jesus Christ is God, then God is really
given in him, and does not have to be sought behind or apart
from him.

2. Because it really is *God* who reveals himself, because God
reveals *himself*, Barth can proceed to say: 'We may sum all
this up in the statement that God reveals Himself as the Lord.
This statement is to be regarded as an analytical judgment.'[57]
Here once again we are in the region of the Anselmian character of revelation as proof. What does Barth mean when he
says that he is making an analytical judgement? In general,
an analytic statement is one whose truth or falsity follows from
the meanings of its terms. But Barth is not concerned with
truths of language. He is rather making the point that the
assertion of the lordship of God in revelation is made necessary
for the theologian by revelation: it follows from the nature of
the event he is describing in a manner similar to that in which
the assertion of 'standard' analytic truth is necessitated by the
meaning of the terms the sentence contains. 'To act as Lord
means to act as God in His revelation acts on man.'[58] It is God

54 *CD* I/1 304.   55 I/1 305.   56 I/1 479.   57 I/1 306.
58 Ibid. My italics.

and not man and his language or conventions who makes this particular statement take the form that it does. The same point can be made in explanation of Barth's apparently problematic assertion that the doctrine of the Trinity arises from an analysis of the concept of revelation.[59] Clearly here he means an analysis of what is understood to happen in the event of revelation. Thus, in marked contrast to what happens in Hartshorne, with his system of *a priori* statements, developed by the exercise of pure reason without the help of any particular observation or revelation, we have in Barth what might almost be called analytic *a posteriori* statements. These statements are grounded in God's proof of himself in revelation, which consists of a number of concrete, individual events in which he is God, and which therefore *must* (rationally must) by the theologian be so described.

3. It is this revelatory realism and necessity that provide the *root* of the Church's doctrine of the Trinity. The doctrine is not identical with statements about revelation, because it purports to be an interpretation of revelation. As a doctrine it aims at being a correct interpretation of revelation, even though the doctrine is not itself in Scripture. 'When we say, then, that the doctrine of the Trinity is the interpretation of revelation or that revelation is the basis of the doctrine of the Trinity, we find revelation itself attested in Holy Scripture in such a way that in relation to this witness our understanding of revelation, or of the God who reveals Himself, must be the doctrine of the Trinity.'[60] The doctrine of the Trinity is what must be true if the biblical witness to revelation is indeed witness to the event that is God. As Jüngel has put it with great precision, the doctrine of the Trinity is *our* interpretation of God's *self-interpretation* of himself to us.[61]

v. *The Triune Becoming* (2)

So far, then, we have seen how Barth characterizes as threefold the events he has called revelation: each requires to be understood in terms of revealer, revelation, and revealing if it is to be understood as the historical event in which God is himself. We have seen, further, that Barth's conception of revelation has a christological centre, and it is from this same centre that he

---

[59] I/1 304, 312, and 332.   [60] I/1 312.   [61] E. Jüngel, loc. cit.

proceeds to a description of the differentiation that can be made between the different aspects of the events. 'Historically considered and stated the three questions answered in the Bible, that of revealer, revelation and revealing, do not have the same importance. The true theme of the biblical witness is the second of the concepts, God's action in His revelation . . .'[62] Above all, that is to say, it is the historical event to which the Bible bears witness; our understanding of the first and third of the concepts, which claim 'equal weight both logically and materially',[63] follow from an answer to the first question. Therefore it is in the discussion of what happens in the event of Jesus Christ that we see the first and crucial development of the notion of *Wiederholung*. 'Revelation in the Bible means the self-unveiling, imparted to men, of the God who by nature cannot be unveiled to men.'[64] Revelation is then not only something that happens, but is also an act of personal initiative, such that—among other things—it informs the one who experiences it of things that he would not be in a position to know of himself. It is also something particular. 'In the historical life of men He takes up a place, and a very specific place at that, and makes Himself the object of human contemplation, human experience, human thought and human speech.'[65] An implication of this is that the *Wiederholung*, the becoming, is part of what it means for God to be God. 'The very fact of revelation tells us that it is proper to Him to distinguish Himself from Himself, i.e. to be God in Himself and in concealment, and yet at the same time to be God a second time in a very different way, namely, in manifestation, i.e. in the form of something He Himself is not.'[66]

And so God becomes. The assertion of the becoming of God leads for Barth to the propounding of what is for him an important principle throughout this argument, indeed, for his theology as a whole, and it is what gives it its wholeheartedly *a posteriori* character.

That God is capable of what the Bible ascribes to Him. . . . that God

---

[62] *CD* I/1 314.   [63] I/1 315.   [64] Ibid.   [65] Ibid.
[66] *CD* I/1 316. Because this is really God's *property*, 'the creation and preservation of the world, and relationship and fellowship with it . . . do not signify an alien or contradictory expression of God's being, but a natural, *the* natural expression of it *ad extra*'. II/1 317.

can become unlike Himself in such a way that He is not tied to His secret eternity and His eternal secrecy but can and will and does in fact take temporal form as well; the fact that God can and will and actually does do this we now understand as a confirmation of our first statement that God reveals Himself as the Lord.[67]

What God does, he can do. 'The God who reveals Himself here can reveal Himself.'[68] R. W. Jenson comments:

As an ontological principle, this principle may seem to hover between obfuscation and utter triviality. But in Barth's thinking the principle is only shorthand for the whole polemic against religion. . . . We are not to say that although God meets us as a figure in our history, it is unworthy of God to become other than himself, that although we meet God living in time, he himself is timeless.[69]

In terms of the discussion with neoclassical theology, Barth's principle can also be understood as an attack on *a priori* theological method. It is impossible to decide in advance of revelation what God can and cannot be, for example, that it is appropriate to speak of 'being' but not of 'becoming' in God, on the ground, say, that 'becoming' entails change and therefore imperfection. This is equally an attack on classical and neoclassical metaphysics. Both Barth and Hartshorne attack the outcome of the classical method, but for Barth the neoclassical metaphysician is simply applying the old method in a different way. Both types of natural theology want to decide in advance what God can and cannot be. Both want to find God *behind* his revelation, to say that he cannot *really* be what he chooses to be. They cannot therefore take God's becoming temporal with full seriousness. This, as we have seen, is the situation with Hartshorne, despite the much vaunted stress on the temporality of God. Neoclassical temporality cannot be a historical and particular temporality.

vi. *The Triune Becoming* (3)

Exactly the same words open the next stage of the inquiry into the divine becoming, but this time the stress is on the second part of the sentence, 'the God who by nature cannot be unveiled to men'.[70] The inscrutability of God 'necessarily means that

[67] I/1 319 f.   [68] I/1 316.   [69] *God After God*, p. 103.
[70] *CD* I/1 320.

even in the form He assumes when He reveals Himself God is free to reveal Himself or not to reveal Himself. . . . It is not the form, but God in the form, that reveals, speaks, comforts, works and aids. . . . God's self-unveiling remains an act of sovereign divine freedom.'[71] Even in the form in which he has in fact chosen to reveal himself—e.g. the humanity of Christ— God retains this freedom.[72] The notion of the freedom in which God reveals himself is crucially important for Barth, and is a constant theme of the doctrine of God. It is this personal, dynamic understanding of revelation, as something that happens at particular times in history, that prevents the inscrutability (*Unenthüllbarkeit*, literally, non-unveilability) from being in contradiction or dialectical opposition to self-unveiling (*Selbstenthüllung*). The image is not of static being lying behind a veil of foreign, material substance that is sometimes swept aside to reveal the mystery beneath. The veiling is a necessary aspect of the unveiling; inscrutability is that without which we could not understand what is meant by self-unveiling: 'the fact that it is the God who by nature cannot be unveiled to man that reveals Himself there has distinct significance for our understanding of His self-unveiling.'[73]

The upshot is that there is no imbalance between God's becoming God in the form of something that he himself is not, and his remaining true to himself in this becoming.[74] This freedom in becoming confirms the Anselmian starting-point in a second way. Here, too, the way things happen shows God to be the Lord.[75] 'God's fatherhood, too, is God's lordship in His revelation.'[76]

The third stage of the inquiry begins with the same sentence as the other two, but again the stress is altered, and is now on the words, 'imparted to men'.[77] Biblically attested revelation is revelation to particular men at particular times. Therefore: 'Part of the concept of the biblically attested revelation is that it is a historical event (*geschichtliche Ereignis*)', though that must not be taken to mean 'apprehensible by a neutral observer or apprehended by such an observer'.[78] What then does Barth mean by *geschichtliches*? He means that there is an analogy, but only an analogy, between revelation and history and it

---

[71] I/1 321.   [72] I/1 322-4.   [73] I/1 321.   [74] I/1 324.
[75] Ibid.   [76] Ibid.   [77] Ibid.   [78] I/1 325.

lies in the fact that 'in revelation as in history the reference is
to a definite event which is different from every other event
and which is thus incomparable and cannot be repeated'.[79]
The interpreter of the biblical revelation is therefore seriously
concerned with Egypt, Babylon, Israel, Cyrenius, Pilate, and
the rest.[80]

Behind this emphasis on concrete particularity and the distinction between revelation and history in the sense of events
apprehensible by a neutral observer lies a concern to prevent
the conception of revelation from degenerating into triviality,
metaphysical generality, or myth. Any merely historical event,
even the empty tomb, is susceptible of a trivial interpretation.[81] On the other hand, the fact that the events we are
describing happened on earth is not enough: so did the events
recorded in the Babylonian myths.[82] Indispensable for its
understanding is the fact that the Bible understands revelation
as 'a concrete relation to concrete men'.[83] It is this that
excludes both its interpretation as myth and its translation into
general metaphysical ideas, the *alter ego* of myth.[84] The point
can be illustrated by a comparison with Hartshorne, whose
theology could perhaps be termed incarnational, in that it
depicts God as happening within the cosmic process. But that
is to reduce the relation between God and the universe to
purely general terms. In fact, Barth might be explicitly con-
testing the neoclassical view of things when he says that the
Bible's method of narration

signifies that when the Bible gives an account of revelation it means
to narrate history, i.e. not to tell of a relation between God and man
that exists generally in every time and place and that is always in
process, but to tell of an event that takes place there and only
there, then and only then, between God and certain very specific
men.[85]

To describe the biblical narratives as mythological is precisely
to mistake their character, because ' "myth" does not intend to
be history but only pretends to be such.'[86] Myth, on Barth's
understanding, uses narrative form to do what Hartshorne is

[79] I/1 329.   [80] I/1 326.   [81] I/1 325.   [82] I/1 324.
[83] I/1 325.   [84] I/1 326-9, cf. Jüngel, *Gottes Sein*, p. 33.   [85] I/1 326.
[86] I/1 327.

doing with his metaphysics: 'to expound what purports to be always and everywhere true.'[87] Revelation is quite different.

The Bible lays such extraordinary stress on the historicity of the revelation recorded by it because by revelation it does not mean a creation of man. It says so emphatically that revelation was imparted to these men in these situations because it is describing it thereby as an impartation to men. This is what the use of the concept of myth rather than saga in relation to the Bible overlooks or denies.[88]

There is, then, a third confirmation of the Anselmian premiss: 'The fact that God can do what the biblical witnesses ascribe to Him, namely, not just take form and not just remain free in this form, but in this form and freedom of His become God to specific men . . . this is the third meaning of His lordship in His revelation.'[89]

In what he has said so far Barth claims not to have produced a doctrine of the Trinity, but to have established its root, 'asking concretely with reference to the biblical texts whether the statement that God reveals Himself as the Lord really has a threefold meaning and yet a simple content in these texts'.[90] The doctrine of the Trinity has true roots in the biblical witness to revelation not in textual evidence of references to Father, Son, and Spirit, but in the Bible's understanding of the historical events in which God is God. That is the basic insight on which all depends.

Before proceeding to the doctrine of the Trinity proper, Barth aims a parting blow at *a priori* methods of doing theology, asking whether there is a second possible root of the doctrine, subsisting in all created reality and providing a kind of natural trinitarian theology.[91] There arises from this discussion the question of the nature and justification of the language the theologian uses in speaking of God. Certainly our theology must make use of ordinary, worldly language. But which language do we use, and on what grounds? Bible, church, and theology certainly believe that their language can describe the reality of revelation. The only question is whether this possibility is to be understood as that of the language and consequently of the world or man, or whether it is to be regarded as a venture which is, as it were,

---

[87] Ibid.   [88] I/1 329.   [89] I/1 331.   [90] I/1 332.
[91] I/1 333–47.

ascribed to the language, and consequently to the world or man, from without, so that it is not really the possibility of the language, the world, or man, but the possibility of revelation . . .[92]

That is to say, do the words and concepts contain in themselves the power of revelation, as manifestly is the case in Hartshorne, or do the words have to obtain their power of true description from outside themselves? Must revelation, and so God, be understood in terms or categories that are brought to them *a priori*, or are they such that they demand rational understanding on their own terms? Barth, of course, takes the second of the alternatives, and for reasons deriving from what we have called his realism of revelation. This is to make the point, as Jüngel has seen, that revelation not only demands understanding in its own right, but *gives* understanding as well. 'Where revelation conquers language, a *Word of God* takes place. The Word of God *brings* the language to its proper expression.'[93]

Barth's suspicion of the *vestigium trinitatis*, of those theories that claim to be able to see the Trinity elsewhere than in the biblical revelation, is therefore derived from the same source as his rejection of natural theology. His fear is that rather than being conquered by revelation, language will conquer it.[94] But the polemic is empowered by the positive view that in revelation God makes our language able to express his triune reality. It is on such grounds that Barth can reject any *analogia entis* so far as that entails the view that a prior understanding of theological language can be brought to revelation. Jüngel sees the issue as being between two approaches to hermeneutics.[95] Because revelation as God's self-interpretation empowers man's interpretation, what he calls a *Signifikationshermeneutik* is rendered both unnecessary and inadmissible. 'An hermeneutic that enquires about God's self-interpretation is essentially different from the Aristotelian *Signifikationshermeneutik*. This is true *despite* the many echoes of this hermeneutic in Barth's *Church Dogmatics*.'[96]

[92] I/1 339.
[93] Jüngel, *Gottes Sein*, p. 26. The translation is a loose one. A more literal rendering would be, '. . . to its true being (*in ihr Wesen*)'.   [94] *CD* I/1 344.
[95] 'Das *vestigium trinitatis* als hermeneutisches Problem', Jüngel, op. cit., pp. 16–27.
[96] Jüngel, op. cit., p. 27. Cf. also the remark of John McIntyre: 'The interpretation . . . is one of the most elaborate exercises in modern hermeneutics that I have ever encountered.' *The Shape of Christology* (London, 1966), pp. 158 f.

The becoming of God has so far been the theme of the exposition of Karl Barth's doctrine of God. Like the neoclassical God, this God becomes *essentially*. There is also in common the fact that the doctrine of God is a dipolar one. In this chapter we have described one pole of the divine reality according to Barth. In the next we shall examine the implications of this threefold becoming for his understanding of the being of God. But only very cautiously can we say that, as with neoclassical thought, the being is abstracted from the becoming. In Hartshorne the terms 'relative' and 'absolute'—and related terms like 'becoming' and 'being'—are both abstract terms, describing respectively the concrete and abstract natures or poles of God. But although the conception of the being of God in Barth will be seen to develop by a process of abstraction (for there is a sense in which all concepts abstract) this is not to say that there is for Barth an abstract pole of the divine reality. It is rather that when we pass to the being of God we shall be concerned with an abstract description of God's actual concrete reality. 'Our theme . . . will be the deity and sovereignty of God—not, of course, in abstraction from His activity, but the being of God Himself in the light of His activity.'[97] The abstract description in fact performs the function of ensuring that we understand the reality of God in His concrete becoming.[98] The two 'poles' of the concept of God are therefore in much more subtle, though equally close, relationship than they are in neoclassical theology. It could be said that both are abstract descriptions of God's concrete reality, though what could be meant by this must await the exposition of the being of God.

[97] *CD* I/2 881.
[98] Jüngel, op. cit., p. 43, makes the point that it is with the help of the doctrines of perichoresis and appropriation that 'the concreteness of the being of God is conceived'.

VI

THE BEING OF GOD: THE TRIUNITY OF GOD

i. *The Divine Unity: Differences of Approach and Method*

Now begins rational theology proper, and with it the more formal use of concepts and general terms. The doctrine of the Trinity is formulated 'In order to achieve the necessary conceptual clarification of the question of the Subject of revelation . . .'[1] Our concern is therefore with the essence of God, with what God really is, what it is that makes him God.[2] But the reference to an essence of God does not imply an essentialist or linguistic approach to the derivation of concepts any more than the description of God's being here implies a negation of the previous emphasis on becoming. Barth's description of the being of God is to be based upon the becoming of God that has already been discerned in the events in which God happens in revelation. Here we can compare Hartshorne's understanding of the essence of a person—or of God—as an abstraction from the occasions that are his reality. The being is abstracted from the becoming. That this comparison is more than merely superficial is shown by the way in which the doctrine of the Trinity is developed here. It was observed that in the case of Hartshorne's God variety or infinite multiplicity is what constitutes his simplicity; the two polar terms are not incompatible, but are both instantiated transcendently and related as concrete to abstract.[3] Something very similar may be said of the relation of threeness and oneness in Barth. 'It may be said of this essence of God that its unity is not only not abrogated by the threeness of the "persons" but rather than its *unity consists in the threeness* of the "persons".'[4] Similarly, in Volume II of the *Church Dogmatics*, when Barth is speaking of the multiplicity of the divine perfections or

---

[1] *CD* I/1 348.   [2] I/1 349.   [3] Above, pp. 32 f.
[4] *CD* I/1 349 f. My italics.

attributes, he argues that God's possession of the many perfections that we attribute to him in no way detracts from his unity. On the contrary, because the perfections are, so to speak, organized around a personal centre, '. . . the very unity of His being consists in the multiplicity, individuality and diversity of His perfections, which since they are His are not capable of any dissolution or separation or non-identity. . . .'⁵

But, as always in the 'dialectical' relationship between the two theologies, the differences also are great. Hartshorne is concerned with abstraction from a temporal succession of occasions. As will become clear, there is an analogy to this in Barth, but not such as to make God dependent upon the time he has himself created. For Hartshorne, indeed, one legitimate motive for the development of the doctrine of the Trinity is that of wishing to allow for temporal succession in God. Speaking of the succession of the divine selves he says: 'A kind of neo-trinitarianism can be worked out . . . with, however, an infinity of Holy Spirits, rather than just one.'⁶ There is no need to labour the point that here Hartshorne and Barth are worlds apart. It is precisely when he is using 'person' language that Barth wishes, in contrast to Hartshorne, to stress the unity rather than the multiplicity of God: 'It is well to note at this early stage that what we today call the "personality" of God belongs to the one unique essence of God which the doctrine of the Trinity does not seek to triple but rather to recognise in its simplicity.'⁷ Three 'personalities' in God 'would be the worst and most extreme expression of tritheism',⁸ whereas here we are concerned from the start with the repetition of the one God.⁹ Moreover, the doctrine of the Trinity, far from requiring reconciliation with monotheism, was in fact developed in its defence.¹⁰ And so for Barth God's unity consists in his multiplicity, and does so because the facts of revelation demand such an understanding. 'If revelation is to be taken seriously as God's presence . . . then in no sense can Christ and the Spirit be subordinate hypostases. . . . Revelation and revealing must be equal to the revealer.'¹¹

A further consequence of the realism of revelation is that we are shown to be not in the realm of logical or metaphysical

---

⁵ II/1 332. ⁶ *LP* 122, cf. *PSG* 227. ⁷ *CD* I/1 350.
⁸ I/1 351. ⁹ I/1 350. ¹⁰ I/1 351 ff. ¹¹ I/1 353.

necessity, where Hartshorne's thinking about the multiplicity and unity of God takes place, but of what might be called theological necessity, where the revealed reality of God imposes upon the thinker the way in which he deploys his concepts. 'God is One, but not in such a way that as such He needs a Second and then a Third in order to be One, nor as though He were alone and had to do without a counterpart . . .'[12] How then is God one? The answer comes from drawing out the implications of the threefold temporal repetition. As it is the repetition of the one God, and as it takes place in time, God himself must be the *repetitio aeternitatis in aeternitate*, the repetition of eternity in eternity.[13] The meaning of this in Barth will only emerge with the exposition of the whole of the doctrine of the Trinity. But this much already has to be said. Barth's conception of the eternity of God is bound up with God's temporality, and does not intend to be its negation as some conception of timelessness. It is not, however, as simple as it is in Hartshorne, where time is absolute. All beings are temporal in the same way, although some last longer than others. Eternity is therefore unending time. For Barth, God is temporal, because revelation *is* God, taking place in time. But God is Lord in his revelation. Therefore

God comes to be understood not as a transcendent thing but as a transcendent happening, and his transcendence therefore understood not as his timelessness, but as his radical temporality. . . . The doctrine of the Trinity identifies God not as the definition of the eternalized time of the past, but as the lord from the future.[14]

The divine repetition is temporal, but not an endless temporal succession from which a concept of God is to be abstracted.

ii. *Analogy and Personality*

As always, the movement of thought is from revelation to the essence of God. The denial of abstract unity and of abstract eternity go hand in hand. Similarly the very fact of repetition entails some kind of real 'inner' distinction and order in the being of God.[15] But this is not simply a repetition of points

---

[12] I/1 354.   [13] I/1 353.
[14] R. W. Jenson, *God After God*, p. 96, cf. the same author's *Alpha and Omega. A Study in the Theology of Karl Barth* (New York, 1963), p. 76, where he says that for Barth God is 'the eminently historical being'.   [15] *CD* I/1 355.

already made, for Barth proceeds: 'This distinction or order is the distinction or order of the three "persons", or, as we prefer to say, the three "ways (or modes) of being" in God.'[16] The phrase 'ways (or modes) of being' translates the German *Seinsweise*.

In regard to *Seinsweise* Karl Barth himself once agreed with us that 'way of being' might be a better rendering in English than 'mode of being,' if only to avoid any hint of 'modalism,' which he completely rejects. Yet his intention here to refer back to the Cappadocian τρόπος ὑπάρξεως and the *modus entis* of Protestant Orthodoxy made it evident that it would be best to preserve the rendering 'mode of being' . . .[17]

However it be translated, the function of the concept in Barth is to help to provide an answer to the question of how the threefold temporal repetition belongs in the unity of the one God. Because of the connotations of the terms 'person' and 'personality' as they are now used he wishes to abandon the traditional designation of the three as 'persons'.[18] Remaining true to his intention of choosing the language to fit the facts, he finds that the term 'person' is more suitable as a description of the one God who exists in three modes of being than for each of the three modes taken individually. There is no doubt at all about his absolute insistence on the personal nature of God. Even when the expression 'mode of being' is employed, it is done with intent 'to express by this term, not absolutely, but relatively better and more simply and clearly the same thing as is meant by "person" '.[19] In fact

. . . we are not introducing a new concept but simply putting in the centre an auxiliary concept which has been used from the very beginning and with great emphasis in the analysis of the concept of person. The statement that God is One in three ways of being, Father, Son and Holy Ghost, means, therefore, that the one God, i.e. the one Lord, the one personal God, is what He is not just in one mode but . . . in the mode of the Father, in the mode of the Son, and in the mode of the Holy Ghost.[20]

Barth's intention is not therefore to detract in any way from the personal nature of God, but to avoid any suggestion of

---

[16] Ibid. [17] 'Editors' Preface' to *CD* I/1 (1974 edn.), p. viii.
[18] I/1 355 f. [19] I/1 359. [20] Ibid., cf. II/1 296 f.

personal independence of the three, and hence of tritheism.[21] Revelation does not give us three gods.

What we have here are God's specific, different and always very distinctive modes of being. This means that God's modes of being are not to be exchanged or confounded. In all three modes of being God is the one God both in Himself and in relation to the world and man. But this one God is God three times in different ways, so different that it is only in this threefold difference that He is God, so different that this difference, this being in these three modes of being, is absolutely essential to Him, so different, then, that this difference is irremovable.[22]

Much of what Barth has here said might suggest that he is doing little more than revise the language of trinitarian theology. But it may be that he is being more radical than he himself believes. Claude Welch has argued that Barth fails to emphasize strongly enough a real difference between his thought and the old theology. In the latter

it is the three persons which subsist. Thus St. Thomas speaks of the *personae* as *res subsistentes in divina natura*, and Calvin formally defines *persona* as *subsistentia in Dei essentia*. This way of speaking was possible because these writers did not have to deal with the conception of the personality of God as such. They spoke of God as a neuter, of *deitas* and of *essentia divina*. Because of this impersonal way of speaking, and the static and almost materialistic conception of substance which it involved, they were able to speak meaningfully of a divine *persona* as that which subsists in the divine nature.[23]

Perhaps it would not be reading too much into Welch's words to suggest that it is the shift from static to dynamic terms, from a substance- to an event-conceptuality that has made the chief difference. He attributes the change to 'the adjustment of our language to the change in the meaning of the term "person" ',[24] and thus himself appears to underestimate the radicality of the change. Jüngel is more aware of what has happened. According to his understanding, Barth's understanding of revelation has made possible a radically different conception of God's independent reality (*Selbständigkeit*), in which God is

[21] I/1 357 f.   [22] I/1 360.
[23] Claude Welch, *The Trinity in Contemporary Theology* (London, 1953), pp. 190 f.
[24] Jüngel, *Gottes Sein*, pp. 103 ff.

seen as *essentially* relational being; in which the being of God *for us* is not something foreign to God's essence but is grounded in his very being.

The being of God is thus *self-related* being. As being, it is relationally structured. The relational structuring of the being of God makes up the being of God, but not in the sense of a neutral structure over against this being itself; rather, the modes of being of God that are distinct from each other are successively related in such a way that each mode of being of God first *becomes* what it *is* together *with* both the other modes of being. . . . God's being is thus, as the being of God, the Father, the Son, and the Holy Spirit, a *being in becoming*.[25]

This 'being in becoming' makes it impossible to conceive God in the old substantial categories.

. . . one will not then be able to conceive God's being as subsistence (*Selbstand*) in the way in which Plato conceives οὐσία, for he ascribes the λόγος τοῦ εἶναι· ἀεὶ ὃ ἔστι, μονοειδὲς ὄν αὐτὸ καθ, αὐτό . . . . ὡσαύτως καὶ κατὰ ταὐτὰ ἔχει καὶ οὐδέποτε οὐδαμῇ οὐδαμῶς ἀλλοίωσιν οὐδεμίαν ἐνδέχεται. Such a being as subsistence excludes *event* from itself, so that such a subsisting being cannot reveal itself.[26]

But what God does, he can do.

The conception of the relational structure of God's being as a being in becoming will now bulk large in the discussion of the being of God. Hartshorne centres his metaphysic on an understanding of the relatedness of all reality, and applies this relatedness, which he has conceived by an act of *a priori* metaphysical analysis, to God in eminent degree. For Barth the notion of relation serves as a means of clarifying the place of the three modes of being in the being of the one personal God. The data that have been deployed so far enable him to say that, 'the distinguishable fact of the three divine modes of being is to be understood in terms of their distinctive relations and indeed their distinctive genetic relations to one another'.[27] Moreover,

If these three names [sc. Father, Son, and Spirit] are really in their threeness the one name of the one God, then it follows that in this

---

[25] Jüngel, op. cit., pp. 76 f.
[26] Op. cit., p. 107. The 'principle of being' of Plato's 'substance' is: 'what always is, being of single form in and through itself, remains the same in the same respect, and never admits of the slightest alteration in any way at all.' Phaedo 78 d.
[27] *CD* I/1 363.

one God there is primarily at least . . . something like fatherhood and sonship, and therefore something like begetting and being begotten, and then a third thing common to both . . . a bringing forth which originates in concert in both begetter and begotten.[28]

It is here that the difference from the neoclassical doctrine of relations is to be seen. In criticizing the attempts that have been made to make God an exception to the 'rule' that all entities are related to other entities—i.e. the attempt to make God 'absolute'—Hartshorne argues that theologians made a gesture to the true doctrine by attributing relation to God within the Trinity, but that this was no more than a device to avoid the full implications of the social doctrine.[29] 'It seems implicit if not explicit in Christianity . . . that the social structure of existence is no mere appearance of something more ultimate, but an aspect of reality itself or as such. The Trinity is one attempt, perhaps none too successful, to express this.'[30] Barth's doctrine of the Trinity is exempt from at least the general point of the criticism, even if it fails to go all the way with neoclassical metaphysics. The whole conception is centred on God's relatedness to what is not himself. But before exposition of this theme and its implications is continued, three points of general clarification can be made.

The first is that the difference between the two theologies is brought out by the fact that the neoclassical metaphysic is the result of the development of an Analogy, a system of concepts by which the whole of reality is to be understood at its different levels. For our purposes, the aspect to be stressed is the relation conceived on the basis of this analogy to hold timelessly between God and that to which he is eminently related, i.e. the world. In Barth at this stage we are concerned with something different, that is, with analogical predication in which personal analogies are cautiously ascribed to God. In particular, he has suggested analogies to the kind of relations that hold between the members of human families.

Second, and this highlights another major difference, Barth's approach is not *a priori*, but *a posteriori*—not 'because the entities in our experience are related, God must be so eminently', but 'the character of God's threeness in revelation

---

[28] *CD* I/1 363.   [29] *DR* 32 f.   [30] *NTOT* 105.

entails a threeness of relation in what he really is'. The relatedness cannot be read off from anything else, for it is unique: 'that
each of these relations as such can also be the One in whom
these relations occur—for this there are no analogies. This is
the unique divine trinity in the unique divine unity.'[31] Of
course the uniqueness and lack of analogies do not entail that
there be no analogical language; if that were so there would be
no theological language at all. The point would rather seem
to be that there is no analogy to the situation taken as a whole,
such that it can easily be encapsulated in ready-made concepts.
The divine relatedness is not a difference in quantity from
other relatedness, but in kind. Therefore the divine unity will
have to be conceived differently from other unities. 'This,
then, is the repetition in God, the *repetitio aeternitatis in aeternitate*, by which the unity of the revealed God is differentiated
from everything else that may be called unity.'[32] And so we
have an analogy of relation, not of being or becoming, that has
to be understood and interpreted on its own terms.

The third point concerns the nature of what Barth is doing
in expounding the doctrine of the Trinity. It is rational theology not only in the sense that have so far been mentioned, but
in the fact that Barth is here concerned with ontology, with
describing the ontological ground for the relation of God to the
creatures. He has shown that in revelation God relates himself
to man. The doctrine of the Trinity as relational being both
follows from that understanding of relation in revelation, and
at the same time shows how it is grounded in the prevenient
reality of God.

iii. *Triunity*

The idea of triunity (*Dreieinigkeit*) brings together the two
aspects of the being of God that have been discussed so far:
unity in trinity and trinity in unity. When either of the two
latter is under discussion, there is bound to be an element of
one-sidedness.[33] And so the further concept is required as a
conflation of the two.

We see on the one side how for those who hear and see revelation
in the Bible the Father, Son and Spirit . . . come together in the
knowledge and concept of the one God. And we see on the other

[31] *CD* I/1 364. [32] I/1 366. [33] I/1 368.

side how for them the source and goal of this knowledge and concept are never a sterile one but are rather the three, whatever we call them. In practice the concept of triunity is the movement of these two thoughts.[34]

We require the concept because of the way in which men have actually come to know God, and because it is required for the rational description of the reality of the revealed God. Further, just as knowledge of the one God is necessarily of him as triune, so it is impossible to know any one of the three without also knowing the other two: '. . . none of the Three may be known without the other Two but each of the Three only with the other Two.'[35] This state of affairs, says Barth, has traditionally been expressed by the doctrine of *perichoresis* or *circuminsessio*, which 'states that the divine modes of being mutually condition and permeate one another so completely that one is always in the other two and the other two in the one'.[36] The value of the doctrine is that it

implies both a confirmation of the distinction in the modes of being, for none would be what it is (not even the Father) without its co-existence with the others, and also a relativisation of this distinction, for none exists as a special individual, but all three 'in-exist' or exist only in concert as modes of being of the one God and Lord who posits Himself from eternity to eternity.[37]

What is the point of all this? It may well appear that after all his insistence on the concreteness of our theological language, Barth is now engaging in speculation of the most irrelevant kind. But that would be to miss the point, for here as always Barth is concerned only with the proper understanding of revelation, with giving rational expression to what Jüngel has called the 'self-interpretation' of God. 'God is what he does among us. All the complicated subtleties of Barth's developed doctrine of the Trinity say this one thing at all the different places where it might be forgotten.'[38] Jüngel makes a similar point. 'In Barth's doctrine of the Trinity the doctrine of perichoresis and the doctrine of appropriations serve to achieve this task [sc. to conceive God in his self-relatedness as *concrete being*]. It is with the help of these doctrines that the concreteness

---

[34] I/1 369.   [35] I/1 370.   [36] Ibid.   [37] Ibid.
[38] R. W. Jenson, *God After God*, p. 113.

of the being of God is to be conceived.'³⁹ The most abstract and speculative appearing doctrines have in fact the opposite function: they keep language about God down to earth.

Having moved in his exposition from the 'outer' revelation to the 'inner' reality of God—though the foregoing account should have shown how metaphorical are those two terms—Barth looks outward again, and uses the picture of God he has built up to throw further light on the historical activity of God. 'To the unity of Father, Son and Spirit among themselves corresponds their unity *ad extra*. God's essence and work are not twofold but one. God's work is His essence in its relation to the reality which is distinct from Him . . .'⁴⁰ There is no conceptual or ontological gulf between the being and the revelation of God, any more than there is an interest in the inner reality of God in abstraction from what he does in history. Why then must there be any distinction at all between outward activity and essence, or between 'economic' and 'immanent' trinity? To use a term suited to the comparison with Hartshorne's conception of God, why is there a need to distinguish between two 'poles' of the divine reality when one seems to be all that we need? An answer to this question brings us to the heart of Barth's doctrine of God. In this dipolar doctrine of God, there is what may be called an asymmetry of understanding, by which God's freedom is preserved. What God does is a sure guide to an understanding of what God really is. 'God's work is, of course, the work of the whole essence of God. God gives Himself entirely to man in His revelation . . .'⁴¹ But God's reality is not exhausted by his acts. If he is to be a gracious God, this giving of himself must be a free, unnecessitated act. 'God gives Himself entirely to man in His revelation, but not in such a way as to make Himself man's prisoner. He remains free in His working, in giving Himself.'⁴²

The asymmetry consists in the fact that while act is indeed a true guide to essence, knowledge of essence does not entail knowledge of the particular acts that God is going to perform. This is directly analogous to our knowledge of human character from action. I may know from his consistent past behaviour that Smith loves his family, but that is not to say that I know which particular loving acts he will perform tomorrow or next

³⁹ E. Jüngel, op. cit., p. 43.   ⁴⁰ *CD* I/1 371.   ⁴¹ Ibid.   ⁴² Ibid.

week. It is analogous to human character, but *only* analogous. The difference between the two cases is significant, and helps to clarify further Barth's conception of the three modes of being as eternal divine events. Jenson puts it thus:

> The doctrine of subsisting relations, and of God as the occurrence of these relations, is manifest nonsense if we insist that an act must be the act of something that is not an act. But why do we insist on this? I suggest that this 'natural' ontology is only a projection on reality of the pattern of our alienated existence: the 'I' that persists *behind* and aloof from my acts is precisely what I *hold back* from my fellows. . . . God has no such lack. He is what he does for the other. God is the occurrence of relation.[43]

iv. *Asymmetry in Barth and Hartshorne*

The asymmetry of understanding in Barth performs a function similar to that performed by the notion of the asymmetry of time in Hartshorne. In the latter it is held that the future is both undetermined and unknown to God. The presence of God in the process ensures that there is an ontological difference between the past and the future. This in its turn ensures that there is room for freedom in the world. Both our theologians are therefore concerned to establish freedom. But there the parallel ends. Hartshorne is not interested in the freedom of God to act graciously but in a general metaphysical freedom—a kind of indeterminacy—in the world process. Because the past alone and not the future is fixed and definite, there is room for each personal event to possess some freedom of its own. Indeed, this creaturely freedom is won at the expense of the freedom of God. Discussing the thought of Schelling, Hartshorne comments: 'A signal achievement . . . is his insight that the freedom of the creatures is not the result of divine choice. . . . God has no choice whatever between there being free creatures and there being no free creatures.'[44] Both we and God can only conjecture on the basis of present trends what the future will bring (a figure of speech that is almost literally applicable in this connection).

Another surface similarity between the two thinkers lies in the fact that both wish to eliminate by means of their dipolar

---

[43] R. W. Jenson, op. cit., p. 112, cf. p. 126, and below, Ch. VIII, § ii.
[44] *PSG* 234, cf. *RSP* 139 f.

conceptuality the divorce between what God is and what he does. There can be no doubt that in this respect Barth is the more successful, if it is true that the neoclassical God can do nothing at all from his seat slightly in the rear of the action. Hartshorne has fallen into exactly the same trap as his classical predecessors, of deciding in advance what is and is not possible for God, and has thus himself achieved a divorce between act and being. The outcome is that what for Barth are sure indicators of the nature of God are of merely secondary importance for Hartshorne. 'Such matters as Anselm's special beliefs about the Church, the Trinity, and the Incarnation are at best subsidiary to the main religious belief . . .'[45] The very things that for Barth declare the being of God for man are for Hartshorne either secondary or obscure, matters of optional interest and concern.

v. *The Meaning of the Doctrine of the Trinity*

Balancing the doctrine of *perichoresis*, and rounding off this part of the exposition, is the doctrine of appropriations. The relationship with *perichoresis* is rather a matter of checks and balances. Once the doctrine of *perichoresis* has set the limits to our understanding of the distinctions in God, the doctrine of appropriations serves to ensure that proper use is made of the 'hint' that we are given in revelation. 'By the specific assigning of a word or deed to this or that person of the Godhead, there should be brought to our awareness . . . the truth of the triunity which is in fact undivided in its work and which still exists in three persons.'[46] Appropriation must not be made in contravention of the rule, 'opera trinitatis ad extra sunt indivisa.'

Per appropriationem this act or this attribute must now be given prominence in relation to this or that mode of being in order that this can be described as such. But only *per appropriationem* may this happen, and in no case, therefore, to the forgetting or denying of God's presence in all His modes of being, in His total being and act even over against us.[47]

Once again it is Jüngel who has seen the point of what Barth is doing here. In his discussion of appropriation in Barth, he states that it is 'a hermeneutical enterprise'.[48] 'Appropriation

---

[45] *AD* 135. Notice that such matters are *at best* subsidiary. One can only wonder what they are at worst.

[46] *CD* I/1 373. [47] I/1 375. [48] E. Jüngel, op. cit., p. 48.

is thus what makes it possible to bring God to speech, for example *as Father*.'[49] As such, it provides a key to the whole of Barth's dogmatic enterprise; he believes it can be shown that 'appropriation and thus the understanding of God as concrete event fundamentally determines Barth's whole dogmatic, and in particular the doctrine of election. . . .'.[50] It can be seen from this that each of the great themes of the *Church Dogmatics* is an exposition of a particular appropriation of the different modes of being of the one triune God, and each is made possible because what happened in Jesus Christ empowers us (simply because it is God's concrete presence among us) to speak in that way. Thus in Volume III there is appropriated to the Father the function of creation, although creation is the act of the whole Trinity, because by so doing we can bring to speech the divine work of creating. Volume IV is about the reconciliation accomplished by the whole Trinity, and yet it is a work that is appropriately ascribed to God the Son. Thus each of the major *loci* is a centre of interest in its own right, but is none the less seen to be a further specification of the event in which God is God in his triune reality.

The doctrine of appropriation is, then, one part of the hermeneutical design which takes its origins in Barth's exposition of the doctrine of the Trinity. What does Barth claim to have achieved so far? In the final section of the discussion of triunity, 'The meaning of the doctrine of the Trinity', Barth says that what he has produced is 'a theologoumenon . . . dogma'.[51] It has been produced by reflection on the biblical text: as such, it is not to be found there but 'belongs to the Church'.[52] The Church has asked the kind of questions that have led her to the doctrine because she is concerned with the problem of who it is that reveals himself in Jesus Christ. The meaning of the doctrine of the Trinity lies largely in the answer it gives about the *identity* of God.

The function of the doctrine is to *identify* which being we are going to be talking about in our theologizing. If we say that God is revealed in Jesus, we raise the question *who* is God, or perhaps the question *which* God is revealed in Jesus. The doctrine of the Trinity

---

[49] Op. cit., p. 49.   [50] Op. cit., p. 53.   [51] *CD* I/1 375.
[52] Ibid.

is an answer. Its logical function is thus closely related to that of a proper name.[53]

Not only is God identified by means of the doctrine of the Trinity, he is identified in a particular way. 'The doctrine of the Trinity tells us . . . how far the One who reveals Himself according to the witness of Scripture can in fact be our *God* and how far He can in fact be *our* God.'[54] Thus there are at work a number of concerns, all centring on the one point: the evangelical concern, that theology serve Church proclamation; the rational concern, that understanding be found of the revelation that both demands and gives rationality; and above all the concern to be true to the reality of God as he makes himself known in what he does.

Barth has given to his doctrine of the Trinity (1932) essentially the same function that the programme of demythologising has in the theology of Rudolf Bultmann. . . . If we understand Bultmann's programme as the quest for appropriate language about God (and therewith about man) and if we view the achievement of this quest in avoiding the objectifying of God as an It or a He and rather bringing God to speech as Thou . . . we shall not be able to overlook a striking parallel to the significance which Barth ascribes (and gives) to the doctrine of the Trinity. For the significance of the doctrine of the Trinity consists for Barth . . . in the fact . . . that God becomes 'no It or He'; 'he remains Thou.'[55]

53 R. W. Jenson, op. cit., pp. 97 f., cf. *CD* I/1 380.   54 *CD* I/1 382 f.
55 E. Jüngel, op. cit., pp. 33 f., citing *KD* I/1 402.

VII

THE BEING OF GOD: APPROPRIATION AND ANALOGOUS PREDICATION

i. *Summary and Introduction*

FROM an account of the becoming of God in revelation, Barth has moved to a description of his being, of what he really is in himself. Because revelation is God taking place, rational theology is forced to the conclusion that his being consists in his becoming: the threefoldness of the becoming of the one God requires interpretation in a doctrine of the Trinity. But, although their ontological grounding in the being of God has been demonstrated, the temporality and variety of the divine actions still require further exposition. The nature of the three modes of being of the one God demands further individual examination, and this provides the subject-matter for this chapter. Chapter VIII will concern itself with the problems arising from Barth's conception of the temporality of God.

An exposition of the Fatherhood, Sonship, and Spirithood of God highlights two features in particular of the relation between this concept of God and the neoclassical. The first concerns the way in which the difficulties raised by Hume about the analogous predication of attributes are countered. Hartshorne, it was noted, supplied one of the two unknowns by arguing to a concept of God from the nature of language and reality as they were conceived *a priori*. Language and reality are such that we know how God would be described were he to exist. All that then remains is to prove that God does in fact exist. Barth's procedure is the reverse of this. God, it is argued, authenticates his existence in threefold revelation events, and thus imposes a certain kind of language upon the interpreter of those events. Once the revelatory character of the events is acknowledged, the interpreter has to speak of God in a certain way, though not with the rigidly prescribed linguistic circle of the rationalist. Theological language becomes open-textured, the limits of the openness being prescribed not by language but by the nature of the object of theology. Analogous predication is both made possible and given its limits by revelation.

The second feature that will receive attention is closely connected with the use of analogous language, and will also reveal crucial differences between the two approaches to theology. This is the notion of relation in God. The relational character of the divine reality according to Barth has already received mention, but will now be developed. Once again, there will be observed a reversal of method. In the case of neoclassical theology a doctrine of relations is read upwards into God. In the case of Barth it is the understanding of God that is held to have far-reaching implications for the way in which we shall understand the nature of reality.

ii. *God the Father*

In this section the function of creation is appropriated to God in his mode of being as the eternal father. The familiar pattern is repeated. Proof establishes becoming, and on the basis of this becoming the being of God is described. It is therefore with a statement about revelation that the exposition of the predication of fatherhood of God begins. By revelation, it is claimed, two errors are removed. When God reveals himself as the Lord it is 'not as a being of the kind and order to which man himself belongs and therefore not as a being over which man for his part might equally well be lord; nor yet as a being which exists and remains in and for itself in its own kind and order'.[1] Behind Barth's claim there clearly lies the conception of the triune God's freedom in revelation—freedom both to reveal himself and to remain true to himself in becoming what he is not. It is this freedom of God that exposes the two errors. In alluding to the first error, the belief that God is of the same kind and order as that to which man belongs, Barth is rejecting the beliefs of those proponents of natural theology whose procedure presupposes that there is between divine and non-divine reality such community of nature that the knowledge of the former can be read off the latter without particular divine

[1] *CD* I/1 384.

initiative. In Hartshorne's theology the community of nature is both close and metaphysically required, because to be real is to be an instance of temporal becoming.

Thus, according to Barth revelation overthrows axiomatic monism of the kind that Hartshorne avows. The reality of God's becoming man paradoxically, perhaps, preserves the distinction between the human and the divine.[2] But it also overthrows the opposite error, which is the propounding of so rigid a dualism that God is logically prevented from becoming man or relating himself to what is not God. Neoclassical theology would agree with Barth in attacking the second error, though for different reasons. If certain doctrines of the classical theists are taken at their face value—for example, the notion of the absolute, as meaning the denial of relativity, or the doctrine of impassibility—then God is indeed confined to his own kind and order. Both Hartshorne and Barth are concerned to develop a concept of God in which he is seen to be really related to the universe without being identified with it. In Barth the crucial proviso is made that God remains free to relate himself or not to do so; that he does relate himself does not entail that he had or has to do so, only that he can do so. He remains the Lord. Behind Barth's thinking there is an evangelical (in the original and best sense of that word) motive operating. He wishes to preserve an understanding of God as one who really does things with, to, and for mankind, but who does them not because of necessitated metaphysical ties but because he freely and graciously chooses to do them. And, it can be observed in passing, Barth may be able to say as much, if not more, about the freedom of man than neoclassical metaphysics, for all the latter's much-vaunted ascription of freedom to the events in the process. 'A God who is dependent on man turns out to be a terrible limitation on man's freedom and creativity. . . . The triumph of Barth's theology is a God who doesn't need man; therefore He can let man live.'[3]

When the analogy of fatherhood is developed, two principles

---

[2] See R. W. Jenson, *God After God*, pp. 113–21. Jenson argues that both in Barth and in Gregory of Nyssa one of the functions of the doctrine of the Trinity is to preserve the fundamental ontological distinction between God and man, in the former case against the Arian doctrines, in the latter in opposition to modern religiosity.

[3] Harvey Cox, *The Secular City* (London, 1966 edn.), p. 82.

can be seen to operate. First, there is the repudiation of essentialist procedures from some general idea of fatherhood, claimed to be known antecedently from elsewhere, to God. The concrete acts of revelation are to control the treatment: as always, language does not possess its ability to express the truth about God, it has to receive it.[4] Second, and related to this, it is the trinitarian doctrine of God which provides the pattern of relations by which the meaning of fatherhood in this case can be made clear.

Before being the father of anyone else, God the Father is the father of Jesus Christ. It is in this that Jesus' divinity, his reality as God, consists. 'The essence of the deity ascribed to Jesus is to make clear and impart and give effect to who God the Father is, who God is in the true sense. . . . It is to represent this God the Father.'[5] Who is this Father? Someone rather different from what we might expect if we followed our own line of thought. Barth derives his conception of God's fatherhood from the events of cross and resurrection, where above all it is shown that he is the Father of Jesus Christ. First, there is death. 'The One whom Jesus reveals as the Father is known absolutely on the death of man, at the end of his existence.'[6] But this is not to say that 'God the Father is identical with death . . .'[7] The fatherhood of God is defined by means of resurrection also: 'He wills death in order to lead our life through it to eternal life.'[8] And so the essential meaning of God's fatherhood is that he 'is the Lord of our existence. He is this in the strict sense to the degree that He is the Lord over the life and death of man.'[9] Therefore his fatherhood means much more than does human fatherhood: 'it is as the Creator that Jesus shows the Father to us.[10] The difference between God's and any other fatherhood is that only God is in total control of existence; all other control can at best be partial. Therefore the *analogy* is real but controlled. 'When Scripture calls God our Father it adopts an analogy only to transcend it at once.'[11]

As our Father, then, God is related to us as Lord of our existence, and yet not bound to be so related. The question then arises of how this can be so. What is the ontological basis of this state of affairs and of the analogical predication it generates?

[4] *CD* I/1 386.   [5] Ibid.   [6] I/1 387.   [7] I/1 388.
[8] Ibid.   [9] Ibid.   [10] I/1 389.   [11] Ibid.

To provide the ontological ground Barth makes the familiar move from becoming to being, from revelatory fatherhood to the eternal triune fatherhood. God's relatedness to us as Lord of our existence is possible because there is already a prior relatedness of God within the Trinity. 'God can be our Father because He is Father in Himself, because fatherhood is an eternal mode of being of the divine essence.'[12] The word fatherhood is here properly used because in the eternal Trinity there is a situation that can only be described by means of an analogy taken from human family relationships. 'God is the eternal Father inasmuch as from eternity and in eternity He is the Father of the Son who from eternity and in eternity participates in the same essence with Him.'[13] Once again we are reminded that this being of God is, in our knowledge, derived from what we know of his becoming; not any becoming or all becoming, from which is derived a 'natural theology' which is then baptized because of Jesus. The doctrine of the creatorhood of God is not an article of natural theology.[14] Rather, 'from the fact that in Jesus and Jesus alone He is manifested as the Creator and therefore as our Father it follows that He already is that which corresponds thereto antecedently and in Himself. . .'.[15]

In sum we can say that the fatherhood of God is an article of faith and not of natural theology because creation is the act of the triune God. We speak of it by appropriation, and, in a sense, it is *only* an appropriation.[16] But it is a necessary ('commanded') appropriation. 'Without making this appropriation we could not even see that it is "only" an appropriation.'[17] We have to make it, because our knowledge of God's fatherhood derives from that revelation in which God really happens as Father.

iii. *God the Son*

The development of the analogy of fatherhood stressed the distinction-in-relatedness between Jesus and the Father. The second leading analogy, that of sonship, centres on the relatedness-in-distinction between the two. The discussion begins with the usual features: the Bible as the place where God's

[12] I/1 390.   [13] I/1 394.   [14] I/1 389 f., 391, III/1 3 ff.
[15] I/1 391.   [16] I/1 394 f.   [17] I/1 395.

reality authenticates itself,[18] and the resulting theological summary:

Jesus is Lord . . . because he has it from God whom he calls His Father to be the Lord, because with this Father of His, as the Son of this Father . . . He *is* the Lord—an 'is' which we deny if we are unable to affirm it with those who first uttered it, yet which cannot be deduced, or proved, or discussed, but can only be affirmed in an analytic proposition as the beginning of all thinking about it.[19]

As a starting-point for rational thought it is not open to question: '. . . who can reveal God except God Himself?'[20] Similarly, the doctrine of the divinity of Christ, which is a dogma interpreting the biblical texts, is an assumption from which theological thinking must start; it cannot be derived by means of reflection.[21]

What reflection can and must do is to ask how the analogy of sonship, the second analogy of relation, obtains its meaning, and what that meaning is. We move now from the topic of God's lordship over our existence to 'God's lordship in the fact that He turns to us, that indeed He comes to us, that He speaks with us, that He wills to be heard by us and to arouse our response'.[22] The idea of sonship, then, can be said to be developed by means of two leading themes that are here adumbrated: the divine initiative in moving toward man and his reconciliation, both of them being almost analytic developments of what Barth means by 'revelation', and showing—if further demonstration were needed—that by that word he means to express far more than a semi-passive divine theophany. Once again, if the event character of revelation is borne in mind, Barth will not be quite so subject to suspicions like those of John McIntyre about the imprecision of Barth's concept of revelation, or rather about the way in which the meaning of the word is allowed to widen.[23] The meaning does here widen but in a controlled way. It is possible to describe any event by means of a large number of statements and from many points of view. The event of revelation is no exception, and when the interest of the interpreter centres on revelation (rather than on

[18] I/1 399–406.   [19] I/1 406.   [20] Ibid.   [21] I/1 414–16.
[22] I/1 407.
[23] John McIntyre, *The Shape of Christology* (London, 1966), p. 165.

its character as including the other two aspects of revealer and revealing) it necessarily appears in the form of God's relating himself to man in reconciliation.[24] Because of this we have to speak of a second mode of the divine activity and being. 'For as we have to say that reconciliation or revelation is not creation or a continuation of creation but rather an inconceivably new work above and beyond creation, so we have also to say that the Son is not the Father but that here, in this work, the one God, though not without the Father, is the Son or Word of the Father.'[25] Moreover, the magnitude of this second work of God demands that 'its subject is identical with God in the full sense of the word'.[26] Thus it is that what happens in revelation licenses—or rather, rationally compels—us to say a second thing about the being of God. God is God in the mode of being of the Son as well as in that of the Father. But once this has been recognized, further questions arise for him who would expound the rationality of the situation. First, how can God be God in this second mode of being? Second, what implications does this have for the language we are to use to describe the reality of God?

'He is the Son or Word of God for us because He is so antecedently in Himself.'[27] When Barth gives his reasons for wishing to hold to the eternal divinity of Christ despite the tendency of much modern thought to dispense with it, the familiar themes of his theology are repeated. Above all, he appeals to the need for grace to be free. If Jesus is God *solely* in his being for us—as related to us—and not 'antecedently in Himself . . . then we turn . . . His being God for us into a necessary attribute of God. . . . Man is thus thought of as indispensable to God. But this destroys God's freedom in the act of revelation and reconciliation, i.e. it destroys the gracious character of this act. It is thus God's nature (*c'est son métier*, Voltaire) to have to forgive us.'[28] Barth is right to insist that a necessary relatedness of God to man cannot be construed as a gracious relationship. A necessitated personal relationship is scarcely, if at all, a personal one. And so while he would share the neoclassical repudiation of a God by definition unrelated to man, he would

---

[24] *CD* I/1 409: '. . . to the extent that in the fact of revelation God's enemies already are actually His friends, revelation is itself reconciliation.'
[25] I/1 410.   [26] Ibid.   [27] I/1 416.   [28] I/1 420 f.

not at all share Hartshorne's solution of the problem. That is not to say that Barth is attempting to mediate between the two extremes of an (alleged) unrelatedness of one God and the necessary relatedness of the other. It is an important part of the findings of this study that the two opposed doctrines represent in this respect not opposites at all, but a kind of *coincidentia oppositorum*, especially in that neoclassical metaphysics appears to be as necessitarian in its doctrines as the classical doctrines it wishes to replace. Barth's position is sharply differentiated by its stress on a personally conceived freedom. Relatedness to what is not himself is indeed part of what it means to be God, but this relatedness is chosen by an act of grace rather than being logically required as is the relatedness of the dipolar deity.

The argument is that because God is in fact related to the world, and to men in particular, through the reconciling activity of Jesus Christ, there is an eternal (and so in a sense necessary) relatedness within the divine reality. The phrase, 'Begotten, not made', is an expression of this eternal divine relatedness, for 'it denotes the real becoming of Jesus Christ, His eternal becoming appropriate to Him as God, His relation of origin and dependence as God in His distinctive mode of being.'[29] This real becoming signifies that there is a difference between the relationship of Father to Son in the eternal Trinity— that is, the God/God relationship—and the relationship between God and the world that is revealed in creation and reconciliation. The Father begets the Son essentially; it is that which makes him to be God. But it is not essential that he should create and reconcile the world, though both of these activities are expressions of what God really is. In fact Barth sometimes hovers on the brink of bringing necessity into God's relationship with the world, so insistent is he on the reality of that relationship. 'God is who He is, not *in abstracto* nor without relationship, but as God for the world.'[30] It is only the dominant theme of freedom that avoids the necessitation, and in fact Barth wants to say that even within the Trinity what is eternally true is so through the exercise of the divine freedom. But it is a different kind of freedom. 'In the superiority of bringing forth from God in God over bringing forth by God,

[29] I/1 430.   [30] IV/3 762.

in the superiority of the freedom in which God posits His own reality over the freedom in which He posits a reality distinct from Himself . . . lies the significance of the "begotten, not created" '.[31]

Thus for Barth, as for neoclassical theism, there is a real relatedness of God to the world. The differences between the two can be illustrated in two ways. The first derives from Barth's statement that, however we are to understand the innertrinitarian freedom, 'God cannot not be God. Therefore—and this is the same thing—He cannot not be Father and cannot be without the Son.'[32] The place of the Son is Barth's doctrine of God is taken by the world in neoclassical theism. Speaking of Ogden, though the remark is even more appropriate for Hartshorne, Jenson says:

It will be seen that this conception of God is very much that of Barth . . . with one great exception: it is not trinitarian. Or rather, it is covertly trinitarian, *with the world where the Son would be*. Everything that Ogden says of God's relatedness is exactly what we want to say of the Father and the Son in the Spirit.[33]

The second feature of the two theologies that brings out the differences between them lies in their doctrines of relations. Neoclassical thought is essentially monistic, in holding that there is only one kind of relation, and that everything that is related is related in essentially the same kind of way. For Barth, on the other hand, there are two kinds of relation. Necessary relatedness is the order within each reality considered in itself. Created beings are necessarily related to other created beings, just as the Father and the Son are necessarily related. But the necessity ends when we come to consider the (none the less real) relation between one order of reality and the other.

No created beings are in fact so independent of each other that . . . they have not also to some extent a certain mutual interdependence, in the sense that none of them would have its being and nature apart from its interlocking with the being and nature of all the others. But God confronts all that is in supreme and utter independence. . . .[34]

[31] I/1 433.
[33] R. W. Jenson, *God After God*, p. 149.
[32] I/1 434.
[34] *CD* II/1 311.

iv. *The Analogy of Sonship*

How is the relation of Father and Son in the triune reality of God to be understood? 'The distinction of way of being in which Jesus Christ is God consists . . . in the relation to another way of being, a relation which the ἐκ [sc. of the Niceno-Constantinopolitan Creed] shows to be a grounding in or proceeding from.'[35] But we must not allow this to convey the impression of 'two autonomous beings in a specific relation of dependence to one another. . .'.[36] That would be to take the analogy beyond the limits laid down by revelation. Rather,

Deus verus and *Deus verus* do not confront one another as autonomous beings but are twofold in one and the same autonomous being.[37] In all its secularity and inadequacy . . . the figure of the Father and the Son says that a similar—not the same but a very different, an inconceivably and inexpressibly different—nevertheless a similar distinction and continuity exists to that between the person of a father and the person of a son in the created world, that there is a similar being of the first for the second and a similar being of the second for the first, that there is a similar twoness and oneness of the same being, between the mode of being in which God is revealed to us in Jesus Christ and the mode of being from which He is as He who is revealed to us in Jesus Christ.[38]

However inadequate this language is to describe the mystery of God—and here Barth proceeds to labour the point by a series of paradoxes in order to express both the adequacy and the inadequacy of analogous language—we can nevertheless be certain that

in naming God thus we are expressing the truth, His truth. In this sense the 'begotten' says precisely what a confession of faith can and should say at the necessary distance from but also in the necessary relation to the object. It explains God's mode of being in Jesus Christ as a real 'Thence' and 'Thither', as the bringing forth from a source which is real in God Himself.[39]

The figure of sonship has the central position that it has in the Christian tradition because of its association with the idea of reconciliation. But there is another figure to be used alongside it to express the revelatory aspect of the divine activity in relation to man. 'We are saying the same thing when we say

[35] I/1 428.   [36] I/1 429.   [37] Ibid.   [38] I/1 431.   [39] I/1 433.

either "Son of God" or "Word of God". . . . One may perhaps say that the first term is more to the point when we understand God's action in Jesus Christ materially as reconciliation and the second is more to the point when we understand the action formally as revelation.'[40] Despite the place given to this figure alongside that of sonship, there can be little doubt that the latter is the prime analogy and crucial for an understanding of what Barth is doing in describing the reality of God. But the additional analogy does provide an illustration of Barth's way with language. Linguistic usage is determined not by what is logically required by the central concepts, as, for example, the divine categories follow logically from the leading category of relativity in Hartshorne. The notion of the divine Word can in no way be read off that of the Son of the Father. Rather, both are determined by the need to describe the revelatory events and their grounding in the prevenient divine reality.

We are now in a position to extend the comparison between the monistic analogy of relation in Hartshorne's system and the Barthian trinitarian analogies. The latter are not so much dualistic as *selective*. The way in which God chooses to relate himself to created reality determines the way in which he is best described. God's being is conceived neither as a transcendent version of the becoming in which everything consists nor as its negation (as in classical theism) but has its own distinctive becoming. This is not only appropriately described in terms of fatherhood and sonship, but also points to those places in the created world where the relationship between the two orders of being can be discerned. 'There is—amid the complete dissimilarity of divine and non-divine—a similarity between the eternal Word of God and the world created by this Word, but also and still more a similarity between the eternal, natural, only-begotten Son and those who are through Him God's adopted sons . . .'[41]

The differences between the two doctrines of relation bring consequences in the areas of ontology and theology. One of the chief implications of trinitarian doctrine for ontology has recently been mentioned.[42] God's free and gracious *choice* of relation with reality that is other than himself is what makes it possible for him to be both fully related and yet ontologically

[40] I/1 434.   [41] I/2 34.   [42] Above, § ii, pp. 153 f.

distinct. By contrast a doctrine of necessary relatedness produces a virtual pantheism, mitigated only by the crypto-concrete 'abstract' pole of the divine reality, upon whose puny shoulders falls, in consequence, the responsibilities traditionally appropriated to the Father (election and creation), Son (reconciliation), and Spirit (redemption, to use the Barthian terminology for God's eschatological activity). Theologically, the outcome is equally problematic.

It is not . . . enough simply to conceive God's being as a being in relation. A conscious or unconscious natural theology does not become evangelical by the mere fact that it makes relation the basic category of its statements. . . . Evangelical theology cannot conceive the purity of the relationship without an origin which *is* as the origin of the relationship in that it *puts itself in relation*.[43]

v. *God the Holy Spirit*

In general, Barth's discussions of the Spirit are not so convincing as his discussions of the Father and the Son. It is hard to see what is said that had not been said before. In contrast to Barth's usual fullness and determination to be understood at all costs, we find here brief concatenations of hints and dicta. One is even tempted to think that the incompletion of the *Church Dogmatics*, with the eschatology and doctrine of the Spirit missing, is not merely a matter of chronology.[44]

The judgement could be glossed by saying that whereas, in his trinitarian thought Barth has satisfactorily laid the ground for the appropriations of fatherhood and sonship, and is therefore in a position to develop doctrines of creation and reconciliation, the same cannot be said for the treatment of the third mode of the divine being. Any weakness in the discussion of the Holy Spirit will militate against a satisfactory expression of the eschatological dimension of Christian theology, with the result that the activity of God will tend to be located in the past rather than in the present and future.

What are the characteristics of the divine events that Barth holds to be appropriable to God the Holy Spirit? First, there is a stress on the Holy Spirit as the subjective side of the event of

---

43 E. Jüngel, *Gottes Sein*, pp. 115 f.
44 R. W. Jenson, *God After God*, op. cit., pp. 173 f.

revelation,[45] as God in his power to be present to the creature.[46] With this go the functions of instruction and guidance,[47] empowering,[48] and the giving of freedom to have faith.[49] Unoriginal as this may appear to be, the shortcomings of Jenson's judgement are revealed by the implications Barth's conception of the Holy Spirit has for a doctrine of the knowledge of God. But where the judgement does succeed is in pointing to the weakness of the second area of discussion, the eschatological function of the Spirit. Difficulties really begin to appear when Barth comes to speak of the futurity of God as the redeemer, and his utterances take on a measure of ambiguity.

In the New Testament sense everything that is to be said about the man who receives the Holy Spirit . . . is an eschatological statement. Eschatological does not mean in an inexact or unreal sense but in relation to the ἔσχατον, i.e. to that which from our standpoint and for our experience and thought has still to come, to the eternal reality of the divine fulfilment and consummation.[50]

The suggestion appears to be that we can speak eschatologically about the man who has the Spirit, but not about God the Spirit himself. 'Only of God Himself, which means at this point the Holy Spirit and His work as such, can one speak non-eschatologically, i.e. without this reference to something other, beyond, and future.'[51] The ambiguity appears as follows. First, Barth sometimes appears to hold that the eschatological future is future only in being so for 'our experience and thought', that it is a matter of ignorance rather than time. The corollary would be that *objectively*, so far as God is concerned, there is no divine futurity, and all has been already decided in a timeless past. There are places in Barth's theology elsewhere to support this suspicion, and some of them will be discussed in Chapter VIII below. Second, there appears at times to be another reason for Barth's wishing to speak 'non-eschatologically' about God, and this is that God's 'essence and work . . . is itself the ἔσχατον'.[52] Even here there is room for doubt as to whether Barth wishes to speak of a real futurity: is the whole essence and work of God—creation, for example—eschatological? But there is at least room for taking him to refer to

[45] *CD* I/1 449.   [46] I/1 450 f., cf. III/2 356.   [47] I/1 454.
[48] I/1 454 f.   [49] I/1 456 ff.   [50] I/1 464.   [51] Ibid.
[52] Ibid.

a real divine futurity, where thea ppropriate function of the Spirit is the anticipation in the present of that which belongs to the end of time, eschatological in the full meaning of the word.[53]

In view of this ambiguity it is not then surprising that although Barth has grounded his statement of the non-identity of the Son and the Spirit in a temporal distinction,[54] the temporality of the becoming fails to have any marked impact upon the doctrine of the being of God in the third mode. Further, the Spirit has a less determinative role than do the Father and the Son in the description of the essence of God. The point is again made by Jenson.

Without the Father there would no Son or Spirit—but it is not said that without the Spirit the Father and the Son would not occur. In every nuance of his formulations, Barth displays the doctrine that the Father is 'the fount of the Trinity.' But that the Trinity also has a goal in the Spirit remains a mere occasional assertion. This gathering to the past, to the Beginning in which all has already been decided, pervades all Barth's thinking.[55]

This orientation to the past was already becoming apparent in Barth's doctrine of the *repetitio aeternitatis in aeternitate*. During his discussion he said of the threefold repetition that: 'He possesses Himself as Father, i.e., pure Giver, as Son, i.e., Receiver and Giver, and as Spirit, i.e. pure Receiver.'[56] Is so passive a role to be attributed to the Spirit, the agent of God's future rule now being realized? The passage continues with words that would appear to confirm the point about the gathering to the past, and the occasional nature of the utterances on the Spirit. 'He is the beginning without which there is no middle and no end, the middle which can only be on the basis of the beginning and without which there would be no end, and the end *which is based wholly and utterly on the beginning*.'[57] There is no suggestion that the middle is in some sense an

---

[53] See especially 2 Cor. i: 21, Rom. viii: 23, and Eph. i: 13 f. In 'Karl Barth and the Development of Christian Doctrine', *Scottish Journal of Theology* 25 (1972) 171–80, I have developed this criticism of Barth in the light of these and certain Johannine statements.

[54] *CD* I/1 451: '. . . we find the Holy Spirit only after the death and resurrection of Jesus Christ or in the form of knowledge of the crucified and risen Lord . . .'

[55] R. W. Jenson, *God After God*, p. 173.   [56] *CD* I/1 364.

[57] Ibid. My italics. Translation altered.

anticipation of the promised end, or that the end is of particular significance in itself. Before, then, the comparison with Hartshorne is continued with an examination of Barth's doctrine of God in *Church Dogmatics* II/1, this aspect of Barth's theology must receive further attention. If the charge is upheld, certain aspects of Barth's concept of God will have been shown to be as necessitarian in their outcome as the classical and neo-classical concepts in their different ways.

VIII

ANALOGY AND FUTURITY IN KARL BARTH'S THEOLOGY

i. *Recapitulation*

G OD's being is *event*, and therefore a becoming. He is what he does. The relational structure of the divine reality, understood as it is on the basis of the divine becoming, 'means . . . that these very relations are not neutral elements of structure in God, but that God's being as being is pure *event*'.[1] One way of conceiving this is with the aid of the metaphor of movement. The incarnation is the movement of God into relation with the world he has created. Because this movement *is* God, there is no unmoved God behind or underlying it; rather it entails that God's being consists in a movement 'outwards' to what is not God. But because this movement is triune, and so not necessitated, it is a movement with a double aspect. God *is* movement towards the other, and this movement is expressed conceptually by the eternal relation of the Son to the Father in the Spirit. In its turn, this inner movement provides the ontological grounding for the outward movement we see to have happened in the life of Jesus.

The outworking of this theory could be illustrated by many aspects of Barth's doctrine of God, and will be illustrated at length in the next chapter. But one particularly illuminating instance of its application is in Barth's doctrine of election, 'the heart of Barth's theology . . .'.[2] What is election for Barth? It is God choosing men for himself by happening among them in Jesus Christ. But this choosing is grounded in an inner-trinitarian decision God made in and toward himself, a decision in which he *is* himself: '. . . in Himself, in the primal and basic decision in which He wills to be and actually is God . . . God is none other than the One who in His Son or Word elects

---

[1] E. Jüngel, *Gottes Sein*, p. 39.

[2] H. Hartwell, *The Theology of Karl Barth: An Introduction* (London, 1964), p. 105.

Himself, and in and with Himself elects His people.'[3] The double movement, within the Trinity and *ad extra*, which is yet one single movement, is well expressed by Jüngel also, when he describes it as God's 'primal decision . . . in which *God* irrevocably determined his being in act. This self-determining of God is an act of his self-relatedness (*Selbstverhält-nisses*) as Father, Son and Holy Spirit. But it is *at the same time* a relating of God to men. . . .'[4] The same writer speaks of the historicality (*Geschichtlichkeit*) of the being of God.[5] Thus the event character of the divine being, God's being in becoming, is expressed in a number of terms all straining to capture the sense of what is being described: decision, act, history, and the relational language expounded in Chapter VII. All of them centre on the events in which God became man in Jesus of Nazareth.

ii. *The Analogy of Becoming*

The most obvious response to so radical a reversal of categories is to express the suspicion that Barth has succumbed to an actualism that is both inconceivable in itself and in any case contrary to the biblical evidence. This response has been made for various reasons and has often taken the form of a claim that the Barthian analogy of becoming requires support from an analogy of being if it is to be in any way credible. The confrontation of analogies will be examined in greater detail below, but first we must clear some of the objections raised to this actualism in itself, apart from any consideration of the analogy of being. Is it either conceivable or correct that God should be described as event?

H. G. Pöhlmann perceives and describes clearly what is happening in this aspect of Barth's theology. He describes the analogy as an analogy of action (*Tätigkeitsanalogie*), and sees the struggle between it and the analogy of being, so clearly documented by the Roman Catholic commentators on Barth, as being between *actualism* and *substantialism*. He describes the actualism as the *Grundprinzip*, the *cantus firmus*—a felicitous and appropriate metaphor—of Barth's theology, as well as the

---

[3] *CD* II/2 76.   [4] E. Jüngel, op. cit., pp. 83 f.
[5] Op. cit., p. 82.

essence and presupposition of his analogy.[6] But he has a number of criticisms to make. First, he claims in contradistinction to Barth that there is a static thread running beneath the dynamism of the biblical concept of God. God becomes static on the cross.[7] Second, there is a theological objection. Barth's actualism endangers the independence of God and the world, and entails an arbitrariness in God's activity.[8] Three points can be made about this kind of objection to Barth's actualism. The first concerns the static thread alleged to be discernible in the biblical understanding of God. Here judgement is very difficult as it involves an appeal to what is the general tendency of Scripture. Much will hang on whether it is right to see creation, incarnation, and cross as things that happen. Certainly, the created order does not have to be understood statically, as Hartshorne has argued. It can also be conceived as that which *happens* in response to the will and word of God.[9] Moreover, there is no question that such a conception endangers the ontological distinction between God and the world, if that is what Pöhlmann means by their independence (*Selbständigkeit*). If it does, Barth's theology of creation has been written in the very teeth of what Pöhlmann sees from the start to be the *cantus firmus* of his theology as a whole.

The second point, in answer to the charge that arbitrariness results from Barth's actualism, is that the being of God, which consists in *triune* and *eternal* becoming, is such that consistency of historical behaviour—expressed in the various appropriations—is conceptualized by it. The God who happens in the incarnation is the same God who upholds all in being and will bring history to its close. Pöhlmann appears to have misunderstood, or failed to notice, the function of the doctrine of the Trinity both in linking the various *loci* of Christian doctrine and in providing a temporality of the divine reality that is positively related to God's eternity.[10] In so doing, he makes precisely the same error as those who accuse Barth of failing to do his ontological homework.[11] Moreover, he appears to wish to

---

[6] H. G. Pöhlmann, *Analogia Entis oder Fidei? Die Frage der Analogie bei Karl Barth* (Göttingen, 1965), pp. 21, 105 f., and 116–19.

[7] Op. cit., pp. 120–6. [8] Op. cit., pp. 122 f.

[9] See e.g. R. Hooykaas, *Religion and the Rise of Modern Science* (Edinburgh, 1972), pp. 12 f. and 24.

[10] See below, § v, pp. 178–81. [11] See below, § iv, pp. 174 f.

return to a conception of a being of God that lies behind and apart from his revelation, and thus to overturn what is most original and interesting in Barth's theology. The real outcome of Pöhlmann's criticism is shown in his suggested solution to the excesses of actualism. A return to an Aristotelian conceptuality would provide a doctrine of being to support the becoming of God, and provide a middle way between Parmenidean substantialism and Heracleitean actualism.[12] The real difficulty with this, apart from the fact that Barth's theology can in no way be described as Heracleitean, is that we do not have merely a static *thread* in that case, but the 'substantial' analogy describes what God *really is* in himself, and the events in which he becomes man cannot be described as God because they are the actions of something timeless and unmoving behind them. Such is not a middle way at all.

The third point concerns the general logical point that may be near the surface, if not on it, that nothing can become without first being. If Pöhlmann is using this argument, he would appear to be the prisoner of the past and of language: of the past, because God has in general been understood by analogy with substance, although it does not follow from that that it has to be so; and of language, because

there is the nonsensical doctrine that any substance would be, or at least contain as its ontic core, a qualityless substratum—qualityless because *it* is what HAS the qualities. Again, people have held that in any change there is 'presupposed' some unchanging element, unchanging precisely because *it* is what *is the subject of* the change. . . . People are pretty clearly being held captive by a gross picture . . . philosophers ask whether an individual is a bundle of qualities or whether there is a 'bare particular' (significant phrase!) 'under' the qualities.[13]

In sum, Pöhlmann has failed to see that in the doctrine of God in Karl Barth there is a consistent divine history, past, present, and future, and that it is in the trinitarian unity of this history that the being of God consists. The transition from this to the next section is made with the aid of a remark of

---

[12] Pöhlmann, op. cit., pp. 124 and 141 f.
[13] P. T. Geach, 'Spinoza and the Divine Attributes', *Reason and Reality* (Royal Institute of Philosophy Lectures V, London, 1972), p. 20. See also the remark of R. W. Jenson quoted at the end of Ch. VI, § iii.

R. W. Jenson. '"Appropriations", therefore, are all those descriptions of God's triune life made possible by the past history of that life. There is nothing "analogous" about them.'[14] As has been argued, there *is* something analogous in our language about God, in the sense that in the sections on fatherhood etc. it was shown that certain descriptive terms are predicated analogously of God. What we have not seen in our study of Barth so far is an Analogy, that is, a system of analogous predication based on a relation held to subsist timelessly between God and the world. From the neoclassical God, precisely because there is such an Analogy, nothing new or surprising can be expected to emerge. It is *logically necessary* that he should continue to be related to the world according to the limits set by the categories, which are therefore his masters, and that the future will continue to be like the past. If Jenson is right, the advantage of the trinitarian conception of God is that necessitation of this metaphysical kind is avoided, without danger to the consistency of the acts in the triune history. God can do new things, as happened in the incarnation, without being any less the God who brought Israel out of Egypt. 'God is free over against the realized actualities of his trinitarian life with us, because he is always ahead of them; he always can be otherwise triune than he has so far been. This freedom *is* his trinitarian life.'[15] But that is to anticipate. First, there is more to be said about Barth and his conception of analogy.

iii. *The 'Analogy of Faith'*

The controversy over Barth's use of the so-called analogy of faith, aspects of which have already been observed in the previous section, has been as intense as it has partly because of Barth's strictures on the analogy of being,[16] and partly because it is on this aspect of Barth's thought that his critics have trained their most withering fire, often selecting the right target, but for the wrong reasons.[17] The controversy centres on

[14] R. W. Jenson, *God After God*, pp. 174 f.

[15] R. W. Jenson, op. cit., p. 174.

[16] See e.g. *CD* I/1 243 f., cf. I/2 43; II/1 81–4. The terms in which Barth describes the dispute are various and imprecise. See also III/1 194 f., III/2 220 f., and 320–4; III/3 102 f.

[17] The literature is vast, and only aspects of it relevant to this discussion can be treated and listed. The following works will be referred to in this chapter by the

two aspects of Barth's doctrine of God, the question of the possibility and/or validity of natural knowledge of God, and the nature of the ontology emerging from the doctrine. By 'ontology' is meant the understanding of the nature of reality, and specifically of the nature of God and his relation to the world, that results from the concept of God. As has already been suggested, and as will become more apparent as the discussion continues, the two are inextricably related. The failure of many of the critics to hit the target derives largely from a failure to appreciate this point.

The discussion of analogy in Barth is also vitiated by the attempt to apply to Barth's usage technical terms that are more appropriate to other ways of doing theology, and indeed by Barth's own use of technical terms. The latter point is well illustrated by Barth's discussion of the analogy of attribution and the analogy of proportionality as he finds it in the theology of Quendstedt.[18] According to McIntyre,[19] Barth here allows himself to be deceived by the terminology into making two errors: first, in appearing to accept that his use of analogy is correctly described as a use of the analogy of attribution, although this does less than justice to the range of his theology;[20]

name of the author alone, with a numeral in parentheses where there is more than one work. H. U. von Balthasar, *The Theology of Karl Barth* (E.T. New York 1971, by J. Drury, of the 1951 work); G. C. Berkouwer, *The Triumph of Grace in the Theology of Karl Barth* (E.T. by H. R. Boer, London, 1956); H. Bouillard, *Karl Barth*, 3 vols., op. cit.; H. Chavannes, *L'Analogie entre Dieu et le monde selon saint Thomas d'Aquin et selon Karl Barth* (Paris, 1969); G. Foley, 'The Catholic Critics of Karl Barth', *Scottish Journal of Theology* 14 (1961) 136–55; R. W. Jenson, (1) *Alpha and Omega: A Study in the Theology of Karl Barth* (New York, 1963); R. W. Jenson, (2) *The Knowledge of Things Hoped For: The Sense of Theological Discourse* (London, 1969); R. W. Jenson, (3) *God After God*, op. cit.; E. Jüngel, (1) 'Die Möglichkeit theologischer Anthropologie auf dem Grund der Analogie', *Evangelische Theologie* 22 (1962) 535–57; E. Jüngel, (2) *Gottes Sein ist im Werden*, op. cit.; W. Kreck, 'Analogia Fidei oder Analogia Entis?', *Antwort. Karl Barth zum 70 Geburtstag am 10 Mai 1956*, ed. E. Wolf (Zürich, 1956), pp. 272–86; J. McIntyre, 'Analogy', *Scottish Journal of Theology* 12 (1959) 1–20; B. Mondin, *The Principle of Analogy in Protestant and Catholic Theology* (2nd edn., The Hague, 1968); H. G. Pöhlmann, *Analogia Entis oder Analogia Fidei?*, op. cit.; R. Prenter, (1) 'Die Lehre vom Menschen bei Karl Barth', *Theologische Zeitschrift* 6 (1950) 211–22; R. Prenter, (2) 'Karl Barths Umbilding der traditionellen Zweinaturlehre in lutherischer Beleuchtung', *Studia Theologica* 11 (1957) 1–88; G. Söhngen, (1) 'Wesen und Akt in der scholastischen Lehre von der participatio und analogia entis', *Studium Generale* 8 (1955) 649–62; G. Söhngen, (2) 'Analogia entis in analogia fidei', *Antwort*, op. cit., pp. 266–71; E. Wildbolz, review of *Karl Barth*, op. cit., by H. U. von Balthasar, *Scottish Journal of Theology* 7 (1954) 108–11.

[18] *CD* II/1 237–43.   [19] McIntyre, pp. 15 f.   [20] Op. cit., p. 15.

and second in failing to see that he does in fact have an analogy of proportionality.[21] We should not therefore lay too much store on Barth's express statements. 'His speech bewrayeth him.'[22] Surely this is correct. The technical language of analogy (attribution, proportion, proportionality, etc.) was developed in exposition and development of the Thomist Analogy, which was essentially concerned to expound the relationship between God and the world in terms of a cause/effect conceptuality. The cause/effect relationship is in Thomas understood timelessly. Thus the Five Ways, from which the concept of God follows analytically,[23] are all designed to establish the causality of God as operating now, and so represent attempts to conceptualise God as the timeless in the midst of time (the unmoved in the midst of motion etc.). Since Barth's programme of theology begins with the assertion of the radical temporality of God in revelation, we should expect to have to use a different set of terms in expounding his conception of the relation of God and the world. However, this is not to deny that there is something like a sustained analogy of proportionality in the doctrine of God proper, as will be evident from the exposition of the following chapter. It is like the analogy of proportionality in that it is concerned to set out which descriptive terms can properly be used of God, and in what sense. It is a use of language like that of Thomas—though the language is very different—but is one based on a very different conception of God and his relation to the world.

This point has been seen by those commentators who have resisted attempts (like that of Pöhlmann discussed in the previous section) to argue that Barth *really needs* an analogy of being in order to found adequately his doctrine of the divine becoming in revelation, or that he presupposes an analogy of being. The definitive expression of the case against Barth is that of von Balthasar:[24] 'While there is agreement between us on the question of the absolute priority of the order of grace over that of nature . . . there can and must, within the all-embracing priority of revelation and faith, also be acknowledged a relative glance back from Adam to Christ and from natural reason to covenant belief.' Here the emphasis is on the

[21] Op. cit., p. 16.   [22] Ibid.   [23] Jenson, (2), pp. 67–72.
[24] Translated from the original edition (1951), p. 313, cf. E.T., p. 245.

side of the controversy concerned with natural theology. The contention is that Barth cannot express his theology of the grace of God without some pre-understanding of an analogy subsisting between God and the world. Grace *presupposes* nature. Now there is a sense in which this is unexceptionable: God's reconciling revelation of himself takes place within created reality. That is Barth's position, as the first part of his doctrine of creation makes abundantly plain.[25] But that is not to say that grace presupposes a fully worked out metaphysic of nature, or indeed one that can be arrived at independently of a knowledge of the triune God. But that is the conclusion that von Balthasar draws, or so it would appear when he equates 'nature' with the *analogia entis*. Quite categorically, he speaks of *the* and not *an* analogy of being.[26] But the point about the analogy of being is that it is expressed by means of an essentially Aristotelian conceptuality that it is the very strength of Barth's trinitarian doctrine to avoid. As McIntyre has pointed out, it is difficult to adopt the Thomistic distinctions without being compelled to accept Thomist metaphysical consequences. 'What we want is this logic without that metaphysic, and I have the feeling that we may be crying for the moon.'[27]

iv. *Ontology in Karl Barth*

What has often been missed in the controversy over analogy is that in his theology Barth is basing his ontology on his understanding of the Trinity, and that his language about God follows from his understanding of this *theological* rather than *metaphysical* analogy. His understanding of the relation between God and the world is based on his doctrine of the Trinity, and not brought to it in order to support it. This has not been understood by von Balthasar, and his failure to do justice to the Barthian understanding of analogy may not be wholly due to the latter's obscurity, but in large part to his looking in the wrong place. That so famed a critic of Barth should express the opinion that the doctrine of the Trinity does not play a central role in the shaping of his (Barth's) theology suggests that in

[25] See especially *CD* III/1 94–228.
[26] Von Balthasar p. 228, cf. original, p. 295. '. . . in der analogia entis'.
[27] McIntyre, p. 20. For other similar criticisms of von Balthasar, see Wildbolz, pp. 110 f., and Foley, p. 152.

some respects at least he has not been listening very hard.[28] The consequences of the oversight reach beyond the pages of von Balthasar alone, and have contributed to what has now become a received opinion about Barth. Thus in a recent study of Barth John Bowden alludes to what he calls the treacherous character of Barth's theological edifice, ascribing it to the fact that 'the way forward from the miracle of knowledge of God is the dubious "analogy of faith" . . . There are no obvious building controls for the structure . . .'[29] That so ludicrously inaccurate a view of what, whether its truth be accepted or not, is a masterpiece of careful thought and construction, should have gained almost the status of axiom almost confounds belief, but is in large part due to the radical rethinking of the relation between faith and reason that Barth has carried out in the company of Anselm.

It is to be acknowledged that Barth often encourages misunderstanding by appearing to take the short way with his critics, especially on the matter of the analogy of being. For instance, when he justifiably contrasts the conception of the creator God with the idea of a world-cause, he says of the latter: 'It is not God. It is a successful or unsuccessful product of the human mind.'[30] Reasons for the rejection of the idea are not spelled out in detail. Only when the place of the Trinity in Barth's scheme of theology is clearly marked out can the revisions in the area of ontology, and their necessary opposition to the 'classical doctrine of God' and its Analogy, be seen for what they are. As has already been suggested, it is E. Jüngel who has really got to the heart of the matter. The ground for his illuminating *Gottes Sein ist im Werden* was earlier laid in a previous work where he pointed out the radical difference between the analogy of being, which compares the being of one order of being with that of another—what we might call a structural analogy—and Barth's analogy, in which the 'Yes' which God speaks to himself—in the Trinity—is compared with the 'Yes' with which God calls into being created reality. This analogy makes it possible to conceptualize a positive and

---

[28] Von Balthasar, pp. 211 f.
[29] J. Bowden, *Karl Barth* (London, 1971), p. 110. The view is shared by J. Macquarrie, *Principles of Christian Theology* (London, 1966), p. 126, and Bouillard, vol. III, pp. 208 ff.
[30] *CD* III/1 11.

gracious relation between God and the world. By contrast, the analogy of being, based as it is upon Aristotelian categories, which are philosophical rather than *offenbarungsmässig* in form, is totally unable to express the 'Yes' of grace.[31] Other commentators have recognized some of the significance of the move without being able to share Jüngel's enthusiasm for it. Thus Pöhlmann recognizes the difference in contents between the two theologies, and that therefore Barth's polemic against the *analogia entis* remains, despite the guarded qualifications made in *CD* II/1 81f.[32] More important, he sees more clearly than do many others what he calls the moment of truth in Barth's attack on Thomist ontology, with its suggestion (as in the Fourth Way) of a neoplatonic pyramid of being in which theocentric thought is replaced by ontocentric.[33]

The over-all importance of the discussion, and the evidence for the contention that here we are faced with a choice between alternative theologies, lie in real differences of theology that appear to be inextricably linked with the different conceptions of analogy. If two concepts of God are seen to be fundamentally different in certain crucial respects, then McIntyre's claim that we cannot have a terminology without metaphysical consequences will be seen to have been correct. Moreover, it will be seen that it is not merely a question of the possibility or otherwise of natural theology, as the dispute between Barth and his critics has sometimes been construed, but of far more fundamental matters.[34] A crucial difference of theology, and one that has already been remarked, is seen in the doctrine of creation. Bouillard observes that Barth's understanding of creation is *aux antipodes* to the Thomist because it makes creation into a temporal action of God, and not merely a relation of dependence. He believes that the difference derives from

---

[31] Jüngel, (1), p. 546. Mondin, p. 168, recognizes what he calls the *toto coelo* differences between Barth and Thomist natural theology in epistemology and ontology, but still, in apparent contradiction, wishes to claim that there is between Barth and Aquinas a difference of emphasis rather than of substance, p. 171.

[32] Pöhlmann, p. 59.

[33] Op. cit., pp. 135–7.

[34] Barth has long—even since the 1920s—conceded the *possibility* of natural theology. See H. M. Rumscheidt, *Revelation and Theology: An Analysis of the Barth–Harnack Correspondence of 1923* (London, 1972), pp. 214 f. What Barth quite rightly questions is the place of any such metaphysical construction as determinative for theology.

a difference in conception of analogy.[35] He is right because in Barth the discussion of analogy is inseparable from the questions of grace and time. The possibility of theological language is grounded on the events in which God graciously became temporal for the reconciliation of the creature. There is therefore at stake in the dispute, as Kreck observes, a deep difference in the understanding of grace rather than a simple choice between being and event language.[36] Grace does not perfect nature, because nature is in need of more radical treatment than that. But that does not for Barth entail a radical discontinuity between creation and reconciliation. In fact the doctrine of the Trinity makes it possible for a different kind of continuity to be established between the two, a continuity of grace. Creation is not a semi-independent sphere but is itself of grace, for it, too, is the act of the triune God. Barth's understanding of the creation derives not from metaphysical analysis, as happens in both Thomas and Hartshorne, but from his understanding of the history of God with man, centred as it is on the incarnation. The incarnation says something not only about reconciliation but also about what the world must be that such an event should be at the heart of God's relations with the creature. It says it because it is the midpoint of a consistent divine history, with a beginning that can be recalled and an end that is expected. On the other hand, metaphysical construction must inevitably conceive in abstract concepts an Analogy, a timelessly subsisting relation between God and the world. This is as true of neoclassical theology as it is of classical. Whatever happens in history, the structure of reality remains essentially the same.

v. *God's Eminent Temporality*

But there are problems of a similar kind in Barth, too, and here we begin to move into an area where Barth's critics have been more successful in diagnosing the ills. What does Barth *mean* when he speaks of the temporality of God? It is an answer to this question that will provide a way into the problem.

Like Hartshorne, Barth is not satisfied with the traditional understanding of eternity as timelessness. The metaphysician's

[35] Bouillard, vol. II, pp. 182 f.   [36] Kreck, p. 281.

point is that 'In the sheerly eternal, what is eternally is, and there is no meaning to the question, "What might have been?" '[37] That, of course, is the *a priori* approach to the matter, and even as such has some impact. Barth, as we might expect, appeals to the presence of God in time. What does revelation tell us about the divine temporality? First it tells us that God has time for us.[38] The pattern of argument is familiar. God is what he is in his revelation. And so since revelation is temporal, the least that can be said is that time is important for God.

If by the statement, 'God reveals Himself' is meant the revelation attested in Holy Scripture, it is a statement about the occurrence of an event. That means it also includes an assertion about a time proper to revelation. If stated with reference to this, it is equivalent to the statement, 'God has time for us.'[39]

He does have time for us, the time of revelation, the time of Jesus Christ. . . . But it is really He Himself who has time for us. He Himself is time for us. For His revelation as Jesus Christ is really God Himself.[40]

The concern of God with time is another implication of the fact that God happens as Jesus Christ.

One implication of the temporality of the revelation event that is worth mentioning for the contrast it introduces between Barthian and neoclassical doctrines of time, is that it will transform our understanding of our own time. We will see that the one who becomes temporal is also the maker of time, which is therefore 'very good'.[41] But it is also *lost* time, with the result that any natural theology of time will suffer from the defects of all natural theology. In particular, it will become mythological, in the sense that eternity will be a projection either of our rejection of time, as is the tendency of classical metaphysics, or of our affirmation of it. But 'The myth of infinite or endless time is shattered by revelation.'[42] In revelation, God reveals his lordship over time and history. To make time absolute, so that even God is subject to it, as happens in neoclassical theism, is from this point of view a form of idolatry.

[37] *PSG* 22.   [38] *CD* I/2 45 ff.   [39] I/2 45.   [40] II/1 611 f.
[41] I/2 53, cf. III/1 125, 130.   [42] I/2 69, cf. II/1 608.

From the temporality of revelation Barth moves cautiously, if not always unambiguously, to an understanding of eternity as eminent temporality. That is to say, he moves towards a conception of eternity in which it is seen not in opposition to or negation of time but both as its affirmation and fulfilment and as its judge, the canon by which the authenticity of what happens in it is to be measured. He expressly contrasts the eternal God of Israel with the timeless God of the Greeks,[43] and, more important, speaks of God's eternity as including time and as being (ontologically) prior to it. Thus, in his discussion of the eternity of the Son, Barth claims that the credal *before all time* 'does not exclude but includes time . . .'[44] This inclusion of created time by divine time is not understood logically and cognitively as in Hartshorne, but in terms of God's capacity to become what he is not. In contrast to classical denials that God can be *potentially* anything, as that is said to imply perfection, Barth, whose conception of perfection is not quantitative, quite openly asserts that God's eternity 'includes . . . the potentiality of time'.[45] 'Because God created time . . . it is not intrinsically alien to Him; for even eternity is His time, in the light of which He created our time.'[46] Therefore eternity is in some sense *prior* to time, so that Barth can even say, pregnantly but obscurely, that the future exists before the present.[47] He would appear to mean that God's future is ontologically prior to our present. As has already been observed, the being of God according to Barth is prevenient.

God's eternity, then, is some kind of time, 'authentic temporality'.[48] How is this eminent temporality to be understood? 'Eternity is the simultaneity of beginning, middle and end, and to what extent it is pure duration. . . . Time is distinguished from eternity by the fact that in it beginning, middle and end are distinct and even opposed as past, present and future. . . . Eternity has and is the duration which is lacking in time.'[49] But what, conceivably, is simultaneity that is pure duration? Duration and simultaneity appear to be (at least) contraries. If a contradiction is being generated, the most

[43] I/2 66.   [44] I/1 426.   [45] II/1 617.   [46] III/1 14.
[47] I/1 464.   [48] III/2 437.
[49] II/1 608. For the notion of simultaneity (*Gleichzeitigkeit*) see also III/1 67 f., where God's eternity is said, significantly, to be the prototype (*Urbild*) of time, and III/2 526 and 558.

likely explanation is that Barth is halting between two opinions. There is evidence for this:

. . . the Bible is interested predominantly, if not exclusively, in this primary and positive quality of eternity, and scarcely or not at all in the secondary quality which is its character as non-temporality. . . . This positive quality of eternity is finely expressed in the definition of Boethius . . . *Aeternitas est interminabilis vitae simul et perfecta possessio.*[50]

An obvious difficulty is that it is not evident that Boethius' definition can be understood to refer to eminent temporality. H. P. Owen, following Aquinas, takes it to be the definitive formulation of classical theology's equation of eternity with timelessness.[51] But whatever the thrust of the definition, Barth's statement as a whole is unclear, if not patently ambiguous. It is difficult to see how eminent temporality can possess 'a secondary quality . . . non-temporality'. If it is primarily a kind of time, how can it be secondarily or in any other way not-time? The truth appears to be that at times Barth defines eternity in the light of (temporal) revelation, while at others he opposes it to time.[52]

Whatever the outcome, Barth's intention is manifestly twofold, to retain the dynamic understanding of God derived from the event character of the 'repetition', and to conceive positively the relation of divine time to created time. 'A correct understanding of the positive side of the concept of eternity . . . is gained only when we are clear that we are speaking about the eternity of the triune God.'[53] Therefore 'God is before, above, and after all things'.[54] Only if God's eminent temporality embraces all of these can it be ensured that

the whole account of the Christian message—creation as the basis of man's existence, established by God, reconciliation as the renewal of his existence accomplished by God, redemption as the revelation of his existence to be consummated by God . . . can be understood as God's Word of truth and not as the myth of a pious or impious self-consciousness. . . . Without God's complete temporality the content of the Christian message has no shape.[55]

The conclusion must be that when Barth is speaking of the threefold divine happening in revelation and of the triune conception of God that follows from it, he makes room for a

[50] II/1 610.   [51] H. P. Owen, *Concepts of Deity* (London, 1971), p. 19.
[52] Cf. Bouillard, vol. II, p. 162.   [53] *CD* II/1 615.   [54] II/1 620.   [55] Ibid.

positive understanding of the relation between God and time. But ambiguity casts a shadow over the whole formulation; indeed, it has been suggested that the difficulties of Barth's theology taken as a whole derive 'from a persisting ambiguity in his talk about "eternity" '.[56] If the close connection claimed to hold in Barth between grace, analogy, and time was rightly discerned, it is scarcely surprising that an ambiguity in one of them should have such universal consequences. Whence, then, does this ambiguity arise? It may well be that despite his insistence upon the historical character of revelation Barth has failed to maintain the full temporal reality of the revelation event. Thus Bouillard expresses the suspicion that in Barth's later work revelation still remains too exterior to time and history, despite the development from earlier emphases,[57] while Jürgen Moltmann marks the spot more closely. Referring to Barth's criticism of his (Barth's) non-eschatological understanding of time in the *Commentary on Romans*, Moltmann wonders whether Barth has been as successful as he might have been in achieving a revision. 'Can the impression then be allowed to stand that "self-revelation of God" means the "pure presence of God", an "eternal presence of God in time", a "present without any future"?'[58] The root of the ambiguity would then seem to be a persistent tendency of Barth's to contaminate the temporality of revelation with a conception of revelation as a timeless theophany, which then reappears in the attempted combination of eminent temporality and timeless eternity. One is even tempted to wonder whether the very word *revelation* is not one of the chief culprits, in that it carries too heavy a load of inherited connotations to be able to bear the radical changes of meaning that Barth wishes to impose upon it. However that may be, we must now move on to a consideration of some of the effects of the ambiguity on Barth's concept of God.

vi. *The Opposition of Time and Eternity in Barth's Theology*

The contention of this chapter is that the most convincing criticisms of Barth's understanding of analogy are not those that wish to foist upon him assistance from a different

---

[56] Jenson, (3), p. 67.   [57] Bouillard, vol. I, p. 238.
[58] J. Moltmann, *Theology of Hope* (E.T. by J. W. Leitch, London, 1967), pp. 57 f.

metaphysical world, but those that hold that at least some of the things that he says reveal his kinship with that very world, and prevent his theology from effectively breaking out of it. If revelation is the breaking in of the timeless, time and eternity are in some sense opposed worlds (rather than simply different ones) and the relation between them must be conceived statically, because the timeless is the static. This section is therefore an attempt to summarize and express systematically the criticisms of Barth's theology that relate to this area of his thought. The points are best summarized under five heads.

1. The orientation of Barth's theology to the past has given many critics the impression that everything has already happened in eternity, and that there is to be no significant future divine history. This would be a direct consequence of the neglect of the third person of the Trinity alleged by R. W. Jenson.[59] If the goal of history in the Holy Spirit is totally subordinate to its origin in the Father, the tendency of a theology will be locate its centre of gravity in the (possibly timeless) past. The effect is felt in many areas of doctrine. Bouillard, for example, asserts that at times the incarnation seems to be snatched from history and located in pretemporality.[60] But the consequences of the orientation are most marked in the doctrine of election which expresses for Barth the heart of the Christian gospel.[61] If the nature of election has already been decided, then it is difficult to avoid teaching either an election in which some men are elect and the rest damned before they are born or some form of universalism. Although Barth wishes to avoid both, there are some who hold that the logic of his position forbids him. 'There is no alternative to concluding that Barth's refusal to accept the apokatastasis cannot be harmonized with the fundamental structure of his doctrine of election.'[62] Suspicions of a fundamental ambiguity in Barth's thought tend to be confirmed by the fact that Barth can also be successfully defended against the charge of teaching the *apokatastasis*.[63]

[59] See above, Ch. VII, § v, referring to Jenson, (3), pp. 173 f.
[60] Bouillard, vol. I, p. 154, cf. pp. 277 f., where Barth is accused of confusing two conceptions of temporality, periodic time, and temporality 'comme forme de l'existence humaine'.   [61] *CD* II/2 13 f.   [62] Berkouwer, p. 116.
[63] See J. D. Bettis, 'Is Karl Barth a Universalist?', *Scottish Journal of Theology* 15 (1967) 423–36.

2. A platonic element has also been observed in Barth's doctrine of God; that is to say, it is sometimes suggested that his concept of God shares some of the abstract timelessness of the Forms. Pöhlmann alleges that although in the period of the *Church Dogmatics* Barth consciously expelled the platonic elements from his theology, there are nevertheless unconscious and subconscious remains. There is at least a relationship of structure between the two, with what Pöhlmann calls the *Christus–Logos* performing in Barth's analogy a comparable function to the *Ideenlogos* in Plato. There are also, he believes, other similarities.[64] Once again it is to the doctrine of election that the critics go for illustration of this theme. Prenter asserts that according to Barth the divine adoption of man, God's humiliation and the consequent elevation of man is seen as an eternal idea, and as such read out of the immanent Trinity.[65] He concludes that there is a noticeably platonic tendency in Barth's thought, and ascribes this in part to Barth's interest in medieval Augustinianism, particularly Anselm, although he does not wish to stress this side of Barth at the expense of the historical actualism. This he believes to be in dialectical relationship with the platonism.[66] In view of the presence of the other straws in the wind, this suggestion must be taken seriously as an aid to the interpretation of parts at least of the *Church Dogmatics*.

3. The upshot of all this is that despite Barth's attempt to see God's eternity as a kind of eminent temporality, the tendency to define eternity in opposition to time, and therefore as a *negation* of the historical orientation of the understanding of revelation, is very marked. Consequently, the history of God with man is telescoped, for the future is not understood eschatologically, as the era when there will take place new triune events, but seen to be merely the vehicle of the repetition of the timeless past. It is possible to construe in this way Barth's discussion of the time of creation and the time of grace, or of Jesus Christ,[67] although it is probably better to say with Pöhlmann that Barth's distinctions between the different types of

---

[64] Pöhlmann, pp. 111 f.
[65] Prenter, (2), pp. 40 f.
[66] Op. cit., pp. 75–8. See also Bouillard, vol. II, p. 162.
[67] *CD* III/1 71 ff.

time are not very clear.[68] The positive thing that Barth has
to say in this passage—Pöhlmann calls it an 'astonishing reversal'[69]—is that we should interpret 'our' time in the light of
the time of grace. It is only when Barth speaks of this time of
grace as a *prototype* (*Urbild*) of 'our' time that suspicions are
aroused.[70] 'It is a perfect temporal present, and for that reason
a perfect temporal past and future.'[71] Does this mean anything?
But what can possibly be the content of saying that God in eternity
is whatever is the prototype of his life in time? Either this sentence
is perfectly empty; or the very form of the statement makes some
sort of comparison between God's own characteristics and his
temporal characteristics. Such a comparison can only be between
timelessness and time.[72]

4. Another variation on the theme is to say that although
Barth has laid the foundations for a breakthrough to a new
way of understanding the eternity of God, and with it God's
relationship with man,[73] he fails to carry his programme
through, and ends up with a doctrine of analogy that collapses
into timelessness. Different commentators have observed the
situation from their different standpoints. Pöhlmann, for
instance, observes that there is in practice a tension between
Barth's kinetic ontology and his concept of analogy, to which
there belongs, from the very fact that it is a concept of analogy,
'*ein immobiles Moment*',[74] and even claims to discern a tendency
in the *Church Dogmatics* to evolution towards what he calls a
true *Analogiemitte*.[75] Bouillard similarly asks whether Barth has
avoided analogy in the way he wanted to, since with him it
remains a generic concept.[76] The situation appears to be that
Barth has *begun* by understanding the relation of the God and
the world not in terms of a static Analogy, but in terms of
correspondences of acts.

Thus Barth understands the creation as God's 'Yes' to the creature,
a 'Yes' with which God interprets the 'Yes' he speaks to himself
in his choice to be what he is. And our self-understanding as
creatures is the 'echo'—here truly a new notion of analogy—we
bring to this promise of God. These are promising beginnings.

---

[68] Pöhlmann, p. 48.   [69] Ibid.   [70] *CD* III/1 73.   [71] III/1 74.
[72] Jenson, (3), p. 153. The reference is to *CD* I/2, but the point is the same.
[73] Jüngel, (1), *passim*; Jenson, (3), pp. 154 f.   [74] Pöhlmann, p. 65.
[75] Op. cit., p. 66.   [76] Bouillard, vol. II, p. 203.

Carrying them through would, however, lead to overcoming the whole notion of resemblance, of imitation and reflection. It would finally destroy the whole scheme of 'analogy' as the scheme in which to cast our understanding of God's eternity. Barth does not achieve this.[77]

5. Why has he failed to achieve it? The chief reason has already been mentioned, and that is the tendency to orientation to the past, and to neglect of the third appropriation of the triune God. Along with this may be adduced Barth's apparent lack of interest in the historical figure of Jesus, who often seems to become an ideal rather than a concrete figure. Therefore, instead of carrying through the radical criticism of classical theology, Barth has merely restructured it, 'putting the historical event of Jesus's existence in the place formerly occupied by changeless "Being" '.[78] It must be stressed again that these criticisms are not of the whole of Barth's theology, but are made possible by the ambiguity in his understanding of time. '. . . the *Church Dogmatics* can be read as the most perfect eternalizing yet achieved of the gospel's themes and story. It is clear that this is the opposite of what Barth intends, and that when we read his theology so we are reading it wrongly—but there is something that compels us to read it wrongly in this way.'[79] Chapter IX will give, with its contrast of Barth to both classical and neoclassical categories, the evidence that Barth's chief tendency is quite other than the one observed in this.

[77] Jenson, (3), p. 155.   [78] Jenson, (1), p. 140.   [79] Jenson, (3), p. 152.

THE DIVINE PERFECTIONS. BARTH, HARTSHORNE, AND THE CLASSICAL CONCEPTION OF GOD

i. *Introduction*

IN most of the foregoing exposition of Barth's doctrine of God we have been concerned with the means by which God authenticates his reality—and thereby gives himself, so to speak, for rational description—and with what God really is in himself. Far from being at the expense of description of God's relations with the world, as some modern writers appear to think must be the inevitable fate of any theology that betrays an interest in God's 'inner' reality, Barth's conception of God is based upon God's becoming man, and so into relation with what is not himself. But it is true that he has not yet ventured upon an account of God's relations with what is 'outside' of himself: that is yet to come, in the doctrines of creation (*Church Dogmatics*, Volume III) and reconciliation (Volume IV). What has been done in the passages covered in Chapters V to VII of this study is the laying of the foundations for descriptive theology: to say what Barth *means* when he uses the word *God*. The account of the Trinity in fact takes the place long taken by natural theology (hence the attraction for some theologians of neoclassical theology, in an age that for the most part rejects classical natural theology.) Its function is at least in part *hermeneutical*.

Between this and the doctrines of creation and reconciliation comes Volume II, which is the doctrine of God proper. In this volume Barth sets out to describe what he calls the *Wirklichkeit* of God, the things we have to say that God *really is* if we are to be true to what happens in revelation. *Wirklichkeit* could be translated either *actuality* or *reality*. A choice between the two is difficult, as both have connotations that express part of Barth's meaning. T. F. Torrance puts it thus:

The word Barth uses throughout this discussion is *Wirklichkeit* which he prefers to render *Aktualität* rather than *Realität* because of the relation between *Aktualität* and *Akt*, actuality and act, which it involves. In English, however, *reality* is sometimes a better rendering of Barth's thought, if we remember that it is a living, active Reality with which we are concerned.[1]

It is to be observed that there are four major sections in Barth's account of the reality of God. We cannot say what God really is according to him unless we are prepared to say what we mean by the knowledge that we really are given of God, and to show clearly the actuality of God in election and command. The triune God happens as both election and command, and if we neglect these two doctrines, then we neglect to say as much as we might about what God is. In this chapter, however, we shall concentrate on those sections from the first part of Volume II which suggest and sometimes even demand comparison with Hartshorne's conception of God. Through the discussion of certain of the divine attributes we shall further elaborate the strange relationship between two theologians who are so different, showing that there really are some things in common despite the utterly incompatible worlds in which they move. Also apparent will be Barth's attack on classical categories; the attack will be shared with Hartshorne, though not the theological grounds for the attack.

The description is dominated by the ideas of love and freedom, two realities that far from being incompatible when predicated of God are held to be inextricably linked. All the descriptive terms that we use of God follow from the fact that God is free in loving, and in being free he loves. That we can say this at all both follows from, and is a development of, the statement that God is Father, Son, and Holy Spirit. God's revelation as Father, Son, and Holy Spirit is the event in which he creates fellowship with man, and it is in doing that that he reveals that he is love. But this is a love that is given freely,

[1] T. F. Torrance, *Karl Barth: An Introduction to his Early Theology, 1910–1931* (London, 1962), p. 151.

for the mode of revelation makes it clear that, first, he is Father as well as Son, and, second, that he is Father, Son, and Spirit independently of his relation to man. Thus all that we shall say about God will continue to be rooted in the hermeneutic of the previous volume, just as the language we use of Hartshorne's God is rooted in the Analogy on which the metaphysic is based.

The discussion of God's 'perfections' (*Vollkommenheiten*)—a term Barth prefers to the traditional 'attributes'—involves a sixfold double dialectic, which is carefully structured to bring out both aspects of the divine event-reality. The first three subheadings, taken as a whole, are perfections of God's love; the second three, those of his freedom. But each of the perfections of love is only to be understood in the light of its freedom counterpart, and vice versa in the case of the perfections of freedom. Twelve attributes or perfections are therefore discussed in a chapter that has been described as being 'of classical significance in modern theological thinking'.[2]

The perfections are all understood in a radically personal way—not *anthropomorphic*, because their meaning is controlled by the triune divine event—and represent a development of the relational concept of God entailed by Barth's understanding of the Trinity. Indeed, it is perhaps worth mentioning that the relational as distinct from the substantial conception of the person may well owe its origin to the Christian doctrine of the Trinity, and came into modern secular thought (e.g. Heidegger) from Christian sources.[3] Moreover, the suggestiveness of Barth's doctrine of God for our conception of what it is to be a human person—made in the image of God—has very likely been obscured by Barth's own anthropology. His rather strained use of the male–female relationship at the heart of his conception of human nature appears to have called attention away from the fact that his position is as radically destructive as any empiricist, existentialist, or neoclassical attack on conceptions of the person as a timeless substance problematically linked to a changing body.

[2] William Nicholls, *Systematic and Philosophical Theology*, *The Pelican Guide to Modern Theology*, vol. I (London, 1969), p. 149.

[3] The suggestion is made by T. F. Torrance, *Theological Science* (London, 1969), pp. 305 f.

ii. *The Being of God in Act*

The way in which we describe God is therefore important. For Barth all centres on the fundamental theological assertion: 'God is.'[4] He sets out to expand this one fundamental statement in the sixth chapter of his *Church Dogmatics*. One qualification—or, better, clarification—that must be made at the outset is that Barth is not recanting of his previous devotion to a dynamic ontology. He is not returning to the heresy much belaboured by Hartshorne, of favouring 'being' at the expense of 'becoming'.[5] Theology does not begin with two concepts, *being* and *becoming*, that have an immutable meaning; rather the terms are seen to mean what they do for the science of theology—if it finds them appropriate words to use—only as it develops its understanding of its subject matter: '. . . we are not concerned with a concept of being that is common, neutral and free to choose, but with one which is from the first filled out in a quite definite way.'[6] Moreover, Barth is quite definite that he has not abandoned his dynamic understanding of the being of God. 'We are dealing with the being of God: but with regard to the being of God, the word "event" or "act" is *final*. . . . To its very deepest depths God's Godhead consists in the fact that it is an event—not any event, not events in general, but the event of His action, in which we have a share in God's revelation.'[7] Any *being* language is controlled by the being of the God who *is* in his particular, individual, becoming for us.

After this rehearsal of the equation of act and being in God that derives from the doctrine of the Trinity, Barth proceeds to discuss it in relation to two themes that are relevant to the comparison with Hartshorne. First, there is the relation to classical conceptuality, and particularly to the doctrine of the *actus purus* or pure actuality of God. In Hartshorne that expression is understood metaphysically and experientially—quantitatively, I have suggested—in distinction from the activist connotations that any Barthian use would entail: actuality refers to possession of reality, rather than as act. Hartshorne accepts the Aristotelian connotations of the expression, but reverses it on logical and ontological grounds to obtain the doctrine of modal coincidence, that God is both

---

[4] *CD* II/1 257.   [5] e.g. *CSPM* 44.   [6] *CD* II/1 260 f.   [7] II/1 263.

actual and potential. Barth, on the other hand, attacks the abstract generality of any such language. 'God is . . . the One who is event, act and life in His own way. . . . God is not merely differentiated from all other actuality as actuality generally and as such, or as its essence and principle . . .'[8] There is no interest in actuality or potentiality as such, as there is in Hartshorne; once again, attention is concentrated on the particular actuality of this particular triune subject. Moreover, if the classical conceptuality entails a dualism of opposites or contraries, as Hartshorne's criticism of it suggests, Barth is in this respect as anti-dualistic as neoclassical thought. The difference is that he conceives the dualism of God and the world differently. While Hartshorne's panpsychism *reduces* the traditional dualities of matter and mind or spirit to a monism of mind, albeit of mind understood concretely and temporally, Barth rejects outright that way of viewing reality. God is for him the creator of both mind and matter—or nature and spirit, as he tends to put it—and is distinct from them both, although at the same time in relation to them both. In his dualism the reality of revelation reveals a more dynamic relationship than any metaphysically conceived dualism, since God is able to identify himself with the reality that he has made.[9] God and the world are ontologically distinct, but this does not entail that they are opposites or contraries. Quite the reverse, and it is this that sets Barth apart both from neoclassical monism and the apparent logical implications of classical dualism.

Second, there arises for further comparison the nature of analogous predication of language in Barth and Hartshorne. Just as for Barth God was earlier shown to be eminently temporal, so here he is eminently personal act. In opposition to the false spiritualizing or false realism of dualist and monist metaphysics, we 'have to understand God's being as "being in person"'. What is meant is certainly not personified being'— or, it might be added, the personified becoming of neoclassical metaphysics—'but the being that in the reality of its person realises and unites in itself the fulness of all being'.[10] The point for comparison is that in both Barth and Hartshorne there is a doctrine of categorical supremacy, even though the categories are different (and in Barth can in any case only be called cate-

[8] II/1 264.   [9] II/1 265.   [10] II/1 268.

gories for the sake of comparison). For Barth God is not merely personal but the supreme instance of personality. 'The real person is not man but God. It is not God who is a person by extension, but we. . . . God lives from and by Himself.'[11] 'The doubtful thing is not whether God is person, but whether we are.'[12] Similarly, 'God alone . . . is properly and adequately to be called Father.'[13] For Hartshorne, only God can truly instantiate the categories, as has already been observed.[14] 'Like everyone, God is both subject and object, but he alone . . . is universal subject, inheriting everything as object; and he alone is universal object, object for every subject.'[15] For both schools the eminent subjectivity of God takes prior place, and for both there is either explicit or implicit a rejection of doctrines of the absolute that make God into an object before he is conceived to be a subject.

. . . it is not the case that this application of the personal manner of speech to God means the recognition of a paradox in the nature of God that we cannot unravel, because on the one hand we must necessarily understand God as the impersonal absolute, but at the same time (and in unavoidable logical contradiction to this) we must also understand him as person.[16]

Barth's expression is almost Hartshornian.

But where he does differ is in the fact that he is more resolutely 'anthropomorphic' than his counterpart in the way in which he describes the divine activity. No language is of itself more suitable than any other to express the nature of God. 'For spiritual—i.e. abstract—concepts are just as anthropomorphic as those which indicate concrete perception.'[17] Therefore metaphysical categories have no *a priori* advantage over the so-called similes and mythical language of the Bible. Indeed, they are suspect precisely because of their generality.

The danger is pressing . . . that we may overemphasise the impropriety of what are in the narrowest sense to be called 'anthropomorphisms,' ascribing in contrast a kind of moderate impropriety to abstract concepts like the being, wisdom, goodness and righteousness of God, and a genuine propriety only to negative concepts

[11] II/1 272, cf 284.   [12] I/1 138.   [13] I/1 393.
[14] See above, p. 78, for Hartshorne's explicit reference to Barth.
[15] *CSPM* 120.   [16] *CD* II/1 286 f.   [17] II/1 222.

like incomprehensibility, immutability, infinity, etc., and therefore thinking that we can speak only uncertainly of the acts of God in His revelation . . .[18]

As always in Barth, language must follow, *a posteriori*, what actually happens. Since what happens is personal event, personal categories are required if we are to describe it correctly.

iii. *The Being of God in Act: Love*

'God is He who in His Son Jesus Christ loves all His children, in His children all men, and in men His whole creation. God's being is His loving.'[19] And the being of God that consists in this loving is one with the essential other-relatedness of the triune God. 'He wills as God to be for us and with us who are not God.'[20] This willing takes the form of a deliberate seeking of fellowship with man, a seeking whose paradigm is the event of election. In election, God ties himself not only to man but to the universe,[21] and ties himself in such a way that not only must he be said to have surrendered his own impassibility[22] but that also we can only speak of this becoming in such terms as these: 'In this primal decision God did not remain satisfied with His own being in Himself. He reached out to something beyond, willing something more than His own being.'[23] In sum, 'That He is God—the Godhead of God—consists in the fact that He loves, and it is the expression of His loving that he seeks and creates fellowship with us.'[24]

In the following pages of Volume II/1 of the *Church Dogmatics* this fundamental identification of being with act, and of act with love, is qualified, and with the help of these qualifications the relationship with neoclassical conceptuality can again be examined. First, Barth rejects the search for a *summum bonum* that is separate from God's love.[25] There is no form of the good that God has to instantiate, but rather 'God is the One who loves, and as such the *Good* and the sum of all good things'.[26] This is the reverse of the neoclassical procedure, which shows

---

[18] Ibid., cf. II/1 221–3, 264 f., 266, 268 f.; IV/1 561.   [19] II/1 351.
[20] II/1 274, cf. 272 ff.   [21] II/2 155 ff.
[22] II/2 163, *something* in common with Hartshorne, though the latter hardly has room for the strongly voluntaristic element.
[23] II/2 168.   [24] II/1 275.   [25] II/1 277.   [26] II/1 276.

its oneness with the traditions of Greek metaphysics in making the forms ontologically prior to and coeternal with God. In Hartshorne relatedness is the universal category or form; since this is equated with value, and since it has to be instantiated by any entity, and eminently by God, there is prior to God a *summum bonum*, an independently established metaphysical category. The supreme good on this understanding is something beyond God: if there is to be a God in the system, he must fit the system, and may therefore only be his love so far as the system permits.

Second, the freedom with which this love is given precludes any suggestion that because God is essentially love, he must always have the creatures around him. The real but free relatedness of Barth's God has already been mentioned, but is of interest here for the polemic against Angelus Silesius's 'Nought is but I and thou, and if we two are not,/Then God is no more God, and Heaven itself is nought.'[27] These words are in close accord with the string of paradoxes quoted with approval by Hartshorne from Whitehead's *Process and Reality*,[28] for example, 'It is as true to say that God creates the world, as that the world creates God.' This mutual need of God and the world in neoclassical theism is in strong contrast with Barth's far more voluntaristic 'He does not need us and yet He finds no enjoyment in His self-enjoyment.'[29] In an interesting aside Barth comments elsewhere that it is the Sabbath rest described at the end of the Genesis account of creation 'which distinguishes God from a world-principle self-developing and self-evolving in infinite sequence'.[30] The rejection of the idea of a God necessarily evolving with the process follows from the fact that if love is to be described as love, it must be given freely. This is not possible in the case of a God who is bound to be related to all that happens.

Having made these qualifications and clarifications, Barth is now able to state a further analytic development of the statement that God is. ' "God is" means "God loves".'[31] 'The statements "God is" and "God loves" are synonymous.'[32] The Johannine assertion that God is love is 'a genuine equation'.[33]

[27] II/1 282.   [28] e.g. *PSG* 280 f.   [29] *CD* II/1 283.   [30] III/1 215.
[31] II/1 283.   [32] IV/2 755.   [33] IV/2 756.

iv. *The Being of God in Act: Freedom*

The freedom of God has already been mentioned in connection both with the *Unenthüllbarkeit* of God and, perhaps more important, with the freedom of the essential Trinity;[34] and, once again, all that is said in this section is a development of and dependent upon the trinitarian freedom there described. Interest now centres on the distinctive way in which God is who he is. If in the previous section we were chiefly concerned with God's *act*, now we concentrate attention on *God*'s act. That is to say, if there the most important feature was the nature of what was described as personal event, now it is the unique character of the actor. But it is only a shift of interest, because of the identification of act and actor.

In discussing the divine freedom Barth comes into greater contact with the traditional and 'metaphysical' categories with which men have attempted to describe God. This would appear to be due to the fact that freedom is often, in some of its aspects, conceived negatively, in terms of absence from limitation etc. and this coincides with the motives of the negative theology, whose method is to negate the alleged limitations of finite reality, and apply the resulting concept to God. Barth's reaction to much of this negative theology is as critical as that of Hartshorne, but his grounds for rejection are his usual ones, that is to say, largely *a posteriori*.

The critique of the past begins with a discussion of the notion of aseity. The positive side of the doctrine of the divine aseity, and that which is worth preserving, is, Barth feels, that expressed by the compounds with the word αὐτός beloved of the Greek fathers: the sense that God contains all his reality in himself, in such a way that he is free to impart himself to what is not himself.[35] Neoclassical thought, with its doctrine that God obtains his concrete actuality from everything *but* himself—a reversal of the old doctrine—would suspect that Barth is succumbing to the attractions of the classical doctrine of the absolute. But this is not so. He rejects a negatively conceived independence. In the shift to the Latin *independentia* began the tendency to error, the tendency for 'the positive aspect of God's freedom to exist in Himself, to be less clearly grasped

---

[34] See above, Ch. VI, §§ iv and v.   [35] *CD* II/1 302.

and considered less important than the negative aspect of God's freedom from all external conditions'.[36] There must be a negative aspect, but 'it was a retrogression when the idea of God's *aseitas* was interpreted, or rather supplanted, by that of *independentia* or *infinitas*, and later by that of the unconditioned or absolute'.[37]

The discussion of aseity leads into the related topic of transcendence. Barth is popularly thought to be very much a teacher of the utter transcendence of God, and in this respect he would seem to be in total opposition to the immanentism of neoclassical theism. In a sense, that is true. But there are ways in which the neoclassical God is transcendent, in that his relativity is a transcendent relativity—or his immanence a transcendent immanence—and certainly ways in which Barth's God is—or better, becomes—immanent. For Hartshorne, God is radically transcendent *in that* he is radically immanent. It could be said of Barth's God, with little exaggeration, that he is radically transcendent *in order to be* radically immanent.[38] Thus, transcendence 'can have "immanence" as its primary connotation . . .'[39]

We may believe that God can and must only be absolute in contrast to all that is relative, exalted in contrast to all that is lowly, active in contrast to all suffering, inviolable in contrast to all temptation, transcendent in contrast to all immanence, and therefore divine in contrast to everything human, in short that He can and must be only the 'Wholly Other.' But such beliefs are shown to be quite untenable, corrupt and pagan, by the fact that God does in fact be and do this [sc. become a creature, man, flesh] in Jesus Christ.[40]

The debate about transcendence and immanence is often as confused as it is because of a failure to understand the variety of meanings of the term *transcendent* and its cognates. At least two are present in this discussion. God can, on the one hand, be considered to be in some sense spatially transcendent— 'the unsubstantial, unprofitable and fundamentally very tedious magnitude known as transcendence . . .'[41]—whether

[36] Ibid.   [37] II/1 303.
[38] Once again, there is a strong voluntarist emphasis.   [39] II/1 303.
[40] IV/1 186. Barth has come a long way from the *Commentary on Romans*.
[41] III/4 479.

this be considered a metaphorical or literal spatiality,[42] and it is here that it is *opposed* to immanence. On the other hand, for God to be God, in even the most attenuated sense of the word, as a superior being of some kind, he must be *ontologically* transcendent of other reality. For Hartshorne, God is ontologically transcendent in both his supreme relativity and his existence or abstract pole. For Barth God's *trinitarian* transcendence provides the ontological basis for the acts in which he becomes (spatially!) immanent. If God were not so supremely transcendent of reality that is other than he, he would not be the God who does the things he does.[43]

From transcendence, Barth moves to a discussion of God's necessity. As in Hartshorne, the idea of necessity is closely connected with God's relatedness to what is not God; but in typically Barthian fashion, our knowledge of God's necessity is seen to derive from what God does in revelation. 'He who begins in this way with Himself in His revelation is . . . the One who properly and necessarily exists.'[44] The differences in the use of the Anselmian proof are thus reflected in the differences of the concept of necessity. For Hartshorne, with his rationalist view of language, logical and ontological necessity are identical. For Barth, noetic necessity, as he calls it, has to *receive* its necessity as a gift from the ontological necessity of God. But for both of them necessity is reconciled with freedom by being centred on one pole of the divine reality, one could almost say on the fact that God exists, in order that in the other pole (his 'accidents') he may be free. God just is, and needs no basis on which to exist: he is *a se*.[45] But that is where the similarities end. According to Barth, God is not necessitated from outside, whether by the necessities of language or of anything else, but 'not needing His own being, simply has being as a matter of empirical fact, thus affirming Himself in fact, although He does not need to, as the One who is'.[46] In their basic meaning the German *notwendig*, Latin *necesse* and its cognates, and Greek ἀνάγκη all imply an external, imposed necessity. 'The case is a good illustration of the fact that our words require a complete

---

[42] See the famous discussion of 'God out There' in J. A. T. Robinson, *Honest to God* (London, 1963), pp. 11 ff.
[43] *CD* II/1 344.   [44] II/1 305.   [45] II/1 306
[46] II/1 307.

change of meaning . . . if in their application to God they are not to lead us astray.'[47]

In this connection Barth is even prepared to speak of God's 'absoluteness' and the connoted 'independence'. This is not in contradiction of his earlier strictures on the notion, but in carefully qualified assertion of the divine freedom over against non-divine reality.[48] It is precisely *because* the absoluteness of God derives from himself, from the one personal centre, and not 'from the mode of His relationship to the world', that 'He can enter into a real relationship with the latter.'[49] Once again it is little, if any, exaggeration to say that God is absolute in order that he might be related.[50] The criticism of the traditional doctrine of the absolute is not that it uses the word, but that it uses it in the wrong sense, and it does so because it does not derive its meaning from God but from an attempt to absolutize human nature.[51] The old concept was defined not positively from the revelation of God but negatively in opposition to non-divine reality, and by that very fact was rendered problematical in relation to it. It is only describable as absolute in virtue of its opposition to what is not itself.[52] As a result, the definition of the absolute will 'hover between two extremes',[53] the one representing the concept that is so vigorously attacked by Hartshorne, the other very nearly that which the latter offers as an alternative. 'On the one hand, it [sc. the absolute defined in opposition to finite reality] may be consistently affirmed, with the result that the existence of the other is rendered problematical and finally destroyed . . .'[54] It is worth mentioning again here that Hartshorne welcomes Spinoza's system, which is what Barth seems to have in mind, because it is there that the denial of contingency implicit in the classical concept of God becomes explicit.[55] 'On the other hand, this other may be inconsistently endowed with a degree of independent reality, so that the so-called absolute is subjected to a certain conditioning by this other and its supposed Godhead to a thoroughgoing determination by the subordinate world.'[56] From Barth's point of view, therefore, the weakness of neoclassical theism is not that it rejects the classical concept, but that it tries to rearrange the same pieces, instead of playing a

[47] Ibid. [48] II/1 308. [49] II/1 309. [50] Ibid. [51] II/1 308 f.
[52] II/1 309. [53] Ibid. [54] Ibid. [55] PSG 189–97. [56] CD, ibid.

different game altogether. It is not a matter of fitting God into
our conception of finite reality, but of beginning with God's
unique subjectivity. The freedom of this subjectivity entails
that there can be no ready-made logical system in which
language can be predicated univocally of God and other
beings.[57] Moreover

... all conceptions of God must be excluded *a limine* and definitively
which take the form of what is called pantheism or panentheism.
God does not form a whole with any other being either in identity
with it or as compounding or merging with it to constitute a
synthesis—the object of that master-concept, so often sought and
found, which comprehends both God and what is not God.[58]

The essential weakness of these systems of cosmological immanence, as distinct from an immanence of particular event, is
that they restrict the freedom of God to be immanent where he
will.[59] But that is in no way to suggest that particularity of
immanence implies arbitrariness. 'For the Son of God who
became flesh in Jesus Christ is, as an eternal mode of the divine
being, nothing more nor less than the principle and basis of
all divine immanence . . .'[60] It is precisely because we learn
there of the faithfulness of God that this faithfulness 'cannot . . .
be reduced to the level of the regularity of a cosmic process'.[61]

In summary we can say that it is the trinitarian grounding of
the divine freedom that enables Barth to conceive as a unity the
acts of love and freedom in which God relates himself to what is
not himself, and yet in doing so remains free. The essential
unity of the two is seen to derive from the fact that God *is*
his act, his becoming. The point is that there are two complementary sides to the divine act. If one side is asserted, the divine
act is not accurately described unless there is at least some
presupposition of the other. Or, as love is described here, it is
not love unless it is seen to be freely given. It is at this point
that the two sides of our comparison are most widely separated,
and in the last two sections far more disagreement than
agreement has emerged. They agree that there is something
radically wrong with the classical tradition. But in their starting-
points for reconstruction they could not be much further apart.

---

[57] II/1 310. Barth quotes the classical tag: 'Deus non est in genere'.
[58] II/1 312, cf. 562.   [59] II/1 313–16.   [60] II/1 317.   [61] II/1 318.

In §§ v–viii below will be expounded some of the analogical language that Barth feels able to develop on the basis of his starting-point. In these analogies he will be seen to have more in common with neoclassical theism than merely an opposition to classical doctrine. Particularly in the discussion of the second group of perfections the two will be shown to go so far together before parting into different worlds, like two ships that almost collide in the darkness and then as if in reaction sheer off in opposite directions.

v. *The Perfections of the Divine Loving: Grace*

In this and the following sections Barth will be treated as being of interest in his own right, though most attention will be given to those predicates that illustrate the likenesses and differences of the two theologies. Some of the perfections that appear in Barth's treatment will receive only brief mention, some none at all. All of them are developments of the theme of God's being in act.

The first set of perfections, those of the divine loving, are introduced by the summary: 'The divinity of the love of God consists and confirms itself in the fact that in Himself and in all His works God is gracious, merciful and patient, and at the same time holy, righteous and wise.'[62] These perfections are then discussed in complementary pairs, the first pair to be treated being the grace and holiness of God. This pair illustrates important facets of Barth's theology and method, without being particularly illuminating for the comparison with Hartshorne.

Grace is not a semi-substantial entity as it sometimes appears to be conceived in theology, but a further specification of the act that God is. God is grace, and there can therefore be said to be in the essence of God a turning to man in condescension. 'Grace denotes, comprehensively, the manner in which God, in His essential being, turns towards us.'[63] Grace is not a 'thing' or substance apart from himself that he gives, but an aspect of the becoming in which God is himself.[64] Here, on the face of

---

[62] II/1 351.   [63] II/1 354.
[64] II/1 356. There cannot be, therefore, 'a higher gift than grace', despite the canonization of that mysterious entity in John Henry Newman's famous hymn.

it, is a problem, for the operation of the divine grace *pre-supposes* the overcoming of opposition.[65] Yet if God really is what he is in his revelation, are we not bound to say that this opposition of the opposition of sin indicates that there is opposition within the Godhead, an opposition that involves a kind of eternal overcoming and struggle—and so an essential disunity—within God? Barth's answer to this is obscure, but does help to throw light on the way in which he conceives the relation between the two 'poles' of the divine reality. 'The form in which grace exists in God Himself and is actual as God is in point of fact hidden from us and incomprehensible to us.'[66] This might be an appeal to mystery that is hardly appropriate in the light of Barth's realism of revelation. But it is not, and the discussion by Jüngel of a related problem in Barth shows clearly why it is not, or at least why it need not be.[67] On the cross God in Jesus Christ suffers the very opposition that God in his grace is concerned to overcome. According to Jüngel, this brings Barth very near to presenting a 'contradiction and conflict' taking place in God himself.[68] But he will not draw the blasphemous conclusion. Jüngel's comment on this is interesting. 'The rejection of this consequence leads in Barth not indeed to a blunting of the doctrine of God's suffering, but on the contrary to a criticism of the traditional metaphysical concept of God, according to which God cannot suffer without running into contradiction with his being.'[69]

Just as the *suffering* of opposition must indicate a real suffering of God without an implied internal contradiction, so it must be with its overcoming. Our understanding of the being of God derives from what happened according to the New Testament in the life of Jesus Christ. This life at least in part must be understood as the overcoming by God of the opposition it met with from evil and sin. Therefore that is part of what we mean by the being of God in act as grace. The triune God is his grace, and in the face of the unaccountable and irrational rejection of God by the creature, that grace must necessarily take the form of opposition and overcoming.

We next come to God's holiness, which is itself an aspect of

---

[65] II/1 355.   [66] II/1 357.
[67] E. Jüngel, *Gottes Sein*, pp. 97–103, 'Gottes Passion'.
[68] E. Jüngel, op. cit., p. 97.   [69] Op. cit., p. 98.

God's grace, and helps to define the latter as the grace of the subject of them both. It involves no 'crucial change of theme', only of emphasis.[70] Stronger light now falls on the freedom, on God's remaining true to himself when he turns to the creature in grace.[71] Moreover, 'The holiness of God consists in the unity of His judgment with His grace.'[72] This is an important theme of Barth's theology and in distinction from the emphasis of his earlier dialectical phase. There is no law/gospel dialectic in Barth, in the sense that the 'No' of judgement is somehow the dialectical opposite or negation of the 'Yes' of grace. Grace and judgement belong together as part of the one gospel, as aspects of the gracious 'Yes' of God to his people that must, if it is to remain grace, sometimes take the form of a denial of some aspects of the life of that people. 'The fact that God does not permit Israel, the righteous, or the Church to perish means that He cannot allow them to go their own way, unaccused, uncondemned, and unpunished, when they are and behave as if they were people who do not participate in this salvation and protection.'[73] His is not an indulgent grace, as must necessarily be that of the passive neoclassical deity.

vi. *The Perfections of the Divine Loving: Mercy and Patience*

While in general it is possible to speak of love without being bound to speak also of mercy, this is not possible when we speak of the love of the triune God: '. . . divine love bears necessarily the character of mercy. The word "necessarily" can and must be understood literally in this connection.'[74] Moreover, this mercy does not belong to the realm of poetry or 'mere simile': it is real, personal mercy, and although in general this vigorous personalism sets Barth at variance with the metaphysical tradition, there is in his language more than an echo of the way in which neoclassical theology speaks. 'The mercy of God lies in His readiness to share in sympathy the distress of another. . . .'[75] God 'participates' in man's distress in a 'concrete' relationship.[76] Indeed, he says, it is precisely in this activity that we can understand the notion of personality when applied to God, and set it against ideas of the impersonal

---

[70] *CD* II/1 359. [71] II/1 360. [72] II/1 363. [73] II/1 366, cf. 363–7.
[74] II/1 369. [75] Ibid. [76] Ibid.

absolute.[77] In particular, it undermines the doctrine of impassibility that is one of the connotations of the notion of the absolute. Barth's language here illustrates both his nearness to and his distance from Hartshorne.

. . . the personal God has a heart. He can feel, and be affected. He is not impassible. He cannot be moved from outside by an extraneous power. But this does not mean that He is not capable of moving Himself. No, God is moved and stirred, yet not like ourselves in powerlessness, but in His own free power, in His innermost being. . . . The 'affection' of God is different from all creaturely affection in that it originates in Himself.[78]

Paradoxical though it may appear to metaphysicians in both classical and neoclassical traditions, God's sympathy is conceived by Barth as essentially active in nature.[79] It is something he does as well as suffers, the act of a totally free agent. For while Barth rejects the doctrine of impassibility, he would not speak, as Hartshorne does, of passivity. Thus he speaks of 'the Lord of history . . . whose *passio* in history is as such *actio*'.[80] The cross is God acting. And so God's suffering is an active suffering, for just as God's grace is holy grace, so this mercy is a righteous mercy. When he is merciful, God maintains his own worth. His mercy is not necessitated.[81]

Thus the second pair repeats the pattern of the first, and a detailed examination of the third—the patience and wisdom of God—would reveal the same basic structure. So far as content is concerned, it has been suggested that there is something in common between the two concepts of God. The differences which keep them firmly apart derive from a twofold but related difference of doctrine and emphasis. First, there is a difference between the conceptions of freedom and necessity. There is in Barth an inner—though chosen—necessity that God be what he is, but this necessity does not extend to God's relations with the world. The neoclassical God is logically bound

[77] II/1 370.
[78] Ibid., cf. IV/2 225 and 357—in the latter passage Barth speaks of the *particula veri* in the teaching of the early Patripassians—IV/3 397, 412, and 420. See also E. Jüngel, op. cit., pp. 97–103, especially p. 100.
[79] *CD* II/1 371–5.
[80] I/1 144, cf. IV/1 245 and 256 for similar language about the action of the Son on the cross.
[81] II/1 376–81.

to be what he is in his relations with the world; there is no room for an active freedom of God. Second, this difference derives from what the two men conceive to be the basis of what they both describe in similar terms: God's 'unsurpassable, unchallengeable perfection'.[82] *Barth's root analogy is of act, in distinction from Hartshorne's root analogy of knowing or experience, conceived passively.* It is for this reason that however near the two may sometimes appear to move, they are bound to end up far apart.

vii. *The Perfections of the Divine Freedom: Unity and Omnipresence*

Those perfections that Barth expounds under the heading of the divine freedom are treated by him at greater length than the perfections of the divine love. They bring him into much closer contact with the classical tradition, and he has therefore to qualify carefully his attribution of these qualities to God, and to make it clear that there are differences between his usage and that of much of the tradition. This is well illustrated in the discussion of the divine unity. As has already been shown, unity for Barth is a triune unity.[83] Here, too, he sets his face against metaphysical or numerical unity; like all the perfections, unity has to be understood personally. This has not always been done in the past, for despite the trinitarian grounding of the concept in the Fathers, 'the development of the conception in the later theology of the Church appears to be of a purely logical and metaphysical kind'.[84] If unity is construed as simplicity, and that is understood in the classical sense of absence of composition, then 'the simple is an utterly unmoved being, remote from this world altogether . . .'[85] Barth wishes to hold a concept of the divine oneness that is distinct from both the classical and the neoclassical conceptions. He shares with the latter the belief that unity consists in variety, but not its continuing to hold a metaphysical, almost numerical, conception of variety. It is a particular, triune variety.

This simplicity has not to be explained as the simplicity of the absolute as compared with the relative, or of the general as compared with the particular. . . . It is the simplicity of the God who is eternally rich in His threefold being . . .[86] It has nothing to do with

---

[82] The words are Barth's, *CD* II/1 376. [83] Above, Ch. VI, § i.
[84] II/1 446, cf. I/2 389.   [85] II/1 449.   [86] III/3 138.

the number 'one', but with this subject in His sheer uniqueness and otherness over against all others, different from all the ridiculous deities whom man invents.[87]

The unity of this God is the unity and uniqueness of the personal act.

The complementary concept is omnipresence. Barth and Hartshorne both believe that God is present everywhere. For the latter, such presence is required by the fact that God is related to all that is real; for Barth, it is the outcome of the relatedness of the three modes of being of the one God. 'God is the One in such a way that He is present: present to Himself in the triunity of His one essence; present to everything else as the Lord of everything else.'[88] There are similarities between the two, in that both ground omnipresence in what can only be called the essential spatiality of God. For Hartshorne, it is a simple matter, for the radical immanence of God in the cosmic process entails that his space is essentially the same as ours, with the exception that it is coterminous with the whole of space, probably understood—in contrast to time—to be finite.[89] For Barth, God's space is a different kind of space. Why does he feel it necessary to speak of a divine spatiality? The justification is a combination of the realism of revelation—God really is *present* to man in revelation—and an examination of the consequences of the alternative, which is to conceive God's relation to space negatively. If God is absolutely non-spatial 'He cannot be conceived in His togetherness with Himself and everything else, but only in His identity with Himself and therefore with everything else as well. . . . Non-spatiality means existence without distance, which means identity.'[90]

How is God's eminent and analogous spatiality to be understood? 'The spatiality of God is to be distinguished from the spatiality of every other being by the fact that it is the spatiality of the divine being. . . . God is spatial as the One who loves in freedom, and therefore as Himself. . . . God possesses His space. He is in Himself as in a space. He creates space.'[91] Thus Barth understands the spatiality of God analogously to the way in

[87] Barth, *Dogmatics in Outline*, E.T. by G. T. Thomson (London, 1949), p. 40.
[88] *CD* II/1 468.
[89] 'I strongly incline to this kind of finitism.' *CSPM* 126.
[90] *CD* II/1 468, cf. 464–8.   [91] II/1 470.

which he understands the temporality, and this enables him to conceive the divine omnipresence as a free and chosen omnipresence. Operating, so to speak, from the base of his inward space, God is able to be actively present in ours, in the space that he has made. Now Barth's argument comes full circle, and ends with God in his revelation. For the final evidence for the freedom of the divine omnipresence is provided by God's special presence. His presence in Jesus Christ

is the one unique and simple presence . . . in which both His special presence in all its diversity and also His general presence with its dynamic identity possess their beginning and their end . . . It is as the One who is present here in this way that He is the God who is specially present in Israel and the Church, and as such generally present in the world as a whole and everywhere.[92]

It is in this conception of the special presence of God in historical events that we see the real difference between the two conceptions of the divine omnipresence. It is there that everything begins for Barth, who proceeds from there to the whole of space; for neoclassical theism, on the other hand, a special presence *may* be allowable once the general presence has been established.[93] Whether it is allowed by the logic of its concept of God is another matter.

viii. *The Perfections of the Divine Freedom: Constancy and Omnipotence*

A preference for *constancy* over *immutability* reflects a common feature of our two theologians: Barth dislikes some of the connotations of *immutability*, while the word *constancy* is appropriately predicated of the neoclassical God, with his necessary and consistent sensitivity to all that takes place in the world process. In fact it is on the basis of the characteristic constancy of experience that Hartshorne claims that his panentheistic conception is well fitted to reflect the biblical teaching that God is without 'shadow of turning', a tag he is fond of quoting.[94] 'Nor is any immutability attributed to deity in the Scriptures save what the context implies is purely ethical. A fixity of ethical principles is one thing, a fixity of a being's whole perceptive-conscious reality is another . . .'[95] This

---

[92] II/1 484, cf. 486 and IV/1 187f.
[94] e.g. *MVG* 159, cf. *LP* 279.
[93] See above, p. 51.
[95] *NTOT* 18 f.

constancy is a constancy of immutable change, as God grows daily in the richness of the cosmic experience. By contrast it would appear that Barth is more in the classical tradition, for his God has no room for 'any deviation, diminution or addition, nor any degeneration or rejuvenation, any alteration or non-identity or discontinuity. The one omnipresent God remains the One He is. This is His constancy.'[96] But this is not the classical conception; all but two of the predicates in this passage could be used of Hartshorne's God. And Barth is as critical as his counterpart of the classical view, drawing from it the same implications.

If it is true . . . that God is not moved either by anything else or by Himself, but that, confined as it were, by His simplicity, infinity and absolute perfection, He is the pure *immobile*, it is quite impossible that there should be any relationship between Himself and a reality distinct from Himself. . . . If . . . the pure *immobile* is God, death is God.[97]

Similarly Barth elsewhere speaks of the 'profoundly unchristian conception of a God whose Godhead is supposed not to be affected at all by its union with humanity.'[98]

However, this constancy is different from that of Hartshorne's God. God is immutable not in the necessity and universality of the relationship with reality other than himself, but in the constancy of his acts of love and freedom. 'He is what He is in eternal actuality. . . . His love cannot cease to be His love nor His freedom His freedom.'[99] There *is* something that can be called immutability, but it is an immutability of love.[1] It is an actively conceived immutability. 'God's constancy . . . is the constancy of His knowing, willing and acting and therefore of His person.'[2] But in other respects Barth is nearer to Hartshorne.

There is such a thing as a holy mutability of God. He is above all ages. But above them as their Lord . . . and therefore as the One who . . . partakes in their alteration, so that there is something corresponding to that alteration in His own essence. *His constancy consists in the fact that He is always the same in every change.*[3]

---

[96] *CD* II/1 491.   [97] II/1 494, cf. IV/1 561.   [98] IV/2 85.
[99] II/1 494.   [1] IV/2 352.   [2] II/1 495.
[3] II/1 496. My italics. Cf. III/3 285 and IV/2 85 f., where Barth prefers not to speak of mutability, but rather of the kind of immutability that does not prevent God from humbling himself. The point is the same.

However, the active construction of the attribute ensures that God's relation to the changes in which he participates is very different from that of the neoclassical God. God remains free both *from* and *in* the changes; the changes depend upon him, and not he upon the changes. Neither creation[4] nor justification[5] imposes changes upon God *from without*. As always, the comparison between the two theologians ends in contrast. The knowledge that God gives in the freedom of his revelation precludes for Barth the kind of monistic speculation that we find in Hartshorne, where 'the world constitutes an integral part of the essence of God'.[6] But it also precludes dualistic speculation, where '*in abstracto* immutability is ascribed to the Creator, and mutability to the creature'.[7] Both kinds of metaphysical speculation are contradicted by the reality of God in his revelation. For while monism leaves no room for freedom, dualism appears to make it impossible for God to love. While classical theology denies one side of the reality of God as both love and freedom in act, neoclassical theology attempts to restore the former, but does so at the expense of the latter, and therefore ultimately at the expense of both. If God cannot be both loving and free, then he is not the God who has revealed himself to us. The heart of the matter is once again christological. 'The truth is that it is by the incarnation that God has revealed His truly immutable being as free love. . . . God is "immutably" the One whose reality is seen in His condescension in Jesus Christ, in His self-offering and self-concealment, in His self-emptying and self-humiliation.'[8]

It is on this basis that Barth can move to a discussion of the divine omnipotence. An immutable being, in the sense of a being that is unmoved and immovable, would be not powerful but powerless. But the God we have been describing 'is not powerless but powerful, indeed all-powerful, with power over everything that He actually wills or could will. God is able, able to do everything: everything, that is, which as His possibility is real possibility'.[9] When Barth comes to elucidate the meaning of this first uncompromising assertion, it is clear that traditional, abstract conceptions of God as, for example, able to do anything but will a contradiction, are beside the

---

point. Unless we ask about the power of this particular subject, there is danger that we shall make power absolute. But, 'Power in itself is evil.'[10] The limit of what is possible for God is set not by self-contradiction but by contradiction of God. Barth is not suggesting that 'we are . . . summoned by God's Word to assert that through God's omnipotence two and two could also be five'.[11] Yet he does want to reject the Thomist definition of omnipotence as saying too little, not too much.

In the last resort we must reject the Thomist limitation of the omnipotence of God to the possible in itself and as such because if we introduce a possible in itself and as such which has in a sense the role of an independent and equal partner and corrective side by side with God, we bring into the realm of creation the very element of disquiet, uncertainty and insecurity which the thesis of Thomas was designed to exclude.[12]

God is the creator of logical possibility.

The heart of Barth's conception of omnipotence is that far from involving a limitation of his power, the personal, and therefore self-limiting character of God's omnipotence ensures that it is wider, not narrower, in scope than the classical definition allows. It is understood positively, in terms of what God is; and what God is, he can be. 'In a positive definition of the divine omnipotence the decisively important thing is that without detriment to His "nature" . . . God is also spirit. Unlike created nature He is not only the theme but also the subject of a knowing and willing.'[13] This association of omnipotence with knowledge and will brings us into the area of the comparison between the two concepts of God. First, there is their common opposition to classical formulations, and here Barth uses similar language to Hartshorne's. 'There is in God both supreme necessity and supreme contingency.'[14] In Hartshorne these apparent opposites are reconciled in the manner of all the polar concepts in this concept of God: God's supreme contingency is a necessary contingency, and the cosmic mind is omniscient in knowing the necessary as necessary, the contingent as contingent. In Barth the reconciliation is trinitarian and voluntaristic, by reference to the free act of God whose act carries necessity with it.[15] Second, there necessarily arises

---

[10] II/1 524, cf. III/4 391.   [11] II/1 537.   [12] II/1 537 f.
[13] II/1 543.   [14] II/1 548.   [15] Ibid.

the question of the relation between God's knowledge and his will. For Hartshorne, because God infallibly knows and therefore contains the past, he can in a sense be said to will, or at least to influence, the future. Both knowledge of and power over the future are limited by the freedom of the process to create itself. In Barth, too, knowing and willing are closely related. As both nature and spirit, God is 'omnipotent in His knowing and willing, and His omnipotence is the omnipotence of His knowing and willing'.[16] In contrast to the neoclassical concept, this is an active knowing, precisely because Barth refuses to be tied to a conception of knowledge derived from the created world. The outcome is that there are sharp differences in the doctrine of omniscience. While in Hartshorne omnipotence is subordinated to omniscence, in Barth the two are held together, as it were in harness. The two are both acts, and as such are what God is.[17] And so a (cautious) equation of the two can be made. 'But . . . the equation cannot mean that God's will is to be reduced to His knowledge if the thinker's taste is intellectualistic, or His knowledge to His will if it is voluntaristic. . . . On the contrary, we have to take quite seriously both that God knows and that God wills.'[18] God's knowledge does not therefore first require the existence of its objects. Being does not determine God's knowledge, as happens in neoclassical theism, but the reverse. 'It is the knowledge of God—and with it His will—which defines the limits of being.'[19] Hartshorne's conception, in which God's knowledge differs from ours only in scope, blurs the distinction between God and the creature. 'The creature who conditions God is no longer God's creature, and the God who is conditioned by the creature is no longer God.'[20] Moreover, on such a conception, prayer is made 'if not impossible, at least superfluous'.[21] In reply to the objection that this is to return to the classical conception of God in which, according to Hartshorne, all is determined by his essence, Barth simply asserts that 'there is no place . . . for the notion that the freedom of our wills is destroyed by this foreordination, or that our choice is not responsible choice, or that our evil choice is thereby excused'.[22]

[16] II/1 543.   [17] II/1 549 f.   [18] II/1 551.   [19] II/1 553.
[20] II/1 580.   [21] II/1 578.
[22] II/1 586, cf. I/2 364 f., 373 f., III/3 93 and 144.

The problem of the relation between God's foreknowledge and human freedom is too complex for full discussion here, but it should be said that Hartshorne, because of his use of the word knowledge in a univocal sense, fails to do justice to the complexity of the situation. If the relationship is between two personal but radically different beings it is a mistake to imagine that it can only be conceived in only mechanical terms as, perhaps, Spinoza did in his radicalizing of the classical concept of God.[23] Barth's 'event' conception of God, in which God is at once a concrete historical happening and a free act of triune sovereignty, sets anew the whole question of the relation between divine grace as determinative and human response as free. God is not now (if he ever was) conceived as the puppet-master operating from outside time, but as the one who exercises both power and knowledge by means of his close relationship with what he knows and creates. The solution is in a sense the classical one; but the relation is conceived personally and not mechanically, and can therefore be understood to have something in common with the relational conceptuality of neoclassical theism, without in any way allowing God's grace to disappear into cosmic indeterminism.

Another area of comparison between the two theologians comes to light when it is seen that for Barth the paradigm of divine omnipotence is God's action on Good Friday.

It is . . . the knowledge of Jesus Christ the Crucified which is the knowledge of the omnipotent knowing and willing of God. It is in Jesus Christ the Crucified that that is loosed which is to be loosed here, and that is bound which is to be bound here. Therefore it is the knowledge of Him and this alone which is the real and incontrovertible knowledge of the omnipotent God.[24]

This 'theodicy of the cross'—if such it be—has been criticized by G. C. Berkouwer. 'It is not possible . . . consistently to retain the cross as the epistemological principle for the understanding of God's "power". The Bible relates the power of God also to the divine act of raising Christ from the dead.'[25] Of course

---

[23] There, of course, the original conception is again different, owing more to the Aristotelian conception of causality.

[24] II/1 607.

[25] G. C. Berkouwer, *The Triumph of Grace in the Theology of Karl Barth*, E.T. by H. R. Boer (London, 1956), p. 312.

it does, but whether or not the consistency Berkouwer wants is possible—and as the history of theology shows, cross and resurrection have tended to vie with each other for supremacy of influence—he appears to have missed the fundamental simplicity of Barth's point. If you wish to see God's omnipotence at work, look at the cross. The triune God does not exercise supremacy in total unrelatedness to his creation, but by freely submitting himself to relationship with it, and in such a way that the creation can reject that relationship if it wishes. What the resurrection does show, perhaps, is that the days of such rejection are numbered. But whatever belongs to the future, that future is in part brought in by the suffering of God. That suffering is omnipotent because it makes things happen, in the way that Good Friday has changed the human situation for ever. Nothing can finally stand in the way of God's suffering love, which is at once passive and active because it is chosen freely. After all, it was Paul who described the crucified Christ as 'the power and the wisdom of God',[26] and so Barth is not without support.

Despite the active character of God's suffering omnipotence, there are parallels between it and the neoclassical conception of power as 'influence'. The parallels highlight perhaps more than anything else the likeness between the two, as well as the fundamental weakness of neoclassical theism. For Hartshorne God's power over others is conceived both in terms of his setting the limits of freedom[27] and as the *product* of his eminent receptivity. 'Power over others consists in this, that one's own reality is rich in value which fits the needs of others and is therefore attractive to them as datum for their awareness'.[28] Like Barth, Hartshorne is interested in the constitutional rather than the absolutistic connotations of the concept of the divine rule. 'Perhaps the most shockingly bad of all theological analogies, or at least the one open to the most dangerous abuses, is that of God as a monarch, a world boss. . . . God is the monarch or king of all only through being in a real sense the slave, nay, the scourged slave, of all . . .'[29] There can be little doubt as to the origins of at least some of Hartshorne's language in this

[26] i Cor. i: 22–5.   [27] *LP* 231.   [28] *LP* 275.
[29] *MVG* 203 f., cf. 294, *DR* 138, *AD* 136, and, for Barth, *CD* III/1 37 f. and III/3 241.

passage. And, speaking of God's sharing of the wealth and the burden of the world, he says: 'the cross is a sublime and match-less symbol of this, partly nullified by theological efforts to restrict suffering and sympathy to God as incarnate.'[30] There is then in neoclassical thought something corresponding to Barth's omnipotence of the cross. Indeed, neoclassical theology might well be understood as a systematized *theologia crucis* or radicalized patripassionism.[31] But if so, it is no more than that, and if a heresy consists in the elevating a part of the Christian view of things to the position of the whole, then it is a true heresy that we find here. Moreover, a God who is so passive that he cannot but be so is no God at all. On this understanding, God's suffering is only *abstractly* active. The suffering of the cross can merely be a symbol of the divine suffering, it cannot *be* it as Barth would have it. On Hartshorne's account the suffering is not chosen, and therefore cannot be gracious. It is the contradiction of an omnipotence of impotence. This God promises no resurrection, for he cannot: merely eternal remembrance in a cosmic graveyard. Death is not conquered, but has the last word.

[30] *MVG* 198, cf. *CSPM* 263.

[31] 'The "patripassionist" consequence in Mr. Hartshorne's theology—that of polarity—reveals as its mythical archetype a mixture of dionysiac elements with the Christian symbol of the cross.' J. Taubes, 'Review Article: Philosophers Speak of God', *Journal of Religion* 34 (1954) 122.

CONCLUSION

X

RECEPTIVITY IS NOT ENOUGH

i. *Neoclassical Theism and the Christian Faith*

IN the works of the two theologians described in the nine previous chapters there are presented two coherent and distinctive concepts of God. They share a common aversion from the classical concept of God, but there are differing grounds for their aversion. These grounds are also the starting-points for their positive proposals, the one purely rationalist, the other perhaps best described as Christian rational autonomy. Despite the deep differences of method and doctrine, a certain amount appears to be held in common, in particular a preference for conceiving God in *becoming* language, in contrast to the deeply engrained tendency of Western thought to speak of God only or chiefly in terms of *being*.

The heart of the differences between the two is best brought out by a survey of the relation in the two between proof and concept of God. Every theologian or philosopher who wishes to speak of God can be expected to provide his reasons for doing so, in some form of proof, in the widest sense of that term. European theological thought has been dominated since the Middle Ages by the cosmological proof of the existence of God, and the concept of God derived from that method of arriving at his existence. That concept centres on the notion of cause, and it is noteworthy that even those philosophers who have used the overtly ontological form of the proof, for example Spinoza, have continued to be dominated by this particular conception of the relation of God to the world. The important point for our purposes is that the concept of God is logically dependent on the kind of way in which his existence is established; that is, on the form of the proof. There is, then, a *logical* relationship between form and content. Thus proof and concept, at least in a rationalist system, and in his natural theology Aquinas must be accounted a rationalist, form a logically related and interdependent system of axioms.

In Hartshorne's theology we have such a system of axioms, and both proof and concept follow logically from the basic insight that reality can be understood panpsychistically as interrelated process, with God playing the parts of the supreme instance of process and at the same time the supreme explanatory factor in a rationalist system. Everything depends upon whether the basic insight that reality is of this character can be accepted as a true description of the universe in which we live *and* on whether the system of axioms holds together as a coherent whole. To come inside this particular circle of belief therefore requires something like an act of faith or of believing intuition in the fundamental metaphysical insight that reality is process. To judge whether the system is true requires an appeal to coherence, as has already been suggested to be the sole possible criterion of truth for such a rationalist metaphysics.[1] There is no conceivable way of standing outside the system in order to judge it from some transcendent perspective, for the very reason that empirical criteria are irrelevant to a system developed purely by means of conceptual analysis and construction. As the exposition of Hartshorne's position should have made clear, neoclassical metaphysics is heavily dependent upon the coherence theory of truth. Moreover, this feature helps to throw some light on why it is so important for Hartshorne to establish the incoherence of the classical metaphysic. This is not to deny that establishing the incoherence of rival theories would be important in the case of any theorist, whether matters empirical or philosophical were at stake. But the situation here is that Hartshorne accepts the validity of the approach and even much of the language of his opponents. Much of the case for his alternative rests upon the claim that it is more coherent than theirs, and therefore has stronger grounds for being accepted as an accurate map of reality.

That fact is, then, that entry into the circle of neoclassical theology has two prerequisites. The first is that the entrant should accept the rationalist doctrines without which there would be no neoclassical theology at all, and particularly those

[1] See above, Ch. IV, § iii.

concerned with the relation of language to reality. At least some of these doctrines are élitist in tendency: that the way to knowledge of God is a matter for the intellect. The second prerequisite is that the entrant judge intuitively that this theology provides a satisfactory view of the universe. That is to say, despite the rationalist nature of the theology, there is no rational way into it. One becomes a neoclassical metaphysician by an act of commitment or faith. What is the difference in principle between making this act of faith and making that in which the starting-point of one's theology is in the dogma of the Word become flesh, as appears to be the fundamental 'given' of Barth's theology?

The appropriateness of the neoclassical system for replacing the widely used Aristotelian conceptuality as a rational basis for Christian theology can also be judged from another angle. To take the neoclassical concept of God as one's 'natural theology' or ante-room for faith appears to demand of the believer two 'acts of faith', one in the neoclassical categories and conception of rationality, and the other in Jesus Christ as the Word of God (or whatever). Christian faith will then require the joint acceptance of a completely abstract, a-historical metaphysic as the prolegomena to belief in the saving significance of a historical figure. The problem is better put otherwise. If Jesus Christ and the gospel about him imply anything at all about the way in which the believer should view the universe, not only does that gospel to a greater or lesser degree exclude metaphysical views which see the universe differently, but in cases such as the one under consideration a clear choice has to be made between some of the things implied by a neoclassical metaphysic and some of the things claimed by the Christian gospel. In this connection R. W. Jenson quotes the remark of an (unnamed) colleague: 'The trouble with Process theology is that it is such an attractive alternative to the Christian faith.'[2] It is, therefore, the contention of this study that, first, Hartshorne's metaphysical system is no more a 'natural' theology than the theology of Karl Barth (if indeed there is such an entity as a natural view of things), and, second, that it in fact represents an *alternative* (and in many respects *competing*) apprehension of the nature of reality

[2] R. W. Jenson, *God After God*, p. 208.

to the Christian one, whether or not that is represented wholly satisfactorily in Barth's theology.

ii. *Karl Barth as a Rational Theologian*

Much has been made of the fact that Barth's theology is of a more *a posteriori* character than Hartshorne's, and indeed the structure of the study has been designed to bring out this feature: that Barth moves from the particular to the general in his theologizing. Thus there is in his thought too a relationship between form and content, but, at least in intention, it is of a more open kind, and is meant to prevent the development of the closed circle that results from the tendency to encapsulate the concept of God in a cluster of logically interrelated categories. Chapter VIII was introduced to show that there is something like a scholarly consensus that Barth has in many respects failed in his attempt to keep his concept of God open to the future, and so open to revision. I would also wish to suggest that R. W. Jenson's diagnosis of the cause is the correct one: that Barth's partial failure—and it is only a partial failure, for the very good reason that most of the attempts to correct the weakness themselves depend upon Barth's own ideas—lies in his not being trinitarian enough at a crucial point in his argument. The third person of the Trinity, whatever additional functions he may have, is the mode of being of the one God by whose activity is anticipated the future redemption of man and the whole created order of which he is a part: see, for example, the eschatological function of the Spirit in Eph. 1: 13 f. and Rom. viii: 23 ff. It is our need to be open always to 'the things that are coming' (John xvi: 13)—another explicit reference to the Spirit—that ensures the openness and provisionality of our ways of speaking about God. For if the meaningful activity of God is already completed in past— or timeless—eternity, the outworking of the divine decision has all the necessity of a timeless concept, and our theology becomes the quest—as it has paradoxically become in the apparently temporalistic neoclassical theology—for timeless truths. The lesson of Barth's doctrine of the Trinity is that if God and so also the creature are to have the freedom proper to their natures, the conception of God as triune, and fully triune, is going to be instrumental in ensuring it. Above all it acts to preclude the

making absolute in any conceptual structure the relation
between God and the creature. That is why Barth's explicit
strictures against classical natural theology, and the implicit
ones against Hartshorne that have here been elicited from his
thought, are totally justified. Whatever the place of a natural
theology, it cannot surely any more consist in the construction
of *a priori* conceptual edifices.

In the light of this, it can be argued that Barth's attempt to
formulate a 'proof' from revelation has the merit of being
rational without being rationalistic. It is concerned to characterize certain events as acts of God because they impose themselves
as such upon the interpreter. The way into this view of reality
is not the acceptance of an analogy as the basis for understanding reality as a whole, but the belief that certain events,
described, remembered, and promised in the biblical books,
are correctly attributable to the agency of God and are such
as to *illumine consistently both human life and the world in which they
happen*. The claim to rationality is very closely connected with
that italicized clause; it is also bound up with a claim to
truth, summed up in the use of the word *correctly*. It is because
there are claims both for truth—however provisional must be
any form of words which attempt to express the claim—and
rationality, and because both are bound up with the events
described by Barth as 'revelation', that there is an inevitable
confrontation with neoclassical metaphysics, which itself
claims both truth and rationality for the revelatory and
comprehensive explanatory power of the categories. Each claims
the truth, but for different reasons, and therefore in so far as
they are considered worthy of attention—and it must be
remembered that for many toughminded contemporary philosophers, neither would be worth so much as a reading—some
kind of choice has to be made. But it is not a choice that can
be made on rational grounds alone, for there are involved, as
should by now be very evident, different conceptions of what it
is to be rational. We are very much in the area of pre-rational
views of the way things are, of which systems of theology and
metaphysics are the outworking in rational terms. It is almost
certainly true that men do not choose their view of the way
things are; in large part, it chooses them. 'Now it is unarguable
that there is a theological circle, that is, that the ultimate

grounds for one's faith cannot be "proved" or even defended by objective criteria separated from the faith itself. In this sense, theology represents a rational explication of what is essentially prerational or believed.'[3] But not all theologies are equally true. The Christian believes that he is in his particular circle not by chance nor by his own efforts, but by the grace of God. It is here that the comprehensiveness and intellectual rigour of Barth's theology puts a fundamental question to neoclassical theology.

iii. *Reasons for the Rejection of Neoclassical Theism*

Hartshorne's theology represents a version of the very ancient philosophical equation of reality and value. In his case the doctrine is that reality is getting better all the time because it is building upon the value of the past which accumulates in the divine memory. Neoclassical theology therefore asks us to take our view of reality from a general doctrine of becoming which is axiomatically optimistic. There is no doubt that in this respect there has to be a choice between the general and the particular becoming of God. We have seen that for Hartshorne christological considerations can be no more than symbolic of deeper truths that have already been decided philosophically. But this theological argument can be supported by a more general point. In his exposition of Barth's trinitarian theology Jüngel says, 'It is not . . . legitimate to confuse the statement, "God's being is in his becoming" with statements like, "God's being is becoming".'[4] One reason for this can be seen in the light of the exposition of Hartshorne's concept of God. It is difficult to accept that the general becoming in which God's reality consists can properly be characterized as love. Merely because God is so constituted that everything that happens must make an impact upon him—a kind of metaphysical sponge, infinitely absorbent—are we to say that he *loves* everthing? If we are going to use words like 'love' and 'grace' when we speak of God must there not be clear connotations of free, active, personal initiative if the existence of this God is going to make any more difference than serving as a validation

---

[3] Langdon Gilkey, *Naming the Whirlwind: the Renewal of God-Language* (Indianapolis and New York, 1969), p. 176.

[4] E. Jüngel, *Gottes Sein*, p. 116, n. 153.

for what man already is? The difficulty with the neoclassical suffering, for all its merits as a pointer to the real concern of God for his creatures, is that it is not also a doing. It is totally automatic and involuntary. It is not under God's control, for he has no choice as to whether or not he suffers with the world; in fact, he is under the control of the cosmic forces which make him what he is.

For the metaphysician, on the other hand, the trouble with Barth's radically personalistic conception will be that it is 'anthropomorphic', or 'mythological' to use the much misused modern cliché. Hartshorne is firmly anchored in that tradition of Western philosophy which regards philosophical abstractions as intellectually more respectable than the allegedly cruder anthropomorphisms of biblical origin. Of course, language has to be qualified when it is used of God and apart from its everyday use, and we have seen how this is done in a controlled way—so that the language is not qualified to death—in both Barth and Hartshorne. But the weakness of neoclassical analogy is that its process of qualification so weakens the personal content of the terms that it virtually disappears. The cause of this is found in the metaphysical assumptions and methods of the system. If God can only be described by means of language that must also be predicable of all other reality, there is a danger—here amply illustrated—of philosophy being a search for a lowest common denominator. The outcome is twofold. On the one hand, such qualities as grace, mercy, and personality have in some sense to be ascribed to all entities before they can be attributed to God in an eminent sense. But, on the other, since what can be attributed to every entity is only personal in the most attenuated sense, the primary category of the philosophy is found to be something less than personal or rather a term sufficiently ambiguous to cover both the personal and the subpersonal, like 'relation'. The philosophy then becomes inevitably procrustean, the attenuation is carried upwards into the concept of God and there follow all the consequences that were set out in the first half of the study. Paradoxically, therefore, in view of the panpsychism of the doctrine, to ascribe personal qualities to God requires a straining of the metaphysical categories in theological special pleading. By appealing to such a metaphysical system as this in support of their theology, Christian theologians are likely to find the problems of demonstrating the meaningfulness of their doctrine compounded. Moreover, and more important, it is not only a question of meaningfulness, for the content of what they are saying is inevitably affected by making unnecessary concessions to ill-founded accusations of anthropomorphism. The theological outcome is the same whether the dependence for metaphysical support be upon classical or neoclassical theoreticians. Therefore

. . . we may and must abandon all conceptions of God which with the help of traditional modes of thought introduce into God a motionless, immutable, abstract invariability and combine it with a motionless and abstract perfection to such an extent that all taking place of God on earth is . . . exposed at the outset [in such a way that] all statements about new decisions, new creations, new acts and words of God must appear the deceptions of a naive anthropomorphism.[5]

That is the lesson for theology of the confrontation between Hartshorne and Barth. It shows clearly that the theology that wishes to stand on the intellectual feet of a philosophy is likely to remain a cripple. Moreover, it demonstrates the lunacy of so much as taking seriously the rationalist dogma that philosophical abstractions are more intellectually appropriate than personal analogies when speaking of God. It makes clear the choice either that the Christian doctrine of the incarnation be relativized and shown to be no more than a pictorial ('mythological') expression of what the philosopher can say better—though, it must be noted, always with a very different meaning—or that the rationalist dogma be itself overcome by the Word's becoming flesh in Jesus of Nazareth.

The case for the rationalistic dogma becomes weaker when it is realized that in the case of neoclassical rationalism at least, the anthropomorphism remains unconquered by philosophical abstraction, even if it is spread thinly throughout the system. Hartshorne's theology is irretrievably anthropomorphic. 'God's "memory" is perfect; His "intentions" are unimpeachable; but does He *really* have "intentions," does He really have

[5] Peter Brunner, 'Die Freiheit des Menschen in Gottes Heilsgeschichte', *Kerygma und Dogma* 5 (1959) 241.

a will, does He really decide anything? "Memory" is no less anthropomorphic than "will" '.[6] That brief sceptical comment sums up many of the internal and other weaknesses of Hartshorne's theology. Most of the problems arise when he tries to elevate universal relatedness, universal passivity, into love, in the hope that the transition from impersonal to personal, from metaphysical to anthropomorphic, will pass unnoticed. Whatever the value of the exposure of the contradictions and moral shortcomings of the classical concept of God, it is of little benefit to overthrow a tyrant if he is replaced by an ineffectual weakling, and that is the impression that remains whatever stress is laid upon the divine influence and persuasion.

This criticism could be put less metaphorically by pointing once more to the particular conception of suffering that dominates this theory of the divine relativity. The essential powerlessness of this deity derives from the way in which he is conceived to be related to the rest of reality, and this itself follows from the basic conception of perception with which this study began. Beings, whether God, man, or molecule perceive what is in their immediate past. Therefore, '. . . God cannot unify the world, since he can prehend the things in it only after their subjective reality or process has ceased to be.'[7] Precisely so: because God 'happens' only after the entities he perceives have happened, they are the real creators of what there is. They it is who, though certainly under the influence of the God who is in their past, make the world to be what it really is. Process theology has been described as a sophisticated form of animism. It is therefore highly mythological, as its God is the projection into timeless truth of a certain conception of human experience. More than that, it represents a superstitious form of idolatry, in that it divinizes the world, both as the creator of itself and God[8] and as the body, coeternal and consubstantial, of God who is its soul. If they had realized some of the implications of these doctrines, modern theologians would

---

[6] Julian Hartt, 'The Logic of Perfection', *Review of Metaphysics* 16 (1963) 762.

[7] R. C. Neville, 'Neoclassical Metaphysics', *International Philosophical Quarterly* 9 (1969) 618.

[8] Cf. A. N. Whitehead, *Process and Reality* (New York, 1929), p. 528: 'It is as true to say that God creates the World, as that the World creates God.'

not perhaps have been quite so eager to employ this philosophy in defence of their faith. But then again, perhaps they would; for the ways of theological fashion in this century are as mysterious as the free choice exercised by Hartshorne's ultimate particles.

SELECT BIBLIOGRAPHY

I. WORKS BY CHARLES HARTSHORNE

1. BOOKS

Beyond Humanism: Essays in the Philosophy of Nature. Lincoln, Nebraska: University of Nebraska Press, 1968 (first published, 1937).

Man's Vision of God and the Logic of Theism, New York: Harper & Brothers, 1941, reprinted Hampden, Connecticut: Archon Books, 1964.

The Divine Relativity: A Social Conception of God, New Haven: Yale University Press, 1948.

(Edited, with W. L. Reese) *Philosophers Speak of God,* Chicago: University of Chicago Press, 1953.

Reality as Social Process: Studies in Metaphysics and Religion, Glencoe, Illinois: Free Press, 1953.

The Logic of Perfection and Other Essays in Neoclassical Metaphysics, La Salle, Illinois: Open Court, 1962.

Anselm's Discovery: A Re-examination of the Ontological Proof of God's Existence, La Salle, Illinois: Open Court, 1965.

A Natural Theology for our Time, La Salle, Illinois: Open Court, 1967.

Creative Synthesis and Philosophic Method, London, SCM Press, 1970.

2. ARTICLES

'Continuity, the Form of Forms in Charles Peirce', *Monist* 39 (Oct. 1929) 521–34.

'Contingency and the New Era in Metaphysics', *Journal of Philosophy* 29 (1932) 421–31 and 457–69.

'Four Principles of Method—with Applications', *Monist* 43 (Jan. 1933) 40–72.

'Metaphysics for Positivists', *Philosophy of Science* 2 (1935) 287–303.

'The Compound Individual', in *Philosophical Essays for Alfred North Whitehead,* New York: Longmans, Green & Co., 1936, pp. 193–220.

'The Reality of the Past, the Unreality of the Future', *Hibbert Journal* 37 (1939) 246–57.

'Anthropomorphic Tendencies in Positivism', *Philosophy of Science* 8 (1941) 184–203.

'A Critique of Peirce's Idea of God', *Philosophical Review* 50 (1941) 516–23.

'Santayana's Doctrine of Essence', in *The Philosophy of George Santayana,* ed. P. Schillp, Evanston and Chicago: Northwestern University, 1941, pp. 135–82.

'Whitehead's Idea of God', in *The Philosophy of Alfred North Whitehead,* ed. P. Schillp, Evanston and Chicago: Northwestern University, 1941, pp. 513–59.

'Elements of Truth in the Group-Mind Concept', *Social Research* 9 (1942) 248–65.

'Reflections on the Strengths and Weakness of Thomism', *Ethics* 54 (1943) 53–7.

'The Formal Validity and Real Significance of the Ontological Argument', *Philosophical Review* 53 (1944) 225–45.

'Philosophy and Orthodoxy', *Ethics* 54 (1944) 295–8.

'Efficient Causality in Aristotle and St. Thomas', *Journal of Religion* 25 (1945) 25–32.

'Ideal Knowledge Defines Reality: What Was True in Idealism', *Journal of Philosophy* 43 (1946) 573–82.

'Reply to Father Meehan', *Journal of Religion* 26 (1946) 54–7.

'The Synthesis of Idealism and Realism', *Theoria* 15 (1949) 90–107.

'Panpsychism', in *A History of Philosophical Systems*, ed. V. Ferm, London: Rider & Co., 1950.

'Whitehead's Metaphysics', in V. Lowe, C. Hartshorne, and A. H. Johnson, *Whitehead and the Modern World*, Boston: Beacon Press, 1950.

'Strict and Genetic Identity: An Illustration of the Relations of Logic to Metaphysics', in *Structure, Method and Meaning: Essays in Honor of Henry M. Sheffer*, edd. P. Henle *et al.*, New York: Liberal Arts Press, 1951, pp. 242–54.

'Tillich's Doctrine of God', in *The Theology of Paul Tillich*, edd. C. W. Kegley and R. W. Bretall, New York: Macmillan, 1952.

'Causal Necessities: An Alternative to Hume', *Philosophical Review* 63 (1954) 479–99.

'Process as Inclusive Category: A Reply', *Journal of Philosophy* 52 (1955) 94–102.

'Omnipotence', 'Panentheism', 'Pantheism', 'God as Personal', 'Transcendence', and other entries in *An Encyclopedia of Religion*, ed. V. Ferm, London: Peter Owen, 1956.

'Whitehead and Beryaev: Is there Tragedy in God', *Journal of Religion* 37 (1957) 71–84.

'The Logical Structure of Givenness', *Philosophical Quarterly* 8 (1958) 307–16.

'Metaphysical Statements as Non-restrictive and Existential', *Review of Metaphysics* 12 (1958) 35–47.

'The Philosophy of Creative Synthesis', *Journal of Philosophy* 55 (1958) 944–53.

'A Philosopher's Assessment of Christianity', in *Religion and Culture: Essays in Honour of Paul Tillich*, ed. W. Leibrecht, London: SCM Press, 1959, pp. 167–80.

'The Logic of the Ontological Argument', *Journal of Philosophy* 58 (1961) 471–3.

'Metaphysics and the Modality of Existential Judgments', in *The Relevance of Whitehead: Philosophical Essays in Commemoration of the Centenary of the Birth of Alfred North Whitehead*, ed. E. Leclerc, London: Allen & Unwin, 1961, pp. 107–21.

'What Did Anselm Discover?', *Union Seminary Quarterly Review* 17 (1962) 213–22.

'Real Possibility', *Journal of Philosophy* 60 (1963) 593–605.

'Is God's Existence a State of Affairs?', in *Faith and the Philosophers*, ed. J. Hick, London: Macmillan, 1964, pp. 26–33.

Replies to 'Interrogation of Charles Hartshorne, conducted by William Alston: I. Process, II. Feeling, III. Morality, IV. God, V. Method', in *Philosophical Interrogations: Interrogations of Martin Buber, John Wild, Jean Wahl, Brand Blanshard, Paul Weiss, Charles Hartshorne, Paul Tillich*, edd. S. and B. Rome, New York: Holt, Rhinehart & Winston, 1964, pp. 321–54.

'What the Ontological Argument Does not Do', *Review of Metaphysics* 17 (1964) 608–9.

'Abstract and Concrete Approaches to Deity', *Union Seminary Quarterly Review* 20 (1965) 265–70.

'The Development of Process Philosophy', Introduction to *Philosophers of Process*, ed. D. Browning, New York: Random House, 1965, pp. v–xii.

'The Meaning of "Is Going to Be" ', *Mind* 74 (1965) 46–58.

'Tillich and the Non-theological Meaning of Theological Terms', *Religion in Life* 35 (1966) 674–85.

'The God of Religion and the God of Philosophy', in *Talk of God*, Royal Institute of Philosophy Lectures II, London: Macmillan, 1969.

II. WORKS ABOUT HARTSHORNE OR RELEVANT TO HIS INTERPRETATION

BROWN, DELWIN, JAMES, RALPH E., and REEVES, GENE, edd., *Process Philosophy and Christian Thought*, Indianapolis and New York: Bobbs-Merrill, 1971.

COBB, JOHN B., Jnr., *Living Options in Protestant Theology*, Philadelphia: Westminster Press, 1962.

—— ' "Perfection Exists": A Critique of Charles Hartshorne', *Religion in Life* 32 (1963) 294–304.

—— *A Christian Natural Theology: Based on the Thought of Alfred North Whitehead*, London: Lutterworth Press, 1966.

FINDLAY, J. N., 'Reflections on Necessary Existence', in *Process and Divinity: the Hartshorne Festschrift*, edd. W. L. Reese and E. Freeman, q.v., pp. 515–27.

GIBSON, A. BOYCE, 'The Two Strands in Natural Theology', in *Process and Divinity: the Hartshorne Festschrift*, edd. W. L. Reese and E. Freeman, q.v., pp. 471–92.

GUNTON, COLIN, Review of Charles Hartshorne, *Creative Synthesis and Philosophic Method*, in *Religious Studies* 7 (1971) 265 f.

—— 'Process Philosophy's Concept of God: An Outline and Assessment', *Expository Times* 84 (1973) 292–300.

HARTT, JULIAN, 'The Logic of Perfection', *Review of Metaphysics* 16 (1963) 749–69.

JAMES, RALPH E., *The Concrete God: A New Beginning for Theology—the Thought of Charles Hartshorne*, Indianapolis and New York: Bobbs-Merrill, 1967.

MEEHAN, F. X., 'Efficient Causality: A Reply and a Comment', *Journal of Religion* 26 (1946) 50–4.

MEYNELL, HUGO, 'The Theology of Hartshorne', *Journal of Theological Studies* N.S. 24 (1973) 143–57.

NEVILLE, ROBERT C., 'Neoclassical Metaphysics and Christianity: A Critical Study of Ogden's *Reality of God*', *International Philosophical Quarterly* 9 (1969) 605–24.

OGDEN, SCHUBERT M., 'Bultmann's Project of Demythologising and the Problem of Theology and Philosophy', *Journal of Religion* 37 (1957) 156–73.

—— *Christ Without Myth: A Study Based on the Theology of Rudolf Bultmann*, London: Collins, 1962.

—— 'Bultmann's Demythologising and Hartshorne's Dipolar Theism', *Process and Divinity: the Hartshorne Festschrift*, edd. W. L. Reese and E. Freeman, q.v., pp. 493–513.

—— 'The Possibility and Task of Philosophical Theology', *Union Seminary Quarterly Review* 20 (1965) 271–9.

—— *The Reality of God and Other Essays*, London: SCM Press, 1967.

—— 'A *Christian* Natural Theology?', in *Process Philosophy and Christian Thought*, edd. D. Brown *et al.*, q.v., pp. 111–15.

PAILIN, DAVID A., 'Some Comments on Hartshorne's Presentation of the Ontological Argument', *Religious Studies* 4 (1968) 103–22.

—— 'The Incarnation as a Continuing Reality', *Religious Studies* 6 (1970) 303–27.

PARSONS, HOWARD L., 'Religious Naturalism and the Philosophy of Charles Hartshorne', in *Process and Divinity: the Hartshorne Festschrift*, edd. W. L. Reese and E. Freeman, q.v., pp. 533–60.

PETERS, EUGENE H., *Hartshorne and Neoclassical Metaphysics*, Lincoln: University of Nebraska Press, 1970.

REESE, WILLIAM L., and FREEMAN, EUGENE, edd., *Process and Divinity: the Hartshorne Festschrift*, La Salle, Illinois: Open Court, 1964.

REEVES, GENE, and BROWN, DELWIN, 'The Development of Process Theology', in *Process Philosophy and Christian Thought*, edd. D. Brown *et al.*, q.v., pp. 21–64.

SCHURR, V., 'Was ist Prozesstheologie', *Theologie der Gegenwart* 13 (1970) 181–3.

TAUBES, JACOB, 'Review Article: *Philosophers Speak of God*', *Journal of Religion* 34 (1954) 120–6.

WESTPHAL, MEROLD, 'Temporality and Finitism in Hartshorne's Theism', *Review of Metaphysics* 19 (1966) 550–64.

WHITEHEAD, A. N., *Religion in the Making*, London: Cambridge University Press, 1926.

—— *Science and the Modern World*, London: Cambridge University Press, 1926.

—— *Process and Reality*, New York: Macmillan, 1929.

—— *Adventures of Ideas*, London: Cambridge University Press, 1933.

—— *Modes of Thought*, London: Cambridge University Press, 1938.

WILCOX, JOHN T., 'A Question from Physics for Certain Theists', *Journal of Religion* 41 (1961) 293–300.

III. WORKS BY KARL BARTH

Anselm: Fides Quaerens Intellectum. Anselm's Proof of the Existence of God in the Context of his Theological Scheme, E.T. of 2nd edn. 1958 (1st edn. 1931) by Ian W. Robertson, London: SCM Press, 1960.

Church Dogmatics, edd. G. W. Bromiley and T. F. Torrance, Edinburgh: T. & T. Clark, 1956–74.

I/1 *The Doctrine of the Word of God*, Prolegomena, Part 1, E.T. by G. W. Bromiley, 1975.

I/2 *The Doctrine of the Word of God*, Prolegomena, Part 2, E.T. by G. T. Thomson and H. Knight, 1956.

II/1 *The Doctrine of God*, Part 1, E.T. by T. H. L. Parker, W. B. Johnston, H. Knight, J. L. M. Haire, 1957.

II/2 *The Doctrine of God*, Part 2, E.T. by G. W. Bromiley, J. C. Campbell, Iain Wilson, J. Strathearn McNab, H. Knight, R. A. Stewart, 1957.

III/1 *The Doctrine of Creation*, Part 1. E.T. by J. W. Edwards, O. Bussey, H. Knight, 1958.

III/2 *The Doctrine of Creation*, Part 2, E.T. by H. Knight, G. W. Bromiley, J. K. S. Reid, R. H. Fuller, 1960.

III/3 *The Doctrine of Creation*, Part 3, E.T. by G. W. Bromiley and R. Ehrlich, 1960.

III/4 *The Doctrine of Creation*, Part 4, E.T. by A. T. Mackay, T. H. L. Parker, H. Knight, H. A. Kennedy, J. Marks, 1961.

IV/1 *The Doctrine of Reconciliation*, Part 1, E.T. by G. W. Bromiley, 1956.

IV/2 *The Doctrine of Reconciliation*, Part 2, E.T. by G. W. Bromiley, 1958.

IV/3 *The Doctrine of Reconciliation*, Part 3, E.T. by G. W. Bromiley, vol. i, 1961, vol. ii, 1962.

IV/4 *The Doctrine of Reconciliation: the Christian Life* (fragment), E.T. by G. W. Bromiley, 1969.

Dogmatics in Outline, E.T. by G. T. Thomson, London: SCM Press, 1949.

Protestant Theology in the Nineteenth Century, E.T. by Brian Cozens and John Bowden, London: SCM Press, 1972.

IV. WORKS ABOUT BARTH, OR RELEVANT TO HIS INTERPRETATION

BALTHASAR, HANS URS VON, *The Theology of Karl Barth*, E.T. by J. Drury of parts of *Karl Barth: Darstellung und Deutung seiner Theologie* (Cologne, 1951), New York: Holt, Rinehart & Winston, 1971.

BERKOUWER, G. C., *The Triumph of Grace in the Theology of Karl Barth*, E.T. by H. R. Boer, London: Paternoster Press, 1956.

BETTIS, JOSEPH DABNEY, 'Is Karl Barth a Universalist?', *Scottish Journal of Theology* 15 (1967) 423–36.

BOUILLARD, HENRI, *Karl Barth. Vol. I: Genèse et évolution de la théologie dialectique. Vols. II and III: Parole de Dieu et existence humaine*, Paris: Aubier, 1957.

BOWDEN, JOHN, *Karl Barth*, London: SCM Press, 1971.

BRUNNER, EMIL, 'The New Barth, Observations on Karl Barth's *Doctrine of Man*', *Scottish Journal of Theology* 4 (1951) 123–35.

CHAVANNES, HENRY, *L'Analogie entre Dieu et le monde selon saint Thomas d'Aquin et selon Karl Barth*, Paris: Les Éditions du Cerf, 1969.

FOLEY, GROVER, 'The Catholic Critics of Karl Barth: in Outline and Analysis', *Scottish Journal of Theology* 14 (1961) 136–55.

GLOEGE, GERHARD, 'Karl Barth', in *Religion in Geschichte und Gegenwart*, 3rd edn. Vol. 1, ed. Kurt Galling, Tübingen: J. C. B. Mohr (Paul Siebeck), 1957, coll. 894–8.

GUNTON, COLIN, 'Karl Barth and the Development of Christian Doctrine', *Scottish Journal of Theology* 25 (1972) 171–80.

HARTMAN, R. S., 'Prolegomena to a Meta-Anselmian Axiomatic', *Review of Metaphysics* 14 (1961) 637–75.

HARTWELL, HERBERT, *The Theology of Karl Barth: An Introduction*, London: Gerald Duckworth, 1964.

JENSON, ROBERT W., *Alpha and Omega: A Study in the Theology of Karl Barth*, New York: Thomas Nelson & Sons, 1963.

—— *The Knowledge of Things Hoped For: the Sense of Theological Discourse*, New York and London: Oxford University Press, 1969.

—— *God After God: the God of the Past and the God of the Future, Seen in the Work of Karl Barth*, Indianapolis and New York: Bobbs-Merrill, 1969.

JÜNGEL, EBERHARD, 'Die Möglichkeit theologischer Anthropologie auf dem Grund der Analogie. Eine Untersuchung zum Analogieverständnis Karl Barths', *Evangelische Theologie* 22 (1962) 535–57.

—— *Gottes Sein ist im Werden*, Tübingen: J. C. B. Mohr (Paul Siebeck), 2nd edn., 1967.

KRECK, W., 'Analogia fidei oder analogia entis?', *Antwort*, ed. E. Wolf, q.v., pp. 272–86.

KUNG, HANS, *Justification. The Doctrine of Karl Barth and a Catholic Reflection*, E.T. by T. Collins *et al.*, London: Burns & Oates, 1964.

McINTYRE, JOHN, 'Analogy', *Scottish Journal of Theology* 12 (1959) 1–20.

MONDON, BATTISTA, *The Principle of Analogy in Protestant and Catholic Theology*, The Hague: Martinus Nijhoff, 2nd edn., 1968.

NICHOLLS, WILLIAM, *Systematic and Philosophical Theology. The Pelican Guide to Modern Theology*, Volume I, London: Penguin Books, 1969.

PARKER, T. H. L., *Karl Barth*, Grand Rapids, Michigan: Eerdmans, 1970.

PÖHLMANN, HORST GEORG, *Analogia entis oder analogia fidei? Dei Frage der Analogie bei Karl Barth*, Göttingen: Vandenhoeck & Ruprecht, 1965.

PRENTER, REGIN, 'Die Lehre vom Menschen bei Karl Barth', *Theologische Zeitschrift* 6 (1950) 211–22.

—— 'Karl Barths Umbildung der traditionellen Zweinaturlehre in lutherischer Beleuchtung', *Studia Theologica* 11 (1957) 1–88.

RUMSCHEIDT, H. MARTIN, *Revelation and Theology. An Analysis of the Barth–Harnack Correspondence of 1923*, London: Cambridge University Press, 1972.

SÖHNGEN, GOTTLIEB, 'Wesen und Akt in der scholastischen Lehre von der participatio und analogia entis', *Studium Generale* 8 (1955) 649–62.

—— 'Analogia entis in analogia fidei', in *Antwort*, ed. E. Wolf, q.v., pp. 266–71.

TORRANCE, THOMAS F., *Karl Barth: An Introduction to his Early Theology*, London: SCM Press, 1962.

—— *Theological Science*, London: Oxford University Press, 1969.

—— *God and Rationality*, London: Oxford University Press, 1971.

WELCH, CLAUDE, *The Trinity in Contemporary Theology*, London: SCM Press, 1953.

WILDBOLZ, EDUARD, 'Review of Hans Urs von Balthasar, *Karl Barth: Darstellung und Deutung seiner Theologie*', in *Scottish Journal of Theology* 7 (1954) 108–11.

WINGREN, GUSTAF, 'Gott und Mensch bei Karl Barth'. *Studia Theologica* 1 (1948) 27–53.

WOLF, E., ed., *Antwort. Karl Barth zum 70 Geburtstag am 10 Mai 1956*, Zollikon-Zurich, 1956.

V. OTHER WORKS REFERRED TO IN FOOTNOTES

AQUINAS, ST. THOMAS, *Summa Theologica*, Questions 1–26.

AYER, A. J., *Language, Truth and Logic*, London: Gollancz, 2nd edn., 1946.

BARNES, JONATHAN, *The Ontological Argument*, London: Macmillan, 1972.

BERKELEY, G., *Three Dialogues Between Hylas and Philonous in Opposition to Sceptics and Atheists*, in *A New Theory of Vision and Other Writings*, London: Everyman, 1910.

BRUNNER, PETER, 'Die Freiheit des Menschen in Gottes Heilsgeschichte', *Kerygma und Dogma* 5 (1959) 238–57.

COX, HARVEY, *The Secular City*, London: SCM Press, 1966 edn.

FINDLAY, J. N., *Hegel: A Re-examination*, London: Allen & Unwin, 1958.

—— 'Can God's Existence be Disproved?' in *New Essays in Philosophical Theology*, edd. A. Flew and A. Macintyre, q.v., pp. 47–56.

FLEW, ANTONY, and MacIntyre, ALASDAIR, edd. *New Essays in Philosophical Theology*, London: SCM Press, 1963 edn.

FOSTER, MICHAEL B., 'The Christian Doctrine of Creation and the Rise of Modern Natural Science', *Mind* 43 (1934) 446–68.

GEACH, P. T., 'Spinoza and the Divine Attributes', in *Reason and Reality*, Royal Institute of Philosophy Lectures V, London: Macmillan, 1972, pp. 15–27.

GILKEY, LANGDON, *Naming the Whirlwind: the Renewal of God-Language*, Indianapolis and New York: Bobbs-Merrill, 1969.

HAMPSHIRE, STUART, *Spinoza*, London: Penguin Books, 1962 edn.

HICK, JOHN, 'God as Necessary Being', *Journal of Philosophy* 57 (1960) 725–34.

HOOYKAAS, R., *Religion and the Rise of Modern Science*, Edinburgh and London: Scottish Academic Press, 1972.

HUME, DAVID, *Dialogues Concerning Natural Religion*, 1779.

KANT, IMMANUEL, *Critique of Pure Reason*, E.T. by F. M. Müller, New York: Anchor Books, 1966.

KENNY, ANTHONY, *The Five Ways*, London: Routledge, 1969.

Locke, John, *An Essay Concerning Human Understanding*, 1690.

Lucas, J. R., *The Freedom of the Will*, Oxford: Clarendon Press, 1970.

McIntyre, John, *The Shape of Christology*, London: SCM Press, 1966.

Macquarrie, John, *Principles of Christian Theology*, London: SCM Press, 1966.

Malcolm, Norman, 'Anselm's Ontological Arguments,' *Philosophical Review* 69 (1960) 40–52.

Mascall, E. L., *He Who Is: A Study in Traditional Theism*, London: Darton, Longman & Todd, 1966.

Moltmann, Jürgen, *Theology of Hope*, E.T. by James W. Leitch, London: SCM Press, 1967.

Owen, H. P., *The Christian Knowledge of God*, London: Athlone Press, 1969.

—— *Concepts of Deity*, London: Macmillan, 1971.

Robinson, J. A. T., *Honest to God*, London: SCM Press, 1963.

—— *Exploration into God*, London: SCM Press, 1968.

Smart, J. J. C., 'The Existence of God', in *New Essays in Philosophical Theology*, edd. A. Flew and A. MacIntyre, q.v., pp. 28–46.

Spinoza, B., *The Ethics*, E.T. by R. H. M. Elmes, New York: Tudor Publishing Co. [no date].

Strawson, P. F., *Individuals: An Essay in Descriptive Metaphysics*, London: University Paperbacks, 1964.

Vesey, G. N. A., 'Foreword' to *Talk of God*, Royal Institute of Philosophy Lectures II, London: Macmillan, 1969, pp. vii–xxiv.

Wiles, M. F., 'Some Reflections on the Origins of the Doctrine of the Trinity', *Journal of Theological Studies* n.s. 8 (1957) 92–106.

INDEX